THE
COMPLETE
KODAK
BOOK OF
PHOTOGRAPHY

THE
COMPLETE
KODAK
BOOK OF
PHOTOGRAPHY

CRESCENT BOOKS
NEW YORK ● AVENEL

This volume was abridged by Thomas Dickey and Don Earnest from the KODAK Library of Creative Photography, a series of books created and designed by Mitchell Beazley International in association with Kodak and Time-Life Books.

Revised and updated by Jonathan Vince

Commissioning Editor Sarah Polden
Art Editor John Grain

Staff for the KODAK Library of Creative Photography

Mitchell Beazley International

Editor-in-Chief
Jack Tresidder

Series Editors
John Roberts, Robert Saxton

Art Editors
Mel Petersen, Mike Brown

Editors
Ian Chilvers, Louise Earwaker, Lucy Lidell, Joss Pearson, Richard Platt, Carolyn Ryden

Designers
Robert Lamb, Marnie Searchwell, Michelle Stamp, Lisa Tai, Ruth Prentice

Assistant Designers
Stewart Moore, Susan Rentoul

Picture Researchers
Brigitte Arora, Jackum Brown, Veneta Bullen, Nicky Hughes, Beverly Tunbridge

Editorial Assistant
Margaret Little

Production
Peter Phillips, Jean Rigby, Androulla Pavlou

Chief Consulting Photographer
Michael Freeman

Consulting Photographers
Michael Busselle, Tony Duffy, Donald Honeyman, Steve Powell, Tim Stephens

Coordinating Editors for Kodak
John Fish, Ken Lassiter, Paul Mulroney, Ken Oberg, Jackie Salitan

Consulting Editor for Time-Life Books
Thomas Dickey

The KODAK Encyclopedia of Creative Photography
© Kodak Limited 1983, 1984, 1985, 1988, 1994

The Complete KODAK Book of Photography
© 1983, 1984, 1985, 1988, 1994 by Kodak Limited, Reed International Books Limited, Salvat Editores, S.A.
Abridged from the KODAK Library of Creative Photography

This 1995 edition published by Crescent Books, distributed by Random House Value Publishing, Inc. 40 Engelhard Avenue, Avenel, New Jersey 07001.

Random House
New York • Toronto • London • Sydney • Auckland

ISBN 0-517-14093-4

A CIP catalog record for this book is available from the Library of Congress.

10, 9, 8, 7, 6, 5, 4, 3, 2, 1

Produced by Mandarin Offset
Printed and bound in China

Kodak is a trade mark of Kodak Limited and its related companies

ABOUT THIS BOOK

The best photographs are simple. They convey a message directly and vividly, whether it be the joy of a family reunion or the splendor of a canyon lit by the evening sky. This same simplicity often applies to the way photographs are taken, especially now that modern cameras and film have made dealing with exposure and other technical problems much easier – freeing the photographer's eye and imagination. The aim of this book is to show that everyone, from novices to experienced enthusiasts, can transform their photography with simple techniques and clear creative principles.

This book thoroughly explores the equipment, techniques and subjects available to you, whatever your interest and level of experience. Throughout, the focus is on taking pictures with a 35mm camera, the tool favored by dedicated amateurs as well as professionals for its versatility and convenience.

The first part of the book, "What Makes A Good Picture," begins by showing you basic compositional principles; understanding them will develop your most important piece of equipment – your eye. You will then learn how to handle a camera, get the right exposure and use color imaginatively.

The second part of the book, "Pictures of Ourselves," is devoted to the favorite subject of most photographers – people – with advice on capturing the likenesses and activities of family and friends, taking formal and candid portraits and photographing nudes.

In "The World Around Us," which explores the popular subjects of travel and nature, you will learn about the tools and techniques for recording landscapes, wildlife and the most pleasurable moments of a trip.

The fourth and final part of the book, "Extending Your Range," covers the techniques you need to explore advanced image-making and the special subjects that interest you. You will become familiar with how to capture action, create special effects, handle special lighting conditions and use basic studio techniques. A section on the home darkroom gives step-by-step instructions on developing and printing your own pictures. And the book concludes by showing you how to present your prints and slides in the most interesting fashion.

In short, you will find – on pages filled with inspiring and informative images – all the practical advice you need to take exciting, memorable pictures of your own.

CONTENTS

PICTURES OF OURSELVES

Page 140

THE WORLD AROUND US

Page 234

EXTENDING YOUR RANGE

Page 320

WHAT MAKES A GOOD PICTURE?

Our response to a picture is guided by the subject matter and by personal taste. But apart from that, two things are fundamentally important in any picture: composition and light. For the picture opposite, the photographer used the massive tree to touchingly frame the child's small figure. Along with this compositional device, the soft light and colors contribute strongly to the picture's mood.

The pictures in the following portfolio exemplify some of the important elements of composition: balance and asymmetry, shape and form, pattern and texture. They are at the core of creative photography, as is light, which is not only necessary to form a photographic image, but is a compositional tool in its own right. To create photographs that have calculated effects, you must know how to vary the quality and direction of light as well as its quantity. Similarly, you can use color to create delight, impact, variety – and you can even make color itself the subject of a picture.

This first part of the book shows you how you can turn these elements into practical ways of improving your pictures. Any good photographer is, of course, familiar with his equipment, and one section will help familiarize you with cameras and film. But good photographers also recognize that much of their work must be done before the shutter is pressed. Ultimately, the ability to produce strong images unerringly, rather than by chance, depends on looking long and hard at your subject, analyzing what you see, and planning what to do.

An expert eye captured this image of a little girl playing in a park. The picture's charm stems largely from the photographer's decision to fill most of the frame with the tree's autumn colors, which are accentuated by diffuse light.

Perfect balance *gives this architectural view a sense of calm elegance. The photographer carefully exploited the symmetry of the paired trees, branched lamp and pilasters behind.*

Deliberate asymmetry here establishes an unsettled mood. The lonely figure, framed so that he crosses the very top of the picture, emphasizes the emptiness of a concrete landscape.

19

Rainy weather, *often thought unsuitable for photography, creates some of the most interesting photographic opportunities. Amateur Luis Huesco took advantage of it when he was on a tour of a Spanish museum. Through a half-open door, he noticed the chance presented by two children playing alone in a drenched courtyard. In spite of their rushing figures, the scene seems charged with an eerie stillness, an effect created by the weather's gray mood in the symmetrical setting.*

The inspired pattern *of this unusual image came from the photographer's simple realization that a plaything such as a badminton shuttlecock can cast fascinating shadows when placed in front of a strong light source. By mating a pair of shuttlecocks in the light of a slide projector, the delicate ribbed wings of a shadow-insect were created.*

The beauty of a woman,
her smile, and her patterned
sweater are brought out by
a setting that reveals the
photographer's eye for the
way colors work together.
The vivid red background
and the frame of dark bricks
complement perfectly the
subtle hues of the sweater.

Pale balloons *float against a somber background of shadowed architecture in a composition that deliberately restricts color to a small area of the frame. The surprising impact of the picture demonstrates the power of color to sway us with the lightest touch.*

Beach umbrellas, *abandoned during a rain shower, sweep in a delicate green arc across the whole picture. The blending and softening of hues on a misty day such as this often creates marvelous opportunities for color photographs.*

Windblown barley *has been blurred here by the choice of a shutter speed too slow to stop the tips of the stalks waving. By this means the photographer has subtly muted the overall color to pale green.*

The sparkle of a smile and the bright red of a sun hat in the picture above lend the simplest of portraits an infectious gaiety. The photographer moved in close to frame the girl against the plain white wall and intensify the impact of the peaked cap above her glowing face.

The yellow rain hat pulled over the child's face makes a telling portrait that needed only an open response to the sudden opportunity. Many photographers would have waited, or asked the boy to lift the hat up again for a clear view, missing the drama of the invisible face.

WHAT MAKES A GOOD PICTURE?

A fast shutter *(left)*
crisply suspends a boy in
midair as he heads a soccer
ball. By also deliberately
underexposing the backlit
subject, the photographer
silhouetted him against the
soft, unfocused background.

A slow shutter *(above)*
helped to convey a child's
imagined speed as he plays
Superman. The long exposure
allowed the camera to follow
the boy as he crossed the
frame, creating streaks of
moving color in the
background. This also blurred
the motion of his legs so that
he seems about to take off.

Blurred water *– achieved by a slow shutter speed – in this somber landscape has smoothed out the one active element of the scene and turned the picture into a hauntingly beautiful still-life. The strange effect was surprisingly easy to create, needing no more than a time exposure of a few seconds.*

A majestic baboon, isolated by a telephoto lens, displays the soft colors and strongly defined patterns of his facial markings. Like many good animal shots, this is not an exotic wildlife picture: the photographer spotted the baboon in the shady doorway of its zoo den, and closed in.

YOU, THE PHOTOGRAPHER

Good photographs come from developing an eye for a picture – not from using banks of powerful studio lights, whirring motor-drives, or two-foot-long telephoto lenses. Success requires no more than the ability to make the essential creative leap from what you see to what will work as a photographic image. The secret of doing this is to train the eye to see images that will give pleasure when they are taken out of the complex, confused, and constantly shifting world and made into photographs isolated by their frames.

Experienced photographers become adept at identifying interesting images largely because they spend a great deal of time looking through the viewfinders of their cameras. Anyone can learn to see pictures in the same way. Look through the viewfinder frequently, even when you do not intend to take a picture. Concentrate on what you can actually see in the frame and how the shapes or colors there work together. You can practice this way of seeing even when you do not have a camera with you – remember the old artist's trick of holding the hands up as a frame? This creative and imaginative process is at the heart of photography, and the pictures on the following pages emphasize how much effective images depend on vision itself.

The viewfinder is your photographic link with the world in front of the camera. Here, the edges of its frame isolate four silhouetted figures from the bustle of a city park. The picture is compelling because the photographer used the camera's special eye to select the right image at the right moment.

Seeing pictures

Distant details, such as the woman walking her dog, may attract the eye, but are not clearly visible. However, with a telephoto lens, the camera can close in on such images.

To begin seeing as the camera sees, you need to recognize its basic powers – and limitations. First, consider the similarities between the camera and the eye. Both use a lens to focus an image on a surface that is sensitive to light. And a camera has ways of controlling the intensity of the incoming light, much as the pupil of the eye does. But, while these parallels are interesting, the differences are actually more relevant when you try to take pictures. In particular, the eye has vastly greater flexibility, working automatically in a way that the most advanced electronic camera cannot emulate.

Because you have two eyes, your brain receives two views of any subject from slightly different angles. Fused together into a single image, they form a picture that gives you a greater sense of depth than any photograph could provide. Moreover, the camera takes in the whole scene with uncritical interest, whereas your eyes concentrate on the parts of the scene you find most interesting.

The focus of the eye can change so swiftly from near to far objects that all appear equally in focus.

A boy playing may move too fast for the eye to capture his actions. But the camera can freeze every detail – even the ball in mid-air.

The eye
The remarkable versatility of human vision stems from the close link between the eye and the brain. Without our being consciously aware of the process, the brain controls the eye as it rapidly scans a scene to build up a complete picture, focusing on various details and adjusting to differing light levels. At the same time, the brain interprets the information received, making sense, for example, of the changes in scale between objects as they appear to diminish in size with distance. Vision extends through a full 160 , compared with the 45 view of a normal camera lens.

Images from the real world
Photographs may look like
the real world – but do not
duplicate the eye's view,
here represented by a hand-
tinted, retouched image.
This scene in a park around
a mansion includes several
photographic subjects, some
of which are reproduced in
the insets. Each inset picture
captures an image different
from one the eye would see.

The camera, however, can focus only a part of the
scene in one picture. The eye is also a great deal
more flexible in handling extreme contrasts in the
light level. Within the same scene, we can distinguish details of objects in deep shadow and in
bright sunlight in a way that is denied to the camera.

On the other hand, the camera has certain powers
that are beyond those of the eye. By framing a small
part of the world and thus engaging our attention,
a photograph can make us see things that might
otherwise go unnoticed. And the camera's ability to
freeze motion can reveal details of moving objects
not always visible to the naked eye.

Perhaps the most essential of all these things to
remember is that your eye can notice instanta-
neously what interests you in a scene and ignore the
rest, shifting attention constantly from the whole to
the smallest detail in a changing stream. The camera,
by contrast, fixes the whole scene in the viewfinder
at the moment you press the shutter. You must
provide the discrimination by so directing the
camera that worthwhile images are selected.

*__The man__ is the subject
for an impromptu portrait.
Notice how the camera has
framed him and isolated him
from his surroundings. The
lens's shallow focus shows
the background as a blur,
removing any distraction.*

The camera
The camera's relative lack of flexibility means that
you must operate it carefully to record effective
images. First, focus must be adjusted for the subject
to appear sharp. The amount of light allowed to fall
on the film must also be just right – and even then
the contrast between light and dark areas in a scene
may be too great for detail to show in both. On the
other hand, the camera records an image fixed in time,
allowing us to keep a record of visual experiences
that we want to remember. Photographs can also show
details of movement the eye could never catch.

Identifying the subject

The first creative step in taking a photograph is to choose the subject. This may seem obvious, but any one situation usually offers a wide range of choices. As a general rule, you should look for a subject that will make a single strong point. The more elements there are in the scene, the more important it is to have a clear idea about what you want the picture to show at the moment you press the shutter. If there are too many details in the viewfinder that do not support the main point, the picture will tend to look untidy – a random snap rather than an effective photograph. As we have just seen, the camera, unlike the eye, is not capable of concentrating on what is interesting and ignoring the rest. Everything in the viewfinder tends to have equal prominence unless the photographer organizes the scene and selects the image to bring out a particular part or aspect of it.

With an inherently disorganized scene – a crowded beach, for example – you need a good deal of skill to produce a broad view that does not look untidy, although the rich variety seen in a panoramic shot may have its own interest. The solution may be to find a viewpoint that allows you to simplify the picture down to a few elements. The photographs on these two pages illustrate three ways of simplifying the picture – moving in on a subject, pointing the camera downward to cut out extraneous background detail, and using a vertical format to concentrate on a single figure.

A conventional panorama of the beach records the overall scene without directing your attention to any feature in particular. The subject is full of other interesting photographic possibilities.

The solitary bather (right) is the subject rather than the confusion of surf. Attention is drawn to her by the footprints the photographer has carefully lined up in the viewfinder before taking the picture.

A downward shot from a hotel balcony produces a forceful picture because the photographer chose as a subject the strong graphic pattern of umbrellas and sunbathers.

A close–up of a little girl's delight as a wave leaves her stranded excludes distracting detail and frames her as the entire subject of the picture within a plain blue background.

Studied images, fleeting moments

Sometimes the world around us moves so fast that we experience moments of action, excitement, or laughter almost as a passing blur. The camera's ability to freeze these moments and record them on film is one of photography's most remarkable attributes and many of the pictures that give greatest pleasure are those that exploit it. But in other photographs what impresses is the sense of absolute stillness and order. This is often the result of the photographer's having had time to think hard about a stationary scene and perhaps rearrange it to make an image that is thoroughly balanced, as in the picture of a hotel balcony on this page.

There are thus two contrasting approaches to taking pictures. On the one hand, an alert photographer can capture those high points and instants in time that may never return – a child's first faltering steps, or a spontaneous burst of laughter in a game. The only way to be sure of catching these fleeting events consistently is to learn to anticipate

them. This means having the camera ready, out of its case, with the film wound on and the controls set to the approximate light conditions and focusing distance. From then on, it is a matter of quick reactions, accurate timing – and a little luck – to be able to capture pictures with the immediacy of the two images at the top of the page opposite.

The other, more considered, approach requires patience together with something of the artist's eye for composition. With time and care, even the simplest objects can be arranged to make an attractive picture and one that perhaps is alive in a different way – because it is charged with atmosphere. The key to successful pictures of this kind is often the lighting, which may be precisely controlled by the photographer. Even natural light can be controlled, if only by standing at a well-judged angle to the subject you are photographing or by waiting for the transformations in a landscape that occur as the sun moves or is covered by clouds.

The warmth and peace of a holiday balcony is evoked precisely in an image that seems as casual as the towel draped on the chair. In fact the photographer carefully studied the angle of the chair, adjusted the louvered doors as a frame, and waited until the sun lit the green slats on one side, leaving the others dark.

Landscapes like the one at right may last only seconds as sunlight bursts through storm clouds. The photographer had forseen the dramatic instant of brilliant contrast.

A gust of wind flips off the cyclist's hat – but the photographer was ready to catch the instant of surprise and amusement. He had preset the camera controls as the cyclist approached a corner.

Spontaneity and contrivance mix in this picture by a photographer who gave the boy the bubble gum so that he would relax for the camera – and then snapped off a remarkably natural and relaxed portrait.

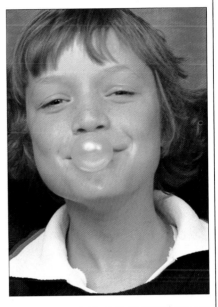

A moment's thought

Many first-time camera users set about taking pictures assuming that everything will fall automatically into place. They aim the lens directly toward the subject, lining up the most important features with the center of the viewfinder as though the camera were a kind of rifle and the subject a target. This approach will certainly record the subject on film, but is unlikely to produce an appealing image. You will achieve better results by thinking for a few seconds and allowing yourself time to study the scene in the viewfinder carefully. Are there distracting elements in the frame that would be better excluded by changing the camera position? Is a vertical format – used for the shot here of the reflected building – more suited to the subject than a horizontal one? Are there patterns – as in the rodeo picture – that can be used to give the picture a bold visual structure? With practice, this self-questioning process becomes automatic, a rapid sequence of mental trial and error. But for the beginner – and even for the expert – a conscious pause for thought can make all the difference between an ordinary snapshot and a picture with real impact.

A few simple ideas can point the way. First, placing the main subject slightly off-center in the frame can create a more balanced and visually satisfying effect than composing directly around the picture's center. The picture of the old woman opposite is a fine example. Pay particular attention to any lines in the scene – they can be used to direct the attention of a viewer around the picture. Strong lines can also affect the mood you want to achieve – diagonals suggest direction and even movement, and are useful for leading the eye into and out of the picture. These are only a few of the elements of composition that you should take into account in making a picture something more than a visual jumble – and many more will become apparent as you begin to develop visual awareness.

Closing in on this row of cowgirls and using a vertical format eliminates the confused background of a rodeo scene – a simple yet often effective compositional technique. The real subject is the central woman, framed by her two similarly dressed companions. Though they are abruptly cropped by the picture's edge, they are still important in providing pattern and balancing the whole image.

Alone in a wheatfield, the child dominates the landscape although occupying only a small part of the picture area. The photographer moved back and up the hill to keep horizon and sky out of the shot and make the wheatfield into a single, simple background of warm color.

Reflections can produce intriguing images. Here, amateur Herb Gustafson used observation and forethought to frame the clock tower of the old Federal Courthouse at St Paul, Minnesota, as a reflected vertical in the glass wall of a modern building opposite.

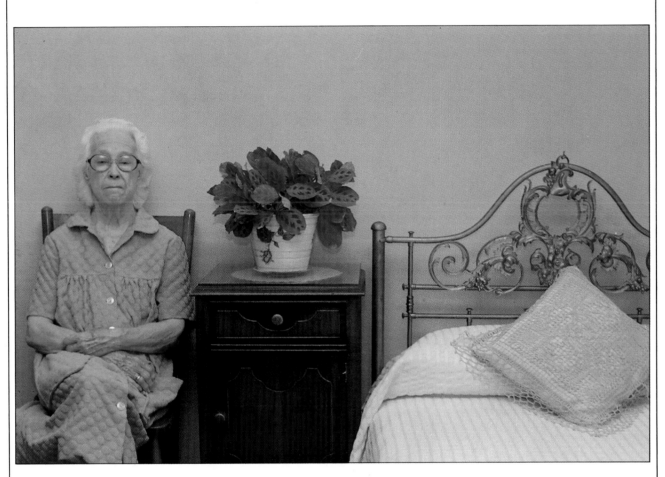

A remarkable portrait of old age, *full of atmosphere, relies for its impact on an imaginative composition in which the subject appears at the very edge of the frame. Center stage is occupied by an unassuming potted plant. The visual balance between the old woman and the bed, with its quilt similar in color to her clothing, helps convey the sense of silence and stillness.*

Choosing the best viewpoint

Changing the viewpoint is a photographer's most important means of controlling the way the picture will look. Sometimes moving the camera only slightly can transform the whole composition. Indeed, one of the easiest ways to improve your pictures is to make a habit of moving around the subject to find the best camera position whenever you spot something you wish to photograph.

Seen from a level camera position, most scenes consist of a foreground, a middle distance and a background. The relative positions of objects on these planes can be altered dramatically by shifting viewpoint. Imagine a scene with a field in the foreground, a house in the middle distance, and a tree behind it in the background. Simply by moving your camera to the right, you will place the house to the left of the tree. A lower viewpoint might bring flowers in the field into the close foreground; a higher view would reduce the amount of sky in the

frame. By moving back, you could make the house appear smaller and perhaps bring extra foreground elements, such as an overhanging branch of a tree, into the photograph.

The photographs below illustrate how very different the same scene can look from various camera angles. Only by exploring all of the possible viewpoints before taking a picture can you hope to arrive at the best one. Of course, any subject may present you with a number of good viewpoints, all of which will produce equally satisfactory images. Then, your choice must depend on the aspects of the scene you find most interesting. An excellent way to learn both the techniques of composition, and the particular approaches to a subject that suit you, is to take a series of photographs from different positions and then compare the results. This might seem to involve a waste of film, but you will very likely gain insights that will save you film in the future.

Four aspects of a single scene
The Acropolis in Athens is one of the world's most photographed landmarks. These photographs demonstrate how moving the position of the camera can radically alter your impressions of the scene. In the first image, the buildings occupy the middle distance as overall shapes against the hills and sky. For the view at far right, the photographer moved in to silhouette the columns. The distant viewpoint below puts the classical monument into the context of a large modern city. Finally, the panoramic photograph, including tiny figures, provides a human scale.

A tennis player throws up a ball to serve. The choice of viewpoint has fully exploited the explosive tension of the sport. When he had posed the subject, the photographer lay on the ground and aimed upward using a wide-angle lens. Thus, the lower half of the server's body appears distorted, emphasizing his leg muscles and long reach.

Deciding the format

Usually one of the major decisions a photographer must make is whether to hold the camera horizontally or vertically. You do not face this choice with cameras that provide a square image. But with a normal 35mm camera, the proportions of the frame are strongly rectangular, and the positioning of this frame is often crucial in terms of both composition and content.

Because holding a camera horizontally is easier than holding it vertically, novices frequently take pictures this way without really considering the alternative. Of course, some subjects naturally suggest a vertical picture – for example, full-length figures, towers or tall buildings. However, even with these subjects there are situations in which you can compose the picture as either a horizontal or an upright image, as demonstrated by the two pictures here of a skyscraper.

Horizontal pictures usually create a more static, peaceful effect than do vertical images, which psychologically suggest vigor – the overcoming of gravity. Sometimes the best images are those that run counter to our expectations. Photographers refer to landscape format to mean a horizontal picture, and portrait format to denote an upright one. Yet a vertically composed landscape may bring interesting foreground or background details into the frame; and a horizontal portrait may be highly effective, as in the example below, in which the off-center placing makes the picture less rigid.

A New York skyscraper, reflected in the mirrored glass of a neighboring building, is intriguingly geometric in the horizontal format above, but gains thrust and impact when viewed vertically in the picture opposite.

The double portrait at left works naturally as an upright composition, the format helping to reinforce the lively upward movement suggested by the pose of the two girls.

A deep-blue door made a perfect background for the man in a blue sweater, and the photographer's first thought was to position him on the axis of the cross-bars in an upright portrait format. However, the effect was too static. By moving slightly to the right and holding the camera horizontally, he achieved a more successful asymmetrical composition.

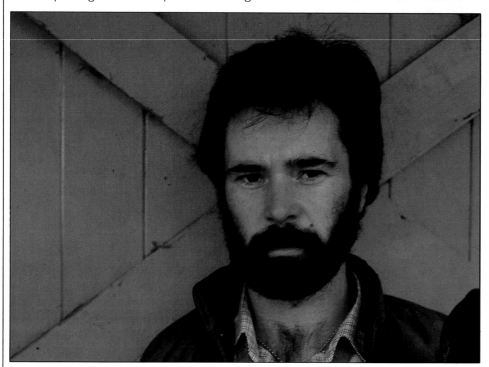

The main point of interest

Whatever the subject, a picture is likely to have greatest impact if there is a main point of interest in the composition. Thus, before you decide how to approach a subject, try to identify the essential focus of attention.

Sometimes the center of interest is easy to spot. For example, the face usually dominates in a portrait, whereas in a landscape a particular tree, hill or stretch of water may provide the key element. When there is no obvious main point, you may have to look harder – or even create one.

Once you have a clear idea of what the main element in the picture should be, start thinking about how you can give prominence to this feature and ensure that other details in the scene do not compete for attention. Three very effective methods – used singly or in combination – will help to achieve this emphasis. First, you can frame the subject in such a way that distracting details are eliminated. In the picture at left below, the photographer excluded the horizon line, which would have marred the effect of the net outlined against the water. Second, you can make use of color or tonal contrasts between the subject and surrounding areas, as in the pictures of the beach sign and the bowler. Third, you can limit the depth of field by selecting a wide aperture and closing in on the main point, so that the subject appears in sharp relief. Both the bowler and the rose at bottom right on the opposite page were picked out in this way.

The strong shapes of both the net and the fisherman required careful framing to limit the picture to these vital elements. The photographer chose a vertical format and aimed the camera downward to eliminate the horizon and obtain a plain background.

The signpost, one small detail in a cluttered beach scene, would lack any impact if photographed from a distance. The photographer spotted the graphic shape and exciting color contrast, and moved in close to isolate the subject from unimportant foreground elements.

At ground level with a 200 mm lens, the photographer was able to combine dramatically this English lawn bowler's white target and his curious pose as he sent down another bowl from 30 yards away. The telephoto lens helped to isolate the subject with its narrow angle of view and a shallow depth of field.

1

2

3

Concentrating on the subject
A general view of a dog-rose bush (1) lacks a definite focus of interest. By closing in and framing one main bloom against green leaves (2), the photographer improved the picture. Opening the aperture wider (3) isolated a single in-focus flower.

Harmony and balance

The basic principles of composition that underlie most successful photographs are not rules to be followed slavishly. But understanding them will help you to produce balanced and pleasing images.

A key principle is that the main subject should occupy a strong position in the frame. One method of locating such a position is to divide the scene in the viewfinder into thirds, horizontally and vertically, as shown in the diagram at bottom right on the opposite page. The four intersecting points are all areas of strength within the frame, and placing the main subject a third of the way across the frame can work well providing there are other elements to balance the image. In pictures with a single point of interest, the "golden section" is a more useful principle. This classical rule governing aesthetic proportions places the subject slightly closer to the center, thus avoiding imbalance if there is a large area of empty frame. The diagrams at the top of the opposite page illustrate the difference between these two approaches. Both principles have the practical effect of placing the subject off-center, so that an image is not too symmetrical and static. However, if a subject depends on symmetry for effect, as in the image below, the central position may be the best.

Another important way to create effective pictures is to use lines or tones to lead the viewer's eye toward the main subject. Converging lines will draw the eye, as will a gradation of tones, with a dark-toned foreground leading back to progressively lighter tones around the main point of interest. The landscape photograph below at right shows both of these techniques.

Color relationships can be used to great effect in balancing an image. For example, a small area of bright color, placed on one division of thirds, could keep the eye from being drawn too heavily toward a main subject positioned on the other third. Conversely, strong colors or highlights near an edge of the frame can spoil a composition by diverting attention away from the main point.

The stylized symmetry of the facade at right would have been less striking had the photographer not carefully centered the subject. The picture at right shows how a human figure, when placed on two of the strong lines, adds interest and prevents the image from being too static.

Positions in the frame

The four diagrams show how the positioning of the subject will affect the balance of the composition.

1–This diagram shows the eye's view of the scene.

2– With the main point of the picture in the center, the image is dull.

3–A more interesting effect emerges.with the scene divided into thirds by the figure and the house on the intersections.

4–With the main subject standing alone, the best position is on the golden section, dividing the frame into proportions of eight to five.

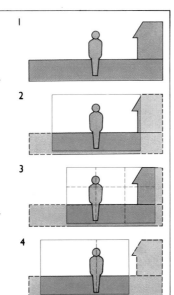

Skeins of wool in perfect visual balance make up a satisfying abstract image. Using a close-up lens, the photographer framed the picture to give more space to the lighter yellow wool, while a loose strand from the weightier blue pulls the elements together.

A tree laden with blossoms commands the horizon. As the diagram below demonstrates, the tree and the yellow field, a supporting subject, both lie on a dividing line of thirds. The slope of the field leads the eye down toward the main point, while the dark foreground draws the viewer into the frame.

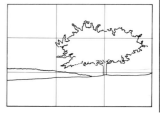

Form and the image

Although shapes alone can make striking images, the information they convey is too limited to show whether an object in a picture has weight, solidity and depth. For this, a viewer needs some indication of form – some variation of light and shade within the outline. Such tonal variations are what give objects the illusion of depth in a photograph.

Light alone governs form, providing the visual clues that convey an object's bumps, hollows, curves or receding surfaces. For example, an orange lit strongly from behind will appear only as a dark, flat disc. But if you soften the light, the shadows on the outer rim will begin to lighten and indicate the orange's curving sides. And if you move the light around so that it falls obliquely on the orange, the gradation of tone from highlights to shadow will reveal the full roundness.

The quality and direction of light best suited to revealing form depends to some extent on the subject. Oblique morning sunlight raking across modern buildings may bring out their angular forms dramatically. But when you want to show more softly rounded curves, as in the picture of weed-covered boulders on the opposite page, the soft light of a cloudy day will give a better impression of form. Bright sun would have thrown a confusing pattern of light and shade over the rocks. For the same reason, moderately diffused light is best for revealing the subtle forms of the face when you want to achieve a balanced effect in portraiture.

Dappled sunlight *models the soft, rounded forms of a polar bear and the ledge it stands on. Flatter light would not have separated bear and background so well.*

Lustrous grapes, *lit obliquely by a low, angled spotlight, have an almost tactile plumpness – an effect created by the play of highlights and shadows.*

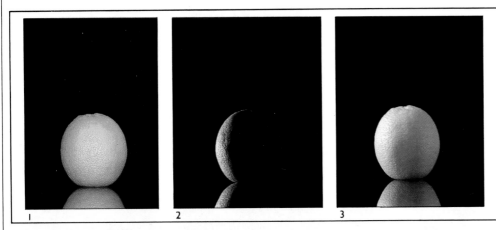

Light and form

Frontal lighting (1) shows relatively little of the orange's form. But harsh sidelighting (2) also may disguise form by picking out only one edge. Softer light from one side (3), and the use of a reflector to direct some light back to the other side, gives a truer picture of the rounded form and the texture of the orange.

1 2 3

Sea-washed boulders in this simple study take on a sculptural power because variations of tone and hue, revealed by diffused light, convey their rounded weight.

Pattern

Patterns depend on the repetition of similar shapes, forms, lines or colors. Because such repetitions attract our instinctive attention, they can be a powerful ingredient in photography. And you can easily compose pictures to bring out patterns by identifying repeated elements in a scene and then isolating the part of the view that contains them. In the three pictures here, close framing of much larger subjects has emphasized the patterns they contained and excluded any distracting elements.

Landscapes make excellent subjects for experiments in photographing patterns. The furrows of a plowed field following the contours of the land, or the regularly planted rows of trees, as in the huge olive grove on the opposite page, give visual structure to scenes that might otherwise appear featureless. You can accentuate such patterns when the light from a low sun at right angles to the camera casts shadows that emphasize the repeated shapes of trees or the snaking lines of ridges and hollows in the land. The higher sun of midday tends to fill in the shadows and make a landscape seem flat. For example, in this kind of light the olive trees would have merged more with the parched ground, and their pattern would have been less striking.

The man-made environment is also full of patterns. Standardization of manufactured objects in bold colors and clean shapes creates infinite possibilities for anyone with an alert eye. The umbrellas below were scattered randomly to dry, but the photographer chose a viewpoint that creates order through repetition of shapes, lines and colors.

A lone couple walking in the forest provide a focus for the pattern created by the rows of tall trees lining their way. The photographer centered the path perfectly and kept the camera level so the trees would appear vertical in the picture.

Gaudy umbrellas lie in a jumble that the photographer organized by framing. A small aperture ensured that the entire depth of the subject would be in focus.

The strength of line

Line is often the basis of composition. Look at a scene through half-closed eyes and you will notice that a few strong lines or contours give definition to everything else. At the same time, lines generate a sense of movement into or around a picture space, because we instinctively follow them with our eyes.

Analyzing a random selection of successful photographs will give you an idea of the many ways of exploiting linear effects to support or enhance subjects. Lines can balance an image, drawing the eye toward the main point of interest and linking other elements together, or they can cause discord. The flowing contours of a figure can suggest a supple roundness, as in the picture at the bottom of this page. And at the right time of day, deep shadows in a landscape can create the kind of strong graphic lines seen in the picture of sand dunes below. Although here the flat, solid tones exaggerate the two-dimensional quality of photography, lines can also be a powerful means of creating an illusion of depth. The converging lines of a street or of an avenue of trees receding into the distance are examples of classic linear perspective. The picture of power lines opposite illustrates a more unusual perspective effect: the lines do not meet in the distance, but sweep up sharply out of the frame.

Often the mood of a picture is affected by the sort of lines that dominate. Angles and jagged edges tend to convey a sense of aggression and restless energy, whereas the gentler rhythms of curves, especially those of the human body, can suggest a soft, romantic mood.

Dense shadows create a sinuous ribbon that divides these dunes into abstract shapes. The photographer obtained these strong lines and dramatic tonal contrasts by taking the picture when the sun was low in the sky.

The gentle contour of a nude woman reclining on her side (right) suggests warmth and sensuousness. Broad, diffused light bounced from a large reflector creates a subtle tonal interplay that helps to soften the contour.

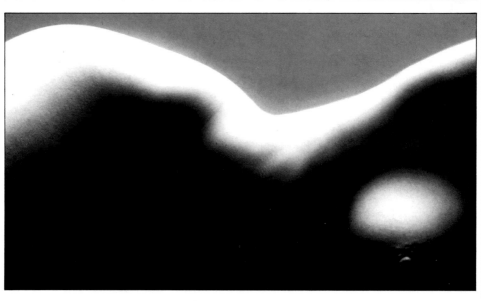

Power cables spanning a deep valley form a network of fine, intricate lines looping upward out of the frame. The effect of the bright sunlight highlighting the cables makes them stand out boldly against the dark background.

Surface texture

With the right lighting, you can pick out rugged surfaces in sharp textural relief or reveal a fine texture in surfaces that seem almost completely smooth to the eye. The photographs on these pages show the importance of lighting in recording the different textural characteristics of a range of subjects.

Generally, to bring out texture the light should come from an oblique angle so as to rake the surface of the subject, highlighting each small relief and creating shadows within the indentations. The lower of the two pictures of sculpture at right shows how shadows bring out the relief. A subject with a very delicate texture, such as an eggshell, needs more acutely angled light than does a coarse-textured subject, such as tree bark.

The quality of light is also important. As a rule of thumb, finely textured surfaces need softer, more diffused lighting to bring out their qualities than do rough surfaces in pictures that seek more dramatic effects. The bright highlights and dense shadows cast by strong light will obscure finer details, although a hard light can suit glossy surfaces, such as the painted door at far right.

Oblique light and low relief
Lighting can accentuate or mask a subject's overall texture, as these pictures of an architectural relief sculpture demonstrate.
(1) The soft, diffused light of early morning shows the design as almost flat.
(2) Late in the day, the sun casts a strong, raking sidelight that picks out the relief and the texture of the old, weathered stone.

1

2

A sleeping owl perches in a tree hollow. Soft, low-angled sunlight picks up the pattern of feathers and creates an extraordinary but illusory resemblance between the harsh texture of the ridged bark and the downy softness of the owl.

Rough and smooth, shiny and mat surfaces make an attractive combination in the still-life on the opposite page. Bright, diffused sidelighting brings out the contrasting textures of the crusty loaves of bread, the wooden surfaces and the ceramic pot.

A smooth surface can be
just as interesting as a rough
one. Here, strongly oblique
light shining on a gloss-painted
door shows up the slick, heavily
coated texture.

Oblique light and high relief
The papery seed pods at
left have rounded forms that
present a higher relief to
an oblique light than do the
fine sculpted ridges opposite.
(1) Soft light shows a delicate
tracery of veins in the seed
pods, but the picture works
mainly as a color pattern.
(2) Hard, oblique light shows
some texture better, and the
shadows bring out the forms
of the pods.

YOU AND YOUR CAMERA

Photography combines two different areas of skill. On the one hand, you need to develop an ability to see creatively, identifying interesting and appealing visual aspects of the world around you. But you also need the ability to translate these photographic ideas into pictures. The camera and film can become efficient servants of your creative impulse – if you learn how to use them.

This is partly a question of mastering essential photographic skills – the principles of camera handling, focusing and exposure that apply to all cameras, however complex or simple. You will handle a camera more confidently if you have a clear understanding of the basic relationship between light, camera and film as explained in the following pages. Try to develop a close familiarity with your own camera also, so that using its controls becomes second nature. The functions and operation of these controls are explained here, but you must study your own camera to see how the principles can be most effectively applied.

Finally, consider your camera in relation to the type of photographs you intend to take. Know the limitations of your equipment and work within them. You will need a camera with a fast shutter to freeze rapid movement, for example. But if you already have one why not go and find some exciting action so as to test the camera's fastest speed? Photography is most enjoyable when you have equipment that extends slightly beyond your current capabilities or needs. As your skill grows, you will value the greater versatility your camera provides.

*Good technique is here
symbolized by a graphic
image that suggests the
photographer's sure-handed
mastery of the camera's
controls in framing and
sharply focusing his subject.*

Light, lens and film

The word photography means "drawing with light," a phrase that conveys both the creative and the chemical nature of the photographic process. A camera is simply a device for bringing together in a sharp image the light reflected from a scene and allowing it briefly to touch a film material so sensitive that the light leaves a trace, which can be developed into a finished picture.

To form an image, light has only to pass through a pinhole into a dark area and fall on a screen. The modern camera uses a lens and variable-size opening, or aperture, instead of a simple hole, and has a shutter that allows light in for fractions of time, which the photographer can control.

The advantage of a lens is that it can gather and focus light into a sharp, bright image. After collecting the light rays scattering out from every point on the subject, the lens bends them through precisely determined angles to meet again as points. These countless points, varying in color and brightness, form an image that is an exact copy of the subject's pattern of light. As shown in the diagram, the rays of light travel through the lens in such a way that this image arrives upside down and reversed, with light from the top of the subject brought to focus at the bottom of the image.

The film lies behind the lens on the plane where the light rays form a sharp image when the lens is focused for distant subjects. As a subject gets closer to the camera, its sharp image falls farther and farther behind the lens; hence, the lens must be moved forward in order to keep the image in focus on the film.

When the photographer opens the shutter, light from the subject begins to act on an emulsion coating on the film that contains crystals of silver halides. These salts of silver are extremely light-sensitive. They darken when exposed to light, much as skin tans in sunlight — but infinitely quicker. The light triggers a chemical change in the salts so that they start to form microscopic grains of black silver. Where more light strikes the film, more crystals are triggered. This process, however, is not visible to the naked eye, and the film requires chemical development before an image of the black silver pattern appears. The lightest areas of the subject — such as the sky — look black because they caused most silver to form, while shadow areas that sent no light to the film appear blank. The result is a *negative* image, which can be reversed in printing to make a *positive* image — recreating the tones (and with color films, the colors) of the original scene.

Anatomy of a camera

The parts of a camera, reduced to a schematic form, show in essence what a simple apparatus it is – a box for gathering and forming an image of the subject. Cameras come in many different shapes and sizes, but they all operate on the basic principles shown below.

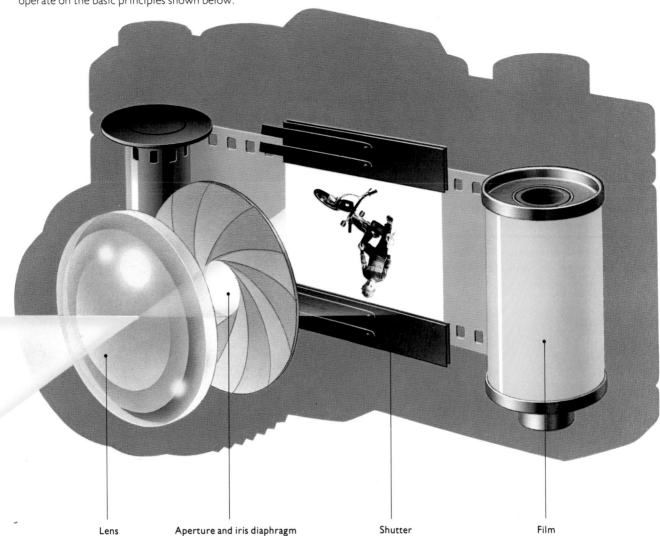

Lens   Aperture and iris diaphragm   Shutter   Film

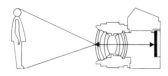

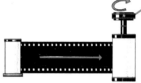

The lens brings the image into sharp focus on the film. Moving the lens forward or back changes the lens-to-film distance, focusing near or far subjects.

The aperture regulates the light entering the camera, usually by means of an iris diaphragm. This is a continuously variable ring of overlapping metal blades.

The shutter controls the length of time light falls onto the film. A common type exposes the film through an opening between two blinds that travel across the film.

The film, held flat at the focal plane, receives the image and records it. The film is wound on after each exposure, permitting a number of shots on each roll.

The camera you use

The variety of camera shapes and sizes may seem bewildering, but there is good reason for this diversity: cameras are designed for different tasks as well as different price brackets. Some are ideal for snapshots, and other, bigger cameras are more suited to applications that demand an image of exceptionally high quality.

Of all the different types, the 35mm camera is the most convenient compromise between image quality and ease of use. The term "35mm" refers to the width of the film, which comes in a long sprocketted strip loaded into a metal cassette. The actual size of a standard 35mm negative is $1 \times 1\frac{1}{2}$ inches – large enough to make quality prints as big as this page, but small enough for the camera that carries it to be reasonably compact.

The most versatile type of 35mm camera is the single lens reflex, or SLR for short. The term refers to the viewing system, which makes the camera extremely easy to use. A mirror reflects light from the single lens up to the viewfinder and shows exactly what is going to appear on film. Focusing and composing the picture is thus made simple. What makes the SLR so versatile is that its lens is removable and can be replaced by others that give different views or perform specialized tasks.

In addition to the SLR, there are other 35mm cameras. Single use cameras come ready loaded with film and can be used only once. Compact cameras have a fixed lens, and a direct viewfinder which gives *approximately* the same view as the camera lens. Most compacts are fully automated and are very easy to use. Hybrid cameras combine the fixed lens and point-and-shoot simplicity of a compact with the through-the-lens (TTL) viewing of an SLR camera.

Medium and large format cameras use film formats larger than 35mm. These cameras produce top quality images and are favoured by professional photographers.

Accessory shoe – five directly coupled contacts link up with corresponding contacts on foot of dedicated flash unit

Built-in, pop up flash unit

LCD panel – shows status of shutter speed, aperture and other camera functions

Electronic input dial – adjusts camera settings

Shutter release

AF illuminator/self-timer indicator – light is projected on to the subject to aid autofocusing when lighting conditions are dim. In self timer mode, lamp starts blinking just before exposure is made

AF lens

35mm SLR

The distinctive body shape of the 35mm SLR is due to its viewing system. The camera is instantly recognizable by the central hump, housing the viewing prism and eyepiece. Modern SLRs are made from lightweight metal and plastic materials, but they still incorporate a reflex mirror behind the lens, so they are generally bigger and heavier than direct vision cameras such as compacts. SLRs range from basic, manually operated types to highly sophisticated electronically controlled models like the one shown here. Modern versions provide advanced features such as accurate autofocus systems and built-in motordrives. Even the simplest, however, incorporates a light-measuring system to advise on exposure.

SLR viewing system

The mirror and pentaprism in an SLR camera (left) let you see the image formed by the lens exactly as it will fall on the film. Light passing through the lens is reflected by the mirror onto a focusing screen, positioned at the same distance from the lens as is the film. This image is then converted by a five-sided prism (the pentaprism) so it can be viewed right way up and right way round. The mirror flips up out of the way when the shutter is released, thus allowing the light to reach the film.

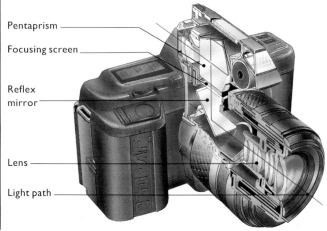

Pentaprism

Focusing screen

Reflex mirror

Lens

Light path

Function buttons and
second electronic input
dial on back of camera

Shooting mode selector
– sets exposure mode

Built-in, pop-up flash

Zoom control –
used to alter
focal length of
zoom lens

Fixed
zoom
lens

Contoured handgrip

Lens release button

Manual focusing ring

Hybrid 35mm camera

These cameras bridge the gap between the versatility offered
by 35mm SLRs and the point-and-shoot simplicity of compact
cameras – hence, they are commonly referred to as 'bridge
cameras'. They are built around a fixed AF zoom lens, with an
extensive focal length range, and are characterized by their
space age styling. The self-contained design of hybrid cameras
incorporates a built-in flash unit and motordrive and an array of
advanced exposure modes and metering patterns.

Single use 35mm camera

These inexpensive cameras
comprise a 35mm film
housed in a small box, which
is fitted with a basic film
advance control and a fixed
aperture, plastic lens on the
front. When the film is
finished, you send the
camera to the lab. You get a
set of prints back but not
the camera. Exposure is
fixed and exposure errors
are corrected at the printing
stage where possible.

Compact camera

Lightweight and fully automated, compacts are perfect for
snapshots. Some models have a single focal length lens – usually
a moderately wide angle, which gives an extensive field of view
and great depth of field. Others have dual lenses, giving you a
choice between a wide angle and a short telephoto. However,
the most versatile compacts, like the one shown above, sport
fixed zoom lenses. You can set any focal length within a limited
range, and the size of the image in the viewfinder changes
accordingly. Some models let you shoot long thin pictures, by
selecting a panoramic mode.

What to do first

Nothing is more disappointing than taking a whole series of pictures and then discovering that the film did not wind through the camera because of incorrect loading in the first place. Happily, the automatic loading mechanisms of most modern cameras make this a rare occurrence, but it can still happen if you don't take sufficient care.

With an unfamiliar camera, always read the instructions to acquaint yourself with the layout and operation of the controls. This is especially important with older cameras like the one in the diagram at the bottom of the page. Loading newer cameras is usually simple, but you should always do it in the shade. Cassettes of 35mm film are not entirely light-proof and direct sun can spoil the first few pictures.

Once you have dropped the cassette into the film compartment you need only draw out the film leader across the camera until it reaches an index mark close to the take-up spool. Closing the camera back advances the film to the first frame, and you are ready to take pictures. Before you do so, though, you should check that the film is loaded correctly, and that there is sufficient battery power. Most cameras have indicators to verify that there are no problems, as shown on the right, and on many the shutter will not fire if the film is loaded incorrectly. However, if your camera is an older model that lacks a film advance symbol, take a look at the rewind knob each time the film advances. If your film is loaded correctly, the rewind knob will turn after each picture.

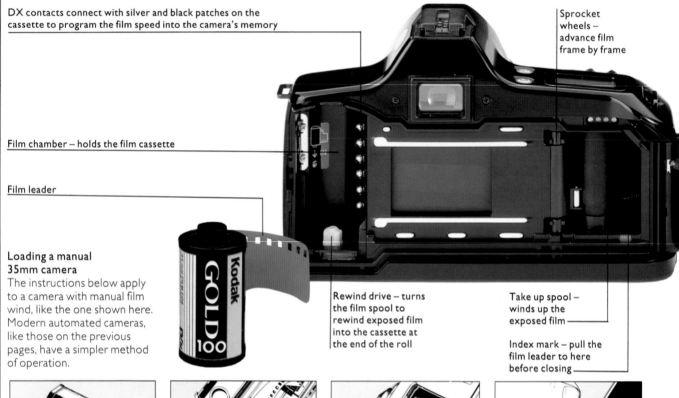

DX contacts connect with silver and black patches on the cassette to program the film speed into the camera's memory

Sprocket wheels – advance film frame by frame

Film chamber – holds the film cassette

Film leader

Loading a manual 35mm camera
The instructions below apply to a camera with manual film wind, like the one shown here. Modern automated cameras, like those on the previous pages, have a simpler method of operation.

Rewind drive – turns the film spool to rewind exposed film into the cassette at the end of the roll

Take up spool – winds up the exposed film

Index mark – pull the film leader to here before closing

1–In the shade, hold the camera firmly by the lens and pull up the rewind knob to open the camera back. Keep the knob raised.

2–Place the film in the left-hand chamber, then push in the rewind knob, turning it until it clicks firmly down into place.

3–Turn the film lip forward and insert the tongue into one of the slits in the take-up spool. Fit the bottom row of holes over the sprockets.

4–Next, click the shutter and wind on to ensure that the sprockets begin to engage both top and bottom rows of perforations.

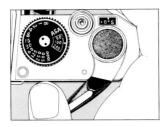

Viewfinder displays

A few cameras provide the photographer with no viewfinder information at all, but most have at least an under/overexposure warning and show the shutter speed. This diagram shows a typical viewfinder display on an autofocus SLR.

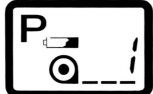

Manual exposure indicator

Shutter speed

Aperture

Autofocus frame – indicates the area on which the camera will focus

In-focus indicator – flashes when camera cannot focus correctly

Flash ready indicator

Exposure compensation indicator

Film and power

Some cameras have a film cassette symbol to show that the film is loaded correctly – if the symbol blinks, the film is loaded incorrectly. On other cameras the frame counter will not advance to '1' when the film is loaded incorrectly.

A battery symbol indicates the camera's power level. The symbol appears full when new batteries are inserted. When the batteries are exhausted and need replacing the symbol appears empty.

Film speed – indicates sensitivity of the film to light

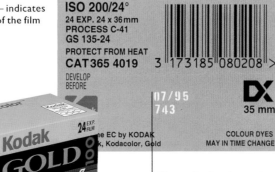

ISO 200/24°
24 EXP. 24 x 36 mm
PROCESS C-41
GS 135-24
PROTECT FROM HEAT
CAT 365 4019   3 173185 080208 >
DEVELOP BEFORE
07/95
743
DX
35 mm
COLOUR DYES
MAY IN TIME CHANGE

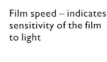

Film expiration date – shows date by which film should be used for best results

5–Close the camera back and continue advancing the film until the number for the first exposure appears in the exposure counter window.

6–To unload, release the rewind catch or button, lift the rewind crank, and turn it clockwise until it suddenly turns more easily.

Setting film speed

The film speed is marked on the film box and on the cassette. Most modern 35mm films are DX-coded. Cameras with DX contacts (as above left) can read the DX code and set the film speed automatically. But older 35mm cameras have a film speed dial (as shown on the right) that must be set manually to match the speed of the film loaded.

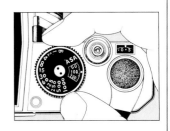

Focusing the image

To achieve sharp images you need to focus the image on the film. To do this you move the lens forwards and backwards to change its distance from the film. Moving the lens farther away from the film brings into focus objects that are closer to the camera.

Except for some of the most basic compacts, all cameras offer some means of controlling the movement of the lens. Manual focus SLRs have a focusing control ring around the barrel of the lens. Turning this ring moves the lens backwards and forwards. Focusing aids at the center of the focusing screen help you judge when the image is in sharp focus. These are often a pair of semicircular prisms – which are together called a split image rangefinder – that split an unsharp image across the middle. When you turn the lens and bring the image into sharp focus, the prisms move together to form a perfectly aligned picture in the camera's viewfinder.

Around the split image rangefinder – or sometimes instead of it – is a ring of tiny prisms of a similar shape. These microprisms break up an unsharp image so that it appears shattered into countless fragments.

Autofocus cameras, as their name suggests, bring a subject to sharp focus automatically, though autofocus lenses for SLRs usually have a manual focusing control ring as well. In most compact cameras, autofocus relies on an infrared beam (or beams) emitted when you press the shutter release. This scans across the subject at the same time as the lens retracts – focusing from near to far. A sensor detects when the beam hits the subject and at the same moment the movement of the lens is stopped. This system, known as an "active" focusing system, works as well in darkness as in daylight.

The system used in most autofocus SLRs is "passive": it depends on sensors behind the lens which detect the sharpness of the image by measuring contrast. This system is very accurate, though it may struggle in poor light or with low contrast subjects – such as a clear sky or a flat wall in shade.

The advantage of the SLR system is that it can focus the lens at any distance. The "active" system is less accurate as it focuses the lens at a series of discrete distances or "steps" – as little as two or as many as 2,000. The more "steps" there are, the more accurately the lens is focused and the sharper the pictures are.

Whatever type of camera you use, in most pictures, a zone that looks acceptably sharp extends behind and in front of the plane you have focused on. The depth of this zone depends on several factors, including the size of the lens aperture, as pages 70-71 explain. But the diagram on the right, here, shows that an important factor is the distance of the subject from the lens. The closer you are to your subject, the more accurately you must focus the image.

The focusing control ring
Turning the wide, knurled ring focuses subjects at varying distances (indicated in feet and meters just under the ring). The ring moves the lens farther from the film for a subject only 3 ft away (left) than for far subjects (right), which are indicated by a symbol representing infinity (∞).

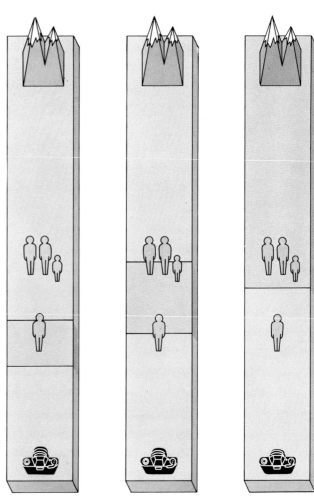

How much is in focus?
At close distances, only a very shallow part of a scene appears sharp (red zone above left). If you are taking a head-and-shoulders portrait, for example, at a range of a few feet, the background will blur (ocher area). The zone of sharp focus becomes progressively wider as you focus on more distant subjects (central group) until eventually the lens brings into focus objects in a zone stretching far back from the middle distance.

SLR manual focusing
The viewfinder contains a split circle in the center. When the subject is out of focus a straight line passing through this circle will be dislocated (right). In focus, the two split halves coincide (below).

Advanced autofocus modes
Most modern cameras, both 35mm SLR and compact, now have autofocus mechanisms that focus the lens for you. There are, however, many different types of autofocus mode, each designed for a different task.

In "one shot" autofocus mode, half pressing the shutter release activates the autofocus mechanism. The camera then focuses on the part of the image covered by the autofocus frame and locks the lens at this setting – provided the shutter release is kept half pressed. A viewfinder symbol indicates that the lens is correctly focused, and the shutter will not fire until the symbol appears.

In "continuous" mode, as long as the shutter release is kept half pressed, the camera constantly adjusts the lens to compensate for a subject's movements – up to the moment the shutter is released. The shutter can be released at any time.

"Predictive" autofocus is a more advanced version of continuous autofocus. The camera calculates the speed and direction in which the subject is travelling. It then predicts where the subject will be at the precise moment the shutter opens, and adjusts focus accordingly.

"Multizone" autofocus uses several focus frames – usually three or five, spread across the viewfinder – enabling you to focus on off-center subjects without moving the camera. The most sophisticated system, known as "eye controlled" autofocus, allows you to select focus frames simply by *looking* at them. A frame lights up when it is selected.

Moving subjects
Modern cameras with "predictive" autofocus mode can focus accurately on fast moving subjects like this skier (left). But for other autofocus cameras a rapid subject can be a problem. The solution may be to pre-focus on a spot in front of the subject and release the shutter just before the subject reaches this point.

Off-center subjects
Cameras with "multizone" autofocus cope well with off-center subjects. But cameras with a central focus frame only (as above) are easily fooled into focusing on the background rather than on the subject. The solution is to put the autofocus frame over the subject, lock the autofocus, then reframe the picture before finally taking the shot.

The shutter

The shutter is the basic picture-taking control on a camera. Releasing it smoothly, at just the right moment, makes all the difference to a shot. Never hurry – the secret of sharp, well-timed pictures is to be ready, and anticipate the moment, squeezing the release gently when you feel everything in the viewfinder is perfect.

Choosing the right shutter speed is just as important. It affects both sharpness and exposure. The numbers on the shutter speed dial or LCD panel are called speeds, but they are actually exposure times – seconds and fractions of a second for which the shutter stays open, exposing the film to the image-forming light projected by the lens. For simplicity, 30 is used to mean 1/30 second, and 60 to mean 1/60 second. The higher the number, the faster the speed and the briefer the exposure. Doubling a shutter number – for example, from 30 to 60 – halves the exposure time. Most SLR cameras have a fastest shutter speed of 1/1000, 1/2000, 1/4000 or 1/8000, but SLRs with a top speed of 1/12,000 are available.

For a sharp picture, the fastest practical shutter speed is the safest to use, because the less time during which light from an image falls onto the film, the less time there is for any subject movement or camera shake to blur the photograph. Camera shake while the shutter is open is probably the commonest cause of disappointing pictures.

A safe working speed for handheld shots with a normal lens is 1/125 second – fast enough to stop camera shake and freeze all except rapid motion. Close-ups and shots with telephoto lenses need faster speeds – 1/250 or 1/500 second – and so do active scenes such as children playing.

In practice, the choice is often limited by the lighting – in dimmer light longer exposures are needed, and this makes it difficult to freeze movement. On dull days or indoors, speeds below 1/60 second may be required for an adequate picture, and then it is necessary to provide the camera with a support – if possible, use a tripod and a cable release.

At slow shutter speeds, any movement blurs the image. *In the picture below of a girl roller skating in a park, a speed of 1/30 dissolves her whole body into streaks of color.*

Setting shutter speed

Shutter speed is set using a variety of controls, depending on the camera make. Generally, an LCD panel shows the shutter speed chosen (1/4000 in this example). Older cameras have a dial to set the speed. Most of the more advanced cameras offer a choice of shutter speeds in the range 30 seconds to 1/8000, though a few models offer faster and slower speeds.

Slow speeds				
4 secs	2 secs	1 sec	1/2	1/4

Camera handling

Slow speeds are suitable not only for static subjects but also when you want to suggest movement impressionistically. The lights of city traffic at night (left) have been blurred into vivid, rushing streaks by using a shutter speed of 1/4.

At medium speeds (here 1/125), *there is still some blur, but it shows mainly in the hands and feet – the parts of the body that are moving at greatest speed.*

Fast shutter speeds will freeze all movement. At 1/500, the girl's body, hands and feet are sharp, even though she is racing toward the camera at full tilt.

		Medium speeds		Fast speeds				
1/8	1/15	1/30	1/60	1/125	1/250	1/500	1/1000	1/2000
Camera support needed		Extra care required with handheld camera		Safe to handhold with standard lenses	Safe to handhold with telephoto lenses			

Medium speeds are the usual choice for everyday scenes, and are also needed for flash pictures, such as the one at left. Most cameras have a top flash synchronization speed of between 1/60 and 1/200. Set this speed or a slower speed when using flash.

Fast speeds of above 1/500 are useful for action pictures or with telephoto lenses, which magnify movement and are difficult to hold steady. The flashing hooves of the racehorses on the left were frozen with a shutter speed of 1/1000.

The aperture

The aperture is the opening of the lens through which light enters the camera. On all but the simplest cameras, you can increase or decrease the opening, usually by means of an iris diaphragm, and this is one of the principal ways of controlling how the picture will look. Widening the aperture allows more light to reach the film. Together with shutter speed (which controls the amount of time during which light can affect the film), this determines the exposure – the total amount of light that reaches the film. The other important function of the aperture is that it affects depth of field – the zone of sharp focus in a scene, extending from the nearest element that is sharp to the farthest. Because wrong focus is less noticeable if the effective lens area is reduced, depth of field increases as aperture size decreases.

Aperture is adjusted in a series of stops, each full stop doubling or halving the amount of light let in. These stops are arranged in a coded numerical series called f-numbers, running in a standard sequence f/1, f/1.4, f/2, f/2.8, f/4, f/5.6, f/8, f/11, f/16, f/22. Some cameras let you set the aperture in third stops or half stops – such as f/13, which indicates an aperture setting halfway between f/11 and f/16. The numbers get bigger as the aperture opening gets smaller. Thus, f/16 is a small aperture and lets in less light than f/2. The system ensures that the same f-number lets the same amount of light reach the film, irrespective of the size and type of lens you use.

A lens's lowest f-number indicates the largest aperture the lens can provide, often between f/1.4 and f/4. To let you view the subject clearly, modern lenses usually stay open at this maximum aperture until you press the shutter release, then the aperture "stops down" to the selected f-number. This means that while you view and focus on the subject, near and far objects may look fuzzy because the aperture has not yet stopped down and improved the depth of field. Many cameras have a depth of field preview button (below). When pressed, it alters the image in the viewfinder to show the actual extent of sharpness.

At maximum aperture, used for the picture below, depth of field is very shallow. Only the main focused subject is sharp. Foreground and background are blurred.

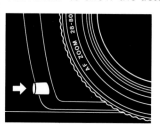

SLR preview button
This is often on, or by, the lens. You simply press it to preview the true depth of field of the aperture.

Aperture scale
The sequence of f-stops is shown at right, light being halved at each setting. The pictures below the scale show the effect on exposure if the aperture is reduced without slowing the shutter speed. By using a preview button, you can see the image darkening at each stop as the aperture steadily cuts the light admitted.

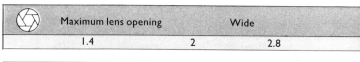

	Maximum lens opening	Wide
	1.4	2	2.8

f/2 Bright image, shallow depth of field

f/2.8 One stop down

At a medium aperture, depth of field is greater. The farthest child and most of the background are sharp. But the boy in the foreground is still out of focus.

At minimum aperture, depth of field is so great that even the foreground boy is sharp. The shot needed a slow shutter speed at this aperture, so any movement would have blurred.

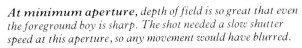

Medium			Small		Minimum lens opening
4	5.6	8	11	16	22

f/4 Two stops down

f/5.6 Three stops down

f/8 Four stops down

f/11 Five stops down, good depth of field

71

How lenses control the image

In its ability to capture and focus the image of a subject on film, the lens is the most important part of the camera. The size and appearance of the image can vary greatly according to the type of lens you are using. And as all 35mm SLRs can be fitted with interchangeable lenses, photographers need to understand some basic lens characteristic.

How much of the scene a lens can capture depends on its angle of view – the way it sees the subject in front of the camera. This is determined by the focal length of the lens – in simple terms the distance from the optical center of the lens to the film plane when focus is set to infinity. Focal length is marked on the front of the lens in millimeters, and this is how lenses are normally described – as 28mm, 50mm or 135mm lenses, for example. Most lenses are within a range from 18mm to about 600mm, although shorter and longer focal lengths can be obtained for more specialized purposes.

Lenses with short focal lengths can convey to the film more of a scene than the eye itself can see when looking through a frame the same size as the viewfinder. They do this by sharply bending the light passing through them, making each object in the scene appear smaller than the eye would see it and, by means of this optical shrinkage, fitting more objects into the frame. For this reason, lenses of short focal length are called wide-angle lenses. The most extreme of them is the so-called fisheye lens, which produces bizarre distortions by compressing an exceptionally wide view onto the relatively small format of the film. At the other end of the scale, telephoto lenses – with long focal lengths – bend the light from the subject relatively little, and produce an enlarged image of a small part of the view, as does a telescope.

From a single camera position, you can thus produce completely different views of the subject by

1 – A 28mm wide-angle lens takes in a broad view of the subject, but makes the distant buildings appear smaller than they would to the eye. This view of the Manhattan skyline from Liberty Island includes a large expanse of the stormy sky that loomed over the city when the shot was taken – and links near and far elements of the scene. But New York's famous skyline looks relatively insignificant.

2 – A 50mm standard lens renders the scene more as the eye would see it. The photographer aimed higher to keep in much of the sky but exclude the foreground. The lens helps to emphasize the city skyline, and the view is relatively wide.

using different lenses. With a wide-angle lens, a human figure can be shown as part of an extensive landscape, or you can close in on the face alone with a telephoto lens. The enormous flexibility gained by having interchangeable lenses is one of the great advantages of the 35mm SLR camera. On the other hand, individual lenses are expensive and also heavy to carry around. One solution is the zoom lens, which has an infinitely variable focal length within a set range, allowing you to achieve a variety of framings and subject enlargements with a single lens. But be careful; top quality zooms are very expensive and they usually have smaller maximum apertures than do equivalent lenses of fixed focal length. Zoom lenses are also heavier than similar lenses of fixed focal length because of their complex construction, and so may be more difficult to handle. The six pages that follow introduce the major types of lenses and the creative uses to which they can be put.

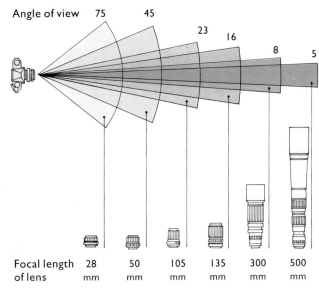

Angle of view	75	45	23	16	8	5
Focal length of lens	28 mm	50 mm	105 mm	135 mm	300 mm	500 mm

Angle of view

The lenses shown above with their angles of view are those most commonly used with 35mm SLRs. Note that the lens with the widest angle of view requires only a short body. Longer lenses can reach out farther to close in on (and enlarge) distant details. But as the focal length increases, the extent of the view decreases, both in width and in height. Cameras with film formats larger than 35mm require lenses of longer focal length to achieve the same results, because more enlargement is needed to cover the larger area of the film itself.

3 – A 135mm telephoto lens brings forward the buildings in the same scene, making the twin towers of the World Trade Center the dominant subject. The sky now takes up a much smaller part of the frame, and the skyline is reduced in width.

The size we see

The 35mm SLR camera comes fitted with a 50mm lens (or sometimes 55mm) – the so-called standard lens. Many photographers never use any other lens, and still take perfectly good pictures.

The most striking feature of the image produced by a standard lens is the naturalness of its perspective. Because wide-angle lenses take in a broad view of the subject, they actually appear to reduce the scale of distant objects in relation to those in the foreground, thus exaggerating the perspective effect by which objects appear smaller the farther away they are. Telephoto lenses have the reverse effect, appearing to compress objects together despite the distance between them. The standard lens, on the other hand, reproduces the scene with its perspective much as the eye sees it. In a sense, photography is most objective with a standard lens – the camera shows the world essentially as we see it.

Because standard lenses are produced in large quantities, they are relatively cheap. They are also extremely versatile. They are suitable for near and distant subjects, accurately focusing subjects at a considerable distance and within two feet of the lens. And they can be used in low light – or with fast shutter speeds in action shots – because they have wide maximum apertures: f/1.8 is common and f/1.4 is not unusual. Taking good pictures with standard lenses needs skill, however. As there is no strong special photographic feature such as dramatic magnification to compensate for poor composition, the image can easily appear bland. More than with any other lens, you must frame the picture accurately and compose it carefully.

Street portraits look more natural when taken with a standard lens – the distortion-free images it forms closely resemble the world as seen with our eyes.

The standard lens
The photographer's work-horse, the 50mm or 55mm lens can give good definition, even in failing light.

A red bicycle, the same shade as the nearby door, establishes a simple but vibrant pattern of line and color. For uncomplicated compositions such as this, the standard lens is ideal.

A tanned back says "summer sun" more eloquently than might a traditional beach scene. The close-focusing capability of the standard lens allowed the photographer to frame the image tightly and eliminate surrounding clutter.

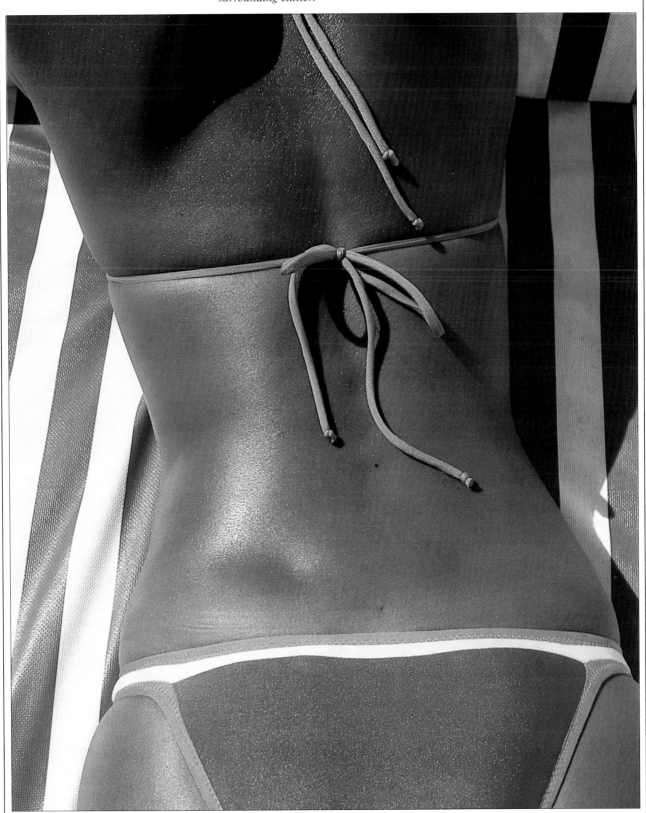

Widening the view

Although a standard lens shows natural perspective, you need a lens of much shorter focal length to get breadth of view. The view of a standard lens is restricted to a viewing angle of about 45°, and to overcome this restriction, you need a lens that can fit more into the same frame – a wide-angle lens. With a 35mm SLR camera, any focal length shorter than about 35mm gives a wide-angle view, although the effects become really noticeable only at 28mm or shorter: many photographers use 35mm lenses in place of a standard lens. Focal lengths shorter than 24mm are available. But while compressing such a broad field of view onto the film format, very wide-angle lenses create distortion, and the more extreme of them are best considered as interesting special-effects devices.

Distortion will be most obvious with scenes involving straight lines, as in architectural photographs.

The most obvious practical use of a wide-angle lens is for pictures in which interesting details cover a wide angle in relation to where you are standing. If you want to show most of your living room in one photograph, for example, your eyes, with an angle of view approaching 160° from left to right, may see the whole room. But it may be impossible to move back far enough to fit everything into the viewfinder frame. A wide-angle lens will help by reducing the image of the objects in the room and squeezing more of them onto the film. In the same way, a wide-angle lens allows you to frame an exterior scene effectively with foreground objects near the frame

Sweeping perspectives and an impressive sense of space give a dramatic look to landscapes shot with a wide-angle lens. Taking advantage of the distortion inherent in a 20mm lens, the photographer of the desert road on the left has turned his picture into a striking landscape, with the road itself forming a shape of startling impact.

Cramped space makes it impossible to move back far enough to show a subject like this adequately without a wide-angle lens. The 35mm lens used here was wide enough to allow the photographer to close in on a furniture restorer and the instrument he is polishing, yet still show his surroundings.

Framed by an arch, and shaded by citrus trees, these Portuguese women make a fascinating folk tableau for the camera. By composing the picture in order to exploit the wide angle of view and great depth of field of the 28mm lens he was using, the photographer was able to include much of the surroundings, and to identify the location as a quiet courtyard. A standard lens would have shown only the group, losing much of the intimacy of this image.

edges, as in the shot here taken through an archway. The result is often to draw the viewer into the picture, creating a feeling of involvement that can give photographs taken with a wide-angle lens a strong sense of immediacy.

As a most useful side-effect, lenses of short focal length produce greater depth of field than do standard lenses at the same aperture. This makes them very useful in poor light and in situations where there is little time to make fine adjustments to the focus. When you are photographing general street scenes with a manual focus camera, for example, a wide-angle lens will let you point the camera and shoot without delaying the moment to adjust the focusing ring.

24mm

28mm

35mm

Wide-angle lenses
These three lenses, which have focal lengths of 24mm, 28mm and 35mm, outwardly resemble standard lenses. But the likeness ends as soon as you fit one to your camera and look through the viewfinder. Cramped views expand, and at small apertures the depth of field makes focusing less critical.

Concentrating the view

Distant subjects that look good in the viewfinder often seem disappointing in the final print, because the attractive details that initially caught the eye occupy only a small area in the middle of the frame. Moving closer is sometimes the answer, but if you are photographing a football game, for example, you cannot intrude on to the playing area. The solution is to use a telephoto lens. This has an effect opposite to that of a wide-angle lens – instead of taking in a wider field of view than a standard lens, it records a much smaller area, and magnifies the subject.

The degree of magnification depends on the focal length of the lens. A 100mm telephoto has a focal length double that of a standard lens, so it doubles the scale at which the eye would perceive a subject. At the same time, the lens's horizontal field of view is half as wide as that of a standard lens.

The most popular telephotos have focal lengths of between 85 and 250mm. The longer focal lengths, although powerful, are much more difficult to handle and to focus. Those of 400mm and longer can pick out subject details missed by the naked eye but require tripod support.

Aside from their magnifying effect, all telephoto lenses have several other common characteristics. The most dramatic of these is the compression of distance that they appear to cause. If you look at a row of objects of equal height and equally spaced – such as telegraph poles – receding into the distance, you will notice that the distant ones seem more tightly packed. When you photograph this scene with a telephoto lens, only the distant poles are included in the frame, and so the picture appears flattened out with its different planes packed together. For example, in the shot of the Grand Canyon on the opposite page, a scene that stretches away from the camera for several miles has been foreshortened startlingly, because a long lens has eliminated the foreground.

Another important characteristic of a telephoto lens is that it gives less depth of field than does a standard lens. As a result, when the lens is focused on a nearby object, the background is unsharp – a useful way of concentrating attention on the principal area of interest. Portraiture with telephoto lenses is often effective for this reason – and also because you do not need to crowd your subject to get a detailed head-and-shoulders shot.

Telephoto lenses

Telephoto lenses magnify the image, filling the frame with a subject that may look like an insignificant detail when seen through a standard lens. These three lenses have focal lengths of 135mm, 200mm and 400mm, magnifying the image 2.7, 4 and 8 times respectively.

400mm

200mm

135mm

Pleasing portraits are easier with a telephoto – its shallow depth of field puts background distractions out of focus. At the same time, magnification of the image allows you to move back to a more comfortable working distance, thus eliminating perspective distortions.

The majesty of landscape is often missing from pictures taken with a standard lens. A telephoto can restore the sense of scale and drama – as in the picture here of the Grand Canyon, taken with a 200mm lens.

The thick of the action at a sports event usually can be captured effectively only with a telephoto lens. The photographer of the football game opposite used a 400mm lens to get close to a player weaving through tacklers on the far side of the field.

79

Recording everything sharply

More often than not you will want your entire image to be sharp from foreground to background – to give a figure a sense of location, for example, to link foreground and background elements, or merely to record the whole of a view. The simplest way to maximize depth of field is to stop down the lens. Stopping down means reducing the aperture of the lens, and the smaller the aperture you use, the greater the depth of field in your photograph. Stopped down to f/16, for example, a standard lens focused on a subject 15 feet away will record sharply everything beyond about eight feet, whereas with the aperture widened to f/2, only the subject itself will be sharply focused, the background and foreground appearing blurred.

Stopping down the lens requires that you also slow the shutter speed to give sufficient exposure. Unless the light is bright, this may limit your freedom to choose an aperture small enough to gain the depth of field you want. Fast film can help or, if the subject is static, you may be able to shoot at a slow shutter speed with the camera steadied – preferably on a tripod. To check how much of your picture will be sharp at a given aperture, you can either refer to the depth of field scale on the lens (see below left) or use the preview button. This closes the lens down to the f-stop you have chosen, allowing you to see through the viewfinder the zone of sharp focus in your image.

Two other factors control the extent to which you can record the whole picture sharply – the lens you use and the camera-to-subject distance. The shorter the focal length of your lens the greater the depth of field. Thus a wide-angle lens has advantages if you want the greatest near-to-far sharpness. Finally, you can extend sharpness by moving back from your subject, since depth of field increases with the distance between the camera and the subject.

Using the depth of field scale

A typical autofocus lens (below) has a focusing distance scale linked by engraved lines to pairs of f-numbers on a depth of field scale. From a chosen f-number, the left-hand line indicates the distance to the nearest point in sharp focus and the right-hand line indicates the farthest point.

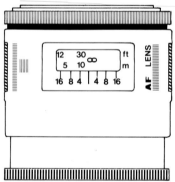

Above, the lens is focused on infinity (marked with a ∞ symbol on the distance scale) and the aperture set at f/8. The line from the "8" on the left points to 16 feet, showing that focus is sharp only beyond this distance. The "8" line on the right, which is well beyond the infinity symbol, indicates that there is depth of field to spare.

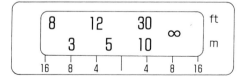

By turning the manual focusing ring to the right so that the ∞ symbol aligns with the "8" line on the right, infinity is still in focus. But depth of field now extends down to 10 feet, so more of the foreground is in focus.

The maternal bond between an ostrich and her eggs makes a striking composition. Focusing on the midground ensured that both were sharp despite the distance dividing them.

Isolating what is important

In photography, you often need to take special measures to focus attention on one center of interest – usually because there are distracting elements in front of or behind your main subject, and you may not be able to get near enough to your subject to cut out the unwanted details. When you are taking a candid portrait, for example, bright colors or strong shapes in the background or foreground may compete for attention with your chosen subject. In such circumstances the best way to simplify the image is to put intrusive elements out of focus by deliberately creating a shallow depth of field. Colors are toned down and shapes reduced to an unobtrusive blur when they are out of focus.

There are three ways of minimizing depth of field: using a wide aperture, a telephoto lens, or a close

viewpoint. Just as you can stop down the lens to achieve maximum depth of field (overleaf), so you can deliberately open up the lens and choose the widest aperture possible to take advantage of the restricted focus it offers. Of course, using a wide aperture makes it crucial that you focus accurately on the part of the scene you want to be sharp, as any slight error will be noticeable. Because telephoto lenses have more limited depth of field than standard lenses, they are well suited for selective focusing, especially when set at a wide aperture. Finally, if the light is too bright for a very wide aperture to be feasible, remember that you can also throw a background out of focus by moving in close to your subject – depth of field is shallower in close-ups than at average focusing distances.

A face in a crowd can be made to stand out. Here, the photographer focused carefully on the girl, then opened up the lens to blur the foreground leaves and soften the background. The blurred elements serve both to emphasize the sharply focused face and to frame it.

Zoo portraits are often spoiled by cage bars and wire netting. Here, however, the photographer concentrated attention on the main subject by holding the camera close to the cage and using a wide aperture to cut depth of field. This throws the bars and netting out of focus, making them less noticeable.

A girl balancing on the bar of her sports bicycle totally dominates the picture here, because a telephoto lens set at a wide aperture has been used in order to soften the intrusive colors and shapes in the busy street behind her. Shooting with a telephoto lens is also a simple way of filling the frame with your main subject without having to get too close.

The right film

In selecting what kind of film to put in the camera, the broad choice lies between film for color prints, for color slides or for pictures in black-and-white (overleaf). Within these categories are many different types of film – it is easier to take successful shots if the film chosen matches the subject and lighting conditions as precisely as possible.

The most important property of a film is its sensitivity to light – the film speed. Slow films need much more light to form a usable image than do fast films, which are highly sensitive. This means that you can more easily take pictures in dim light with fast film. In brighter light, fast film allows you to select a fast shutter speed or a small aperture if needed. However, fast films have one drawback: the grains that make up the image have to be large so that they react quickly to a limited amount of light, and when the picture is blown up they show as gritty texture. Slow films have smaller grains and can record finer detail, but unless the light is bright, they may force the photographer to use an unsuitably slow shutter speed or too wide an aperture. In average daylight, films of medium or medium-fast speed offer a good compromise. Fast films are an advantage in poor light or for action photographs requiring fast shutter speeds. Slow films are useful for static, detailed subjects, such as still-life or architecture.

Film speed used to be indicated by an ASA (American Standards Association) or DIN (Deutsche Industrie Norm) number, but nowadays it is designated by the ISO (International Standards Organization) system whereby the ASA number appears first, then the DIN number. Thus, ISO 100/21° (or simply ISO 100) indicates ASA 100 or 21°DIN – a medium speed. Each doubling or halving of the ISO number indicates a doubling or halving of speed, changing the exposure required by one full stop on either the aperture or shutter speed controls.

Film speed
The film speed rating is clearly marked on the box, as at left. Kodak Ektar 100 film – a medium film for color prints – takes its name from the ISO speed rating, which is numerically the same as the old ASA rating. New cameras set the speed automatically when you load the film. On older cameras, you need to set a control to the correct ISO number (bottom left). The guide to film speeds (right) shows the range and differing sensitivities.

For fine detail, as in this shot of a tub of chilies in a market stall, slow film is best. The Kodachrome 25 film for slides used here has extremely fine grain (seen in the inset microscopic enlargement).

In average light, medium-speed film works well, needing not too wide an aperture and showing little grain (inset). This picture of the interior of a partly inflated hot-air balloon was shot on Ektachrome 64 film for slides.

	ISO Slow			Medium	
Color prints	25				100
Color slides	25	50		64	100
Black-and-white	25	50			100

Slow films (ISO 25-50) are the ideal choice whenever fine detail and saturated color is important, provided the light is bright or you can set a long exposure.

Medium speed films (ISO 64-200) are designed for everyday photography. They offer fine quality results, but can be used under overcast lighting conditions.

			Fast					Ultra Fast		
(125)	160	200		400				1000	1600	(3200)
	160	200	320	400	(640)	800			1600	
125				400					1600	3200

Fast films (ISO 320-800) are useful in a wide range of situations, from poor light outdoors to artificial light indoors. Image quality is high with modern films.

Ultra fast films (ISO 1000-3200) tend to give grainy images, but are useful when light is very dim. With these films, you can take pictures by candlelight.

Note to table: brackets signify that films at this speed rating are available only from manufacturers other than Kodak.

Choosing black-and-white film

Why should anyone use black-and-white film? After all, it is now only slightly cheaper than color and the bright hues of nature seem a lot to sacrifice. But black-and-white clearly does have a great appeal, and is the chosen medium of many good photographers. What this film lacks in color, it gains in dramatic impact. Whereas the variety and vibrancy of color sometimes complicate the appearance of a scene, black-and-white has a graphic simplicity that is well shown in the picture on the opposite page – an ability to convey mood, form, and pattern solely in tones of light and dark. You can learn important lessons in photography by using this film, because it is one step farther removed from the real world. Without color you can more easily concentrate on composing with light, developing a new and valuable way of seeing the world around you.

Black-and-white film has other, more practical advantages. Processing is simple, allowing both development and printing to be carried out at home with relative ease. The equipment needed is neither expensive nor complicated. And home processing allows total control over the final image, including subtle adjustment to the quality of the print.

Black-and-white film is available in a wide range of speeds which adds to its versatility. Slow film (ISO 25) is useful for copying prints onto a new negative or for photography requiring fine detail. Using such film, big enlargements can be made without graininess appearing. At the other end of the scale, ultra-fast film of ISO 3200 will cope with very dim light or fast-moving subjects.

Manipulating prints from a black-and-white negative is relatively easy. Here, selective cropping and enlargement during printing have produced several quite different portraits of a boy from a single negative.

Difficult lighting conditions are much less of a problem in black-and-white than in color. The superb versatility of monochrome is evident in the evocative portrait of a little girl (left) taken on fast film in low light. The print still contains a full range of delicate tones.

Tone and texture create a powerful abstract image in this high-contrast picture of sand dunes (right). Black-and-white concentrates attention on such qualities.

Choosing color film

Most photographers simply want the film they use to record accurately the colors they see. Thus it may seem surprising that such a range of color film is available. For 35mm cameras, there are several dozen types of daylight and indoor films. The reason for this diversity is that each film has its own characteristics, and you may want to choose different films for different purposes.

The initial choice, of course, lies between films for slides (transparencies) or for negatives from which you can make prints. Beyond this, a film's sensitivity to light is the main consideration. Fast films are very sensitive, and give the photographer great versatility, but slower, less sensitive films have other advantages. For example, they provide a good range of tones between light and dark. And because they make use of finer grains of light-sensitive silver salts to form an image, they can look sharper and are less grainy in big enlargements than photographs taken on faster film.

Although grain size is a consideration when choosing color film, the film's color rendition is often more important. A photograph of the same scene taken on different types of film will vary slightly but distinctly in color, as the pictures below show. One film may record reds with special intensity. Another may distinguish more clearly colors that are closely similar. Yet another film may give the picture a warmer or cooler appearance overall – this is particularly noticeable in neutral color areas such as black, white and gray, and in skin tones. In photographs, it is often in the skin tones that we are most sensitive to variations in color values and most disturbed by unnaturalness.

Variations of color are usually quite subtle, and are most obvious when you make comparisons between slide films; the printing process tends to reduce the differences between negative films. In general, photographers form their own preferences for color film. The best way to make a choice is to try out a number of films, and decide which you like most. You may even want to use two different films, choosing for portraits a type that produces very natural skin tones, but preferring a different film for landscapes, where you may feel that the rendition of blues and greens is more important. The difference in the qualities of the blues is one of the features of the color films shown below.

The color characteristics of film
This garden still-life incorporates a wide range of colors. Shot on different types of slide film, the colors show slight but distinct differences – for example, in some the blue is stronger, in others the red. The green is particularly strong in the image second from right. However there is no "best", because color judgments are largely subjective.

Subtle colors and flowing movement emphasize the grace and beauty of dance. Here, the photographer chose fast film to cope with the dim light of the rehearsal room. This film has helped to soften the colors.

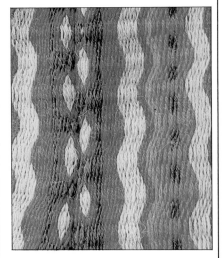

A vivid piece of woven fabric relies for its impact on the juxtaposition of primary colors. The photographer took the picture with slow transparency film, which has moderate contrast and good color fidelity, suited to the reproduction of vibrant hues.

How color film works

Color print film is like a layer cake (above) made of gelatin containing grains of silver salts. Each layer records a different part of the visible spectrum – red, green or blue light. Processing creates a silver image where light was absorbed in each layer. At the same time, a dye image appears in color exactly opposite to the color for which the layer is sensitized. For example, the blue-sensitive layer forms a yellow dye image. After bleach and fix have removed the silver image, the dye layers (visible in the magnified cross-section above) form the negative from which a positive print is made. Processing of color slides is more complex because the film must form a positive picture. During processing, a second development introduces transparent dyes that form the image, subtracting appropriate colors from the light that passes through the slide.

Slide film

To achieve precision and brilliance of color, many photographers prefer to use color slide film – often called transparency or color reversal film. Because this produces a positive film image directly, without an intermediate printing process, any adjustment the photographer makes to the camera's controls leads directly to a corresponding change in the appearance of the final picture.

Although color slides need projection or enlargement to be seen properly, they display great brilliance and color saturation. We see slides by transmitted, rather than reflected, light. Therefore, the range of brightness is higher – a slide usually has more snap than a print (see overleaf).

This impact derives partly from the higher contrast of slide films – they allow little latitude for over- or underexposure. On a dull day, or under flat lighting, this is an advantage, but on a bright sunny day, when the shadows are very dark, and the highlights bright, high contrast can prove a problem. At worst you can lose highlight and shadow detail altogether, depending on how you set the exposure.

As a general rule, blank highlights – for example pale, washed-out features in a portrait – are more likely to spoil a picture than are murky shadows. For this reason, if you are uncertain about the light, some underexposure of color slide film is better than overexposure.

Regular users of color transparency film often deliberately underexpose all their pictures to take account of this – usually by a third or half a stop. Even in low or flat lighting conditions, slight underexposure leads to richer, more saturated colors. You can also underexpose by setting your camera's film speed control to a slightly higher speed – say ISO 80 if you are using ISO 64 film.

When the contrast between highlights and shadows is very high – in strong sunlight or when shooting into the sun – bracketing exposures increases the chance of getting just the picture you want. For the sunset pictures shown below, the photographer used this simple technique, making exposures at intervals of one stop above and below the setting indicated by the camera's meter.

The sunset looks different in this picture than in the three on the right, because the photographer varied or bracketed the exposure so that he could choose the best. The image above received two stops more exposure than the meter indicated. The result is pale but pleasing, with a satisfying balance of tones.

One stop overexposure gives the best balanced result. There is more detail in the sand spit and clouds compared with the pictures on the right.

Underexposure of color slide film can add to color saturation and avoid the burned-out appearance of sunlit highlights. For the picture of a flower bed (right), the photographer deliberately set the camera to give half a stop less exposure than the meter indicated. The inset shows the "correct" exposure setting (above).

At the metered setting, most of the cloud and sea areas are left as broad masses, but in compensation the red sky is particularly rich.

One stop underexposure produces an image that loses almost all the detail, but is still acceptable because of its dramatic effect.

91

Print film

While slide films have the advantage of brilliance and color intensity, you need to project them onto a screen or use a small viewer to see them at their best. Many people prefer to see their pictures in the form of a print which they can hold in their hands. And because of the brilliance of the original, a paper print made from a transparency rarely seems as satisfactory. If your principal aim is prints, then color negative film may be your best choice.

Because a print is viewed in different conditions to a slide, its colors may appear more muted, and some photographers prefer to work with color negative film because they consider that the hues and tones of a print have more subtlety than those of a slide. Another significant difference is the low contrast of a negative compared with a slide. If you hold a negative up to the light it will look relatively dull. However, because the negative is only an intermediate step on the way to a print, low contrast is not the disadvantage it may seem. It means that negative film can be corrected for some over- or underexposure. As a result the film is ideal for

simple cameras that do not have sophisticated ways of avoiding exposure errors. Even when loaded into an SLR camera, negative film needs less care in assessing exposure than does slide film because to a certain extent exposure errors can be corrected during printing.

Printing a color negative can be much more than just the mechanical process of reversing colors to their normal hues. First, a color-correcting mask that gives the negative an orange tint has to be removed. Then, and more significantly, printing provides the opportunity to control selectively the overall or local color of the picture, and to correct for errors in color balance as well as exposure.

For the many photographers who print their own negatives in home darkrooms, the printing process can, in fact, be just as creative as actually taking photographs. Even if you do not have a home darkroom, you can exert some measure of control over the appearance of the final print by examining a contact sheet (see opposite) and giving appropriate directions to the color laboratory.

*The **unreal hues** of a color negative (right) are little help in judging the final color of the print (above). Part of the problem is the orange dye mask that covers the whole of the negative. This helps to produce more accurate colors in the print, but makes interpretation of the reversed colors more difficult. The best general guide to how a negative will print is its density. A thin negative – one that is underexposed – has little visible detail and will produce a dark, muddy print. By comparison, a dense negative – one that is overexposed – creates fewer problems for the printer.*

Purple in the negative will appear as yellow in the print – the orange mask has combined with blue (the complementary of yellow) to give the purple appearance.

Yellow in the negative also forms its complementary color – blue – on the print. The orange mask distorts yellow only slightly.

Green in the negative will print as red – the gloves in the girl's pocket.

A contact sheet, on which
an entire roll of film has
been printed, provides you
with a convenient working
guide to the appearance of
all the pictures on the roll.
Some laboratories can make
a contact sheet, from which
you can then choose which
images to enlarge, say how
they should be cropped to
improve the composition, and
decide if color correction
is needed. From this roll,
the photographer picked out
the image of the boat, and
asked the printer to bring
out an overall warm color
and crop the picture on the
left-hand side. Both these
changes would be simple to
make in a home darkroom.

94

MAKE LIGHT WORK FOR YOU

Modern cameras simplify exposure control. Their automatic systems of measuring and regulating the light that enters the camera do most of the work for you. But the camera will not always get it right, because no amount of technological wizardry or computerized circuitry can produce just the picture you want in every situation. Camera systems work to fixed rules, whereas exposing the film often involves a creative choice. In the final analysis, you must yourself decide how you would like the picture to look and, if necessary, overrule the automatic system.

A good camera metering system aims to provide an exposure that is technically correct – one that offers a compromise between the amount of light needed for dark and light areas of the scene. Usually, the result will look fine. Sometimes, however, a particular part of a scene is more important to you than the rest. The camera cannot deduce this, and in settling for an average exposure it may over- or underexpose the key area of your composition. That is where your creative choice comes in. This section not only explains how to determine the exposure you want, but looks at different types of light, the effects they can create in a picture, and the extent to which you can control them.

Sun behind the subject makes exposure hard to judge. The camera's meter is bound to read the bright sky and indicate an exposure setting that will cut down the light. In such situations you have to override the meter – as the photographer did here. The amount of light is just right for the three figures, although the meter needle indicates overexposure. With less light, they would have appeared only as silhouettes.

Controlling light

The light reflected from the world around us varies enormously in intensity. On a sunny day, the scene may be several hundred times as bright outdoors as indoors. Our eyes quickly adjust to these different levels of brightness, but film is not as versatile – it needs a precisely fixed amount of light to form a good image. To get correctly exposed pictures you have to control the light that enters the camera, by first measuring the brightness of the scene and then adjusting your aperture and shutter speed until the quantity of light hitting the film exactly matches the film's sensitivity.

Both shutter and aperture halve or double the amount of light reaching the film each time you adjust their control scales by one full step. Thus, controlling the light is a simple matter of increasing or decreasing either the shutter speed or the size of the aperture. If you balance an increase of shutter speed against a decrease of aperture (or vice versa) the total amount of light reaching the film remains constant. As the diagrams below make clear, several different combinations of aperture and shutter speed can give you the same effective exposure.

This is not to say that each combination will produce the same image. In the picture of wine flowing into a glass at bottom left, a fast shutter freezes the movement, but a wide aperture throws the background out of focus. Conversely, as the shutter speed slows and the aperture narrows, the decanter in the background comes into focus but the flowing liquid blurs. Varying the aperture and shutter speed thus gives you creative control over the picture.

In very bright light, there may be a wide range of possible shutter and aperture combinations. But in dim light your choice will be more restricted. The photographer of the mother and child at the foot of the opposite page, for example, could not use too slow a shutter without blurring the picture, and had to choose the widest possible aperture to deliver enough light to the film.

Aperture and shutter speed
These two controls determine exposure in much the same way as length and diameter affect volume: though the disc representing light on the left is short and fat, it has exactly the same volume as the long, thin stick of light on the right – a long exposure at a small aperture.

Think of exposure as an hourglass – just as the same amount of sand runs more quickly through the hourglass on the left, so doubling the aperture lets through the same amount of light in half the time.

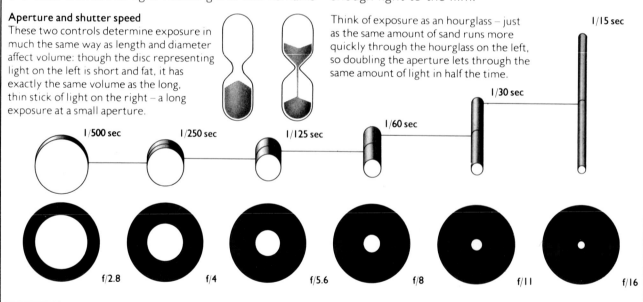

1/500 sec   1/250 sec   1/125 sec   1/60 sec   1/30 sec   1/15 sec

f/2.8   f/4   f/5.6   f/8   f/11   f/16

Wine splashing into a glass appears motionless at 1/500, but the brief exposure forces the use of a wide aperture, so there is little depth of field.

1/60 at f/8 is a good compromise – the film gets the same exposure, and the decanter is sharper, although the wine now shows signs of movement.

At f/16, the whole image is in focus, but getting correct exposure at this small aperture means using a speed of 1/15 – so the pouring wine is blurred.

Summer shadows cut a bold pattern of lines on the road, and draw your eye toward the car in the middle distance. The bright light gave the photographer plenty of freedom to choose shutter speed and aperture, so it was possible to keep the picture sharp from foreground to background by using a shutter speed of 1/250 and an aperture of f/11.

At a firework display there are far fewer choices – here the photographer needed a shutter speed of 1/125 to keep the group sharp, so he set the lens to its widest aperture to make the most of the dim light. He had to forgo depth of field.

Measuring light

Most modern cameras have some form of built-in light metering system that measures the brightness of the scene by means of light-sensitive cells, relates this to the film speed you have set, and either makes or recommends an appropriate exposure setting. When you point the camera at a subject and trigger the meter, you may see a viewfinder display of the shutter speed or aperture – or both – that the camera has set. Simpler automatic cameras generally warn you only if there is a risk of over- or underexposure. And on cameras with manual metering, a needle, or a digital display, indicates how you should change the camera's controls to get the right exposure. Most SLRs have through-the-lens (TTL) metering: cells inside the camera which read the brightness of the light after it has passed through the lens.

Meters indicate "correct" exposure as one that will record the subject in a mid-tone, between light and dark. The intention is to provide maximum detail, and an exposure suitable for most subjects. As a result, if you aim the camera at a sunlit wall the meter will select an exposure that will show the wall mid-gray in tone. If you point it at the same wall in deep shadow, the meter will recommend more exposure – again trying to show the wall mid-gray. Normally, however, in a scene of sun and shadow, the highlights are almost white, shady areas are dark and only some areas are mid-gray. Meters vary in the way they cope with this. They may simply average out the brightness of the whole image, but often they weight the average toward areas of the frame that are usually most important in pictures – the center and lower half. Some allow "spot metering," taking the reading from a small central area of the viewfinder, giving that the most detail.

The secret of successful exposure decisions is to understand how your particular meter reads a scene and to visualize in advance how you want the picture to look. No matter how sophisticated your camera, you alone can make the creative decisions.

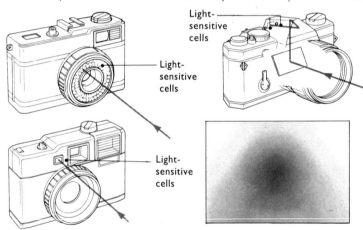

Light-sensitive cells

Light-sensitive cells

Light-sensitive cells

Light-sensitive cells

External metering (above)
Simple cameras incorporate the light-sensitive cells of the metering system either on the lens or in a window on the body to read reflected light.

Center-weighted metering (above)
Many SLRs measure the light reflected from the whole subject, but give extra emphasis to the brightness of the central area.

Through-the-lens metering (left)
Most SLR cameras have cells that measure the brightness of the light entering the camera through the lens. This provides a more accurate estimate of correct exposure than external metering.

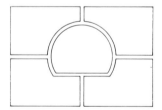

Intelligent metering (above)
Some cameras meter from several areas of the frame, comparing the readings with stored brightness patterns of typical photo subjects.

Handheld meters

Handheld incident meters give very accurate readings, as they measure the light falling onto a subject, rather than the reflected light. This means that the reading is not influenced by the subject's tones – under even lighting, dark, light and mid tones are all recorded faithfully. To take a reading, the meter is held in front of the subject, pointing at the camera. The meter then displays the recommended aperture and shutter speed settings.

Understanding your meter
A center-weighted meter gave perfect exposure for the skin tones opposite right, because the subject's face and arms filled the area of the frame given priority in this type of meter's system of averaging light. With a meter that measures light equally over the whole scene. This kind of shot is harder to get right. The bright sky behind the subject may influence the meter to indicate less exposure than the main subject needs. To avoid making errors you must know your own meter.

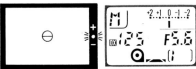

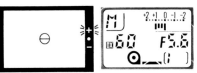

Underexposure
When the minus sign glows, or the bar pattern on the LCD shows a negative value, your pictures will be dark.

Correct exposure
When the zero in the viewfinder glows, or the LCD shows "0", your pictures will be correctly exposed.

Overexposure
When the plus sign glows, or the bar pattern on the LCD shows a positive value, your pictures will be too light.

Manual or automatic/1

All but the most basic new cameras have some method of automatic exposure control, and many have a wide choice of exposure modes. The quickest and simplest way of setting shutter speed and aperture is programmed exposure mode. If it is set to "program", the camera automatically chooses an appropriate combination of shutter speed and aperture according to the film speed and the brightness of the light reflected by the subject. In the dimmest conditions, the camera sets the lens to its maximum aperture and chooses the slowest shutter speed available. With progressively brighter subjects, the program sets faster and faster shutter speeds until it is able to set a shutter speed that will eliminate the effects of camera-shake (usually 1/60 or 1/125). The program then sets a combination of faster shutter speeds and smaller apertures as the light gets brighter.

Some programmed exposure modes take into consideration the focal length of the lens. When a telephoto lens is fitted to the camera, the program sets faster shutter speeds as there is a greater risk of camera-shake. With a short focal length lens, the risk of camera-shake is less, so instead of setting fast shutter speeds the program sets narrow apertures, which give greater depth of field.

The main drawback of programmed exposure is that the camera assumes complete control over the exposure settings. However, some cameras feature "program shift", which can be used to alter the exposure settings chosen by the camera.

Many cameras have advanced programmed exposure modes that are designed for particular types of photography. For example, speed programs (often known as sports programs) favor fast shutter speeds and choose smaller apertures only when the top shutter speed has been set. On some modern autofocus cameras, the speed program automatically selects continuous focus mode.

Semi-automatic exposure gives the photographer more control than programmed exposure, but is still quick to use. There are two modes: shutter priority and aperture priority. In shutter priority mode, the photographer chooses a shutter speed and the camera selects an appropriate aperture. Conversely, in aperture priority mode, the photographer selects an aperture setting and the camera sets an appropriate shutter speed.

Manual exposure provides maximum control, because the photographer sets both shutter speed and aperture, but it is the slowest exposure mode to use. A display in the viewfinder – and on the LCD panel, if the camera has one – shows that the selected combination of settings will give a correct exposure, or indicates how to alter the settings to get the exposure right.

Programmed exposure
In program mode the camera measures the subject brightness and the program sets an appropriate aperture and shutter speed combination, based on the focal length of the lens and the film speed. As the light level changes, the program automatically adjusts the exposure settings to maintain

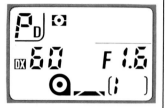

a correct exposure. It may also select the autofocus. Program modes are ideal for candid photography.

Semi-automatic exposure
The two semi-automatic exposure modes give the photographer more creative control over exposure. In shutter priority mode, as right, you set the shutter speed and the camera sets the aperture, giving you control over the sharpness of the image. In aperture priority mode you set the

aperture and the camera selects an appropriate shutter speed, giving you control over depth of field.

Manual exposure
Manual exposure is slow to use but offers the most control. You can experiment with a wide range of aperture and shutter speed combinations for different effects.

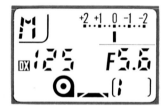

Creative control is needed with some subjects. Using a manual camera, the photographer could set the controls to overexpose the pavement and stop the little boy appearing as a silhouette.

Depth of field is important in the tranquil park scene above. The photographer wanted to show everything in sharp detail from the dappled foreground to the distant background figures. Aperture priority exposure mode, or a depth program, suits this type of scene.

Movement and timing are the crucial elements of the shot on the left. A fast shutter speed, and a quick response, have caught the flying spray and sense of fun perfectly. A shutter priority mode enabled the photographer to set the speed and then concentrate on the action.

Manual and automatic/2

When can you trust your camera meter, and when should you override it? If scenes with an average distribution of tones are lit from the front or the side, the camera's meter will probably serve well enough. But if the light is coming from behind the subject, for example, the meter may give a reading for the bright background so that the subject itself is underexposed and appears as a silhouette. Exposure often involves a creative decision and the meter's reading should be seen as a starting point. Identify the part of the scene you consider the main subject of the picture. If this is much lighter or darker than the rest, you should adjust the exposure to show good detail there, rather than accepting an average of the whole scene.

An effective way of basing exposure on the most important area is to take a "key reading" close to the main subject before moving back to your shooting position. You can do this readily with manual exposure controls but need some other method with automatic systems, such as a memory lock, which allows you to set the exposure and then hold it while you move to another camera position. Alternatively, you can use a compensation control, which allows you to choose several stops more or less exposure than the meter suggested.

Mixed light and dark areas in the same shot require care. If you think a light background such as the sky is biasing the meter, compensate by giving one or two stops extra exposure. Conversely, if you have a small, light subject against a dark background, give slightly less exposure than is indicated. For scenes with important detail in both light and dark areas, take readings for each and pick the midway setting.

When you are in doubt, "bracketing" offers a solution. Take the same shot three or five times, changing the exposure in either third- or half-stop increments around the setting you think is correct. Cameras with an autobracketing function can do this for you. When you press the shutter release, the camera takes a series of shots (usually three), at, above, and below the exposure reading.

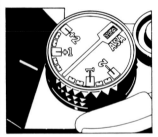

Exposure compensation
Automatic cameras often have an exposure control. A light subject (right) may appear dull at the automatic exposure, but plus one stop on the control restores the true brightness (far right).

Reading from a face

1 – When you need to set the exposure for an important element such as a face, move close so that the face fills the whole frame, and set the exposure.

2 – Then move back to your chosen camera position and take the shot at the same setting. Some automatic cameras have a memory lock to help you do this.

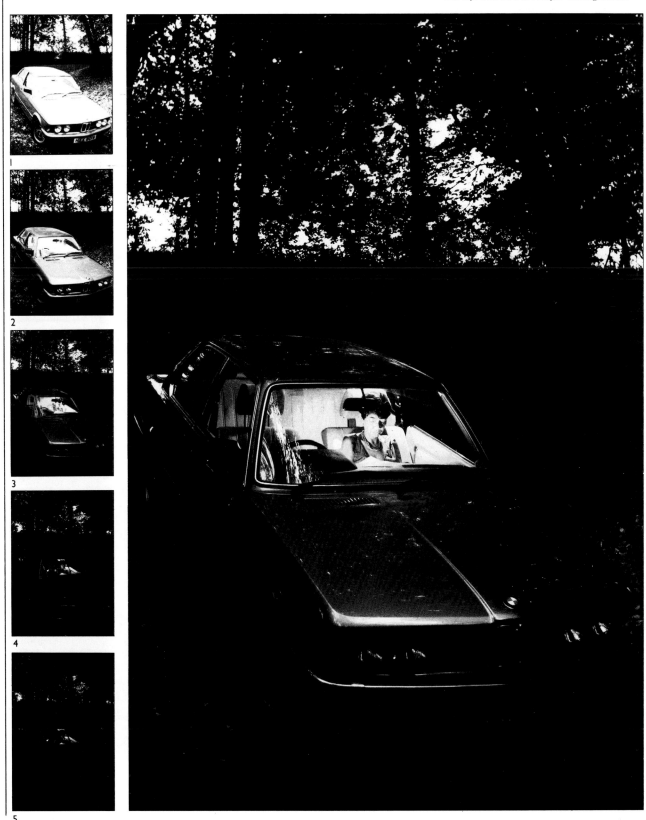

Bracketing is advisable when you are unsure of a reading. The meter alone could not determine the right balance in the scene below. The photographer made five varying exposures and selected the third frame as the best for enlargement.

1

2

3

4

5

The exposure you want

Despite all the sophistication of through-the-lens meters, accurate exposure is still technically the most difficult part of photography. Because film can reproduce only a part of the enormous brightness range the eye sees on a sunny day, exposure meters can suggest a setting suitable only for an average of the main tones in the picture. They take no account of the photographer's wish to show clearly all the details in a particular shadow or highlight area.

A useful way to look at a scene is to imagine that a bright sunlit view contains ten main levels of brightness. (One such view is diagrammed at the top of the opposite page.) Different films vary in the brightness range they can handle, but in practice you can assume that the image on the film will show good detail in only five or six of these levels. Parts

of the scene beyond these limits will show as entirely dark or light, with no visible detail. Therefore, with high-contrast subjects, you have to decide which parts of the scene you consider most important and adjust the exposure to make sure that they fall within the range of the film. This is a creative decision, and the examples on these two pages show that you often have to sacrifice some of what the eye can see. If the most important detail is in a portion of the subject that is significantly brighter than the rest of the scene, give one or two stops less exposure than that indicated by the average reading, to avoid overexposing this detail. Conversely, if the important detail is in a dark part of a predominantly light scene, increase the metered exposure by one or two stops.

Sunlight *streaming through a window creates a brightness range too great for the film. Setting exposure for the light area records detail only in the garden.*

Giving two stops extra exposure *shows the foreground detail fully, but the highlights around the window are burned out, unbalancing the composition.*

The tonal range of the scene
(above) covers nine out of a
possible ten brightness levels –
represented diagrammatically
by the spots. Because only six
of these levels will show good,
clear detail on the film, the
photographer must select the
most important area.

A simplified tonal range
divides the scene into three
main areas: first, the bright
garden, then a well lit middle
portion and finally the darkest
parts of the foreground. This
foreground clearly needs some
extra exposure for the picture
to have visual interest.

With one stop more exposure than
the averaged meter reading, the detail
in the garden vanishes but the strongest
areas of interest show up well.

Into the light

Keeping the light source behind the camera almost always guarantees a clear, detailed image. However, to realize the full potential of different subjects, you need to accept the challenge of taking pictures in less conventional lighting conditions. Several of the pictures on these two pages show how you can bring sparkle to otherwise ordinary scenes by photographing into the light.

Backlighting always accentuates shape. A solid object with the sun directly behind will be reduced to a black outline. But if the subject lets some light through, the effect will be quite different. In the picture of the ruined abbey at left below, pale sunlight passing through small gaps between the stones casts a radiating pattern on the grass, yet the

contrast is low enough for an exposure that also shows clearly the texture of the shadowed walls. With transparent and translucent subjects, backlighting can often intensify colors and reveal hidden structures. For example, in the photograph at the bottom of this page, the rimlit red and yellow leaves at the ends of the branches glow with color, while shadows within the lacy pattern of green leaves show the complex structure of the branches.

In strongly backlit scenes, the contrast between bright highlights and dark shadows needs to be taken into account when calculating exposure. As a general rule, if you want to record shadow details clearly, you should take a close-up reading from the most important area.

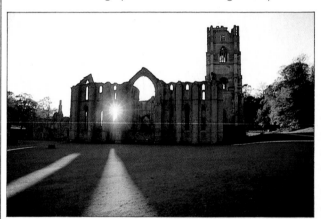

Coppery backlighting burnishes the leaves of a plant. The photographer shone a reading lamp on the wall behind the plant and took the picture on daylight film, using a No. 10 red filter to intensify the warm color of the tungsten light. Room lighting reveals some of the decorative detail on the pot.

Low sun streaming through a narrow arched window is the dazzling focal point for the image of an ancient abbey, above. Shadows cast by the acutely angled rays create perspective lines that lead the viewer into the picture and convey a sense of depth.

Strong light directly behind a spreading tree picks out shapes, patterns and colors against the dark background. The contrast between bright highlights, on the outermost leaves, and solid shadows, where branches and foliage block the light, adds to the impact of the composition.

A fine spray striking a surfer disperses the sun's rays into thousands of tiny particles, stippling the whole scene with sparkling light. With plenty of reflected light in the shadow areas, the photographer based exposure on an average reading.

Raking light

Many photographers are wary of taking photographs in bright sun because of the problems of high contrast. But at the right time of day, clear sunlight offers marvelous photographic opportunities.

In midmorning, and again in the afternoon and early evening, the low sun sends oblique shafts of light across a scene, picking out textural details that are lost in flatter lighting. As the position of the sun moves more to the side of the subject, shadows become larger and longer. Yet because the light is less intense than at midday, these shadows are soft-edged rather than harsh. This sets up a subtle play of light and shade often exploited by landscape photographers to give modeling and depth, as in the pastoral scene opposite. You can use the same lighting effect to give drama and atmosphere to any subject. Viewed from the side, a figure facing a low-angled sun will be outlined with a golden light that appears both warm and flattering. The profiled girl at far right is an example.

Going out with a camera and observing how the colors, forms and moods of a scene change according to the sun's position is by far the best way to discover lighting effects. Sometimes, returning to your subject an hour later can make a surprising difference. But you do not always have to wait for the sun to move. To get the striking picture at the bottom of this page, the photographer changed his viewpoint by walking around the corner of the block and took the second picture with the slanting sunlight falling across the subject.

Moving the camera
Altering the direction of the light resulted in two very different images of the same subject (right). Harsh frontal lighting registered the old man, the plants and the wrought-iron balcony in equally sharp detail (1). By walking around the corner, the photographer got a far more atmospheric view (2). Bright sunlight from one side casts a halo around the man's white hair and transforms the ornate metalwork into glittering silver filigree.

Low evening sun rakes across a hilly landscape dotted with sheep. The lengthy shadows cast at this time on a bright day, together with the warmth and clarity of the light, are perfect for bringing out form and texture in such scenes. Here, sunlight catching the poplars makes an interesting contrast with the dark line of firs standing high on the horizon.

Oblique rays from late afternoon sun skate over a craggy rock and gently gild the profile of a girl gazing out to sea. Light reflected off the sand and water creates a hazy background that adds to the strong romantic mood of the picture.

Sunlight controlled

Strong sunshine tends to produce such extreme contrast that deep shadows or blank highlights may spoil your pictures, regardless of how well you judge the exposure. But you can radically improve photographs by using simple techniques to modify the light falling on a subject – especially if the subject is of a manageable size.

The simplest way to reduce high contrast is to move the subject into the shade. If you are photographing people in a landscape setting, the shade of a tree will provide a much more even tone on their faces than if they stand in the open. Be careful to take the exposure reading close to the subject so that the meter is not influenced unduly by the bright sunshine beyond. Another technique is to reduce the intensity of the light by rigging up a diffuser between the sun and the subject. For example, if you shield a flower with a piece of translucent paper or a

sheet of thin white cloth, the highlights will be less bright and the shadows softer.

A more practical solution may be to fill-in the shadows with flash at reduced power. Advanced flash units control fill-in lighting automatically, but with more basic automatic units set the ISO rating on the flash at double that of the film in use. With a manual flash set the unit to half power or wrap a paper tissue over the front. For fill-in flash in bright, sunny conditions, a powerful flash unit is required.

You can also reduce contrast by reflecting natural light back into the shadows. A reflective surface, such as a white wall, acts as an excellent balancing light source. Alternatively, you can introduce special reflectors such as those shown below and in the diagrams on the opposite page – or simply use a hand mirror, carefully angled to reflect a beam of light into a specific area of shadow.

White clothes gleam brightly in the light from a flash unit in this outdoor fashion picture. The photographer set the exposure for the shaded building behind, then halved the flash power.

Special reflectors

You can use any bright, reflective surface to throw light into shadow areas, but portable reflectors are standard equipment for portrait and still-life photography. Several bought or home-made types are shown below. Umbrella reflectors can be folded for transport.

Folding silvered umbrella

Crumpled cooking foil on board

White card or polystyrene

Daylight from a window shines strongly on this informal still-life arrangement on a basketwork surface, as diagrammed above. The directional light shows up shape and texture well.

A large white card, placed in front of the subject and to the right, reflects some light back into the deep shadow on the hat, adding foreground detail.

A large mirror replacing the card fills the shadow completely. With the card moved to the left, the jug is lit as well, and the emphasis of the picture shifts to the bright foreground.

Handling limited light

Low light produces some of the most evocative and spectacular photographs you can take – from sunsets and dimly lit interiors to street scenes at night with illuminated signs and floodlit buildings. In order to use limited lighting effectively, you need first of all to escape from the idea that the only acceptable image is one that is evenly and brightly lit. At night or in a dark interior, for example, there is often too little light or too much contrast between highlights and shadows to obtain full detail over the whole image. Make a virtue of necessity, and take advantage of the way low light simplifies an image. You may be able to create a strong silhouette or take a shot in which the light forms an interesting rim around the subject. A good time to experiment is at dusk, when there is still enough light for a relatively short exposure, but street and house lights evoke a nocturnal mood.

To obtain enough light for exposure in low lighting situations, you often need to use both wide apertures and slow shutter speeds. You can shoot some subjects with a handheld camera if you have fast film and a lens with a wide maximum aperture – at least f/2.8. But many subjects demand a slow exposure, requiring a tripod or other form of camera support. When using a wide-angle or standard 50mm lens, support the camera for exposures slower than 1/60; with a long lens, 1/125 is about the slowest safe speed for handheld shots. One great advantage of a tripod and a long exposure is that you can use a very small aperture and so increase the overall sharpness of your image. However, very long exposures in dim light can produce unpredictable effects, especially with color film, so you may need to try several different exposures to get the picture right.

Low light exposure guide
Exposure readings tend to be misleading in low light, but you can use this chart for typical subjects as a rough guide.

FILM IN USE	ISO 100		ISO 400	
Brightly lit shop windows	1/30	f/2.8	1/60	f/4
Well-lit street scenes	1/30	f/2	1/60	f/2.8
Fireworks	1/8	f/2.8	1/30	f/4
Floodlit buildings	2 secs	f/5.6	1/2	f/5.6
Street lights	1/4	f/2	1/15	f/2
Neon signs	1/30	f/4	1/125	f/4
Dim church interior	10 secs	f/4	$2\frac{1}{2}$ secs	f/4
Landscape at full moon	20 secs	f/2.8	5 secs	f/2.8

Making a time exposure
For exposures longer than 1 sec, use the "B" or time setting. This keeps the shutter open for as long as the release is pressed. A tripod and cable release will prevent camera shake.

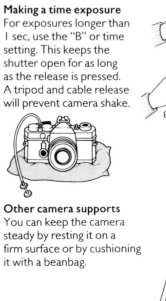

Other camera supports
You can keep the camera steady by resting it on a firm surface or by cushioning it with a beanbag.

Snaking streaks of light (left) were created by a time exposure that recorded the head and tail lights of cars moving across the bridge. The evening sky provided the meter reading to show the bridge in silhouette.

Delicate rimlighting traces the monk's profile to produce a powerful portrait – the photographer metered the light on the monk's forehead, and gave one stop more exposure.

Shimmering water reflects light from the evening sun, backlighting the figures and foreground. To reduce the foreground to silhouettes, the photographer metered the bright area of water.

Using flash

The most portable and convenient means of providing extra light for photography is an electronic flash unit. This fits onto an accessory slot – known as the hotshoe – on top of the camera. When you release the shutter, the flash unit discharges a brief, intense flash of light.

The duration of the flash – between 1/1000 and 1/50,000 – determines the length of the exposure. You need to adjust the shutter speed only to ensure that when the flash fires the entire frame is exposed. This means setting the camera's flash synchronization speed, or a slower speed.

There are three categories of flash unit: manual, self-regulating and dedicated TTL. Manual units are the most basic – they discharge the same brightness of light on every flash, leaving you to control the

exposure using the aperture settings on the lens. An exposure chart indicates which aperture to use for different flash-to-subject distances and film speeds.

Self-regulating units offer a degree of automatic exposure control. A sensor cell measures the light reflected from a subject, and the unit quenches flash output automatically when the subject has received enough light. A chart or dial shows which aperture, or apertures, you can set.

Dedicated TTL units offer advanced features and are designed for use with particular cameras. They link up with a camera's through-the-lens (TTL) metering system to control exposure automatically.

Most compacts, and some SLRs, have a built-in flash unit. These units are low powered, but many have a range of advanced features.

Power control

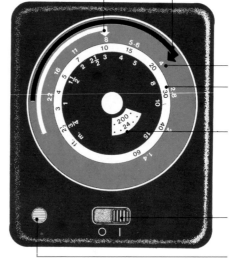

Aperture choice indicator arrows

Aperture scale

Scale of maximum flash-to-subject distances

Film speed window

On-off switch

Ready light

Using a self-regulating flash
The on-camera flash unit above has a calculator dial (enlarged above right) on its top surface. As an example, the dial has been set to show which f-stops you may choose if you are using ISO 200 film. You have a choice of f/4 or f/8 – the white and black arrows point to these f-numbers, and the maximum working distances appear alongside. In the operating sequence explained at the right, you select the correct power output with a switch elsewhere on the unit – again marked in white and black to correspond with the chosen aperture.

1 – Turn the calculator dial until the speed of the film in use appears in the window.

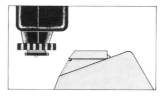

2 – Slide the foot of the flash unit into the camera's hot shoe.

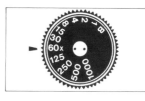

3 – Set the shutter speed to the camera's flash synchronization speed.

4 – Gauge the distance to the subject. Then choose the f-stop – here f/4 for 20 feet.

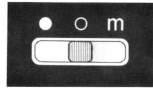

5 – Slide power control to the setting that corresponds with the aperture chosen.

6 – Switch on flash unit. You can take pictures soon after the ready light glows.

Self-regulating flash (left)

Units such as the one at left give a choice of automatic aperture settings. The flash head can be tilted to bounce light off a ceiling.

Dedicated TTL flash
(below left)

The flash unit below links up with the electronics in particular cameras to give fully automatic exposure control. It calculates the duration of each flash by analysing light readings from the camera's through-the-lens (TTL) metering system, and camera-to-subject distance information from special autofocus lenses. An automatic zoom head mechanism matches flash coverage to the field of view of the lens. The AF auxiliary light, positioned below the flash head, emits an infra-red beam in dim light to facilitate autofocusing.

Hammerhead flash
(below)

The powerful flash unit at right is attached to the camera by means of a bracket and a cord. The flash head can be tilted upwards to provide bounce flash.

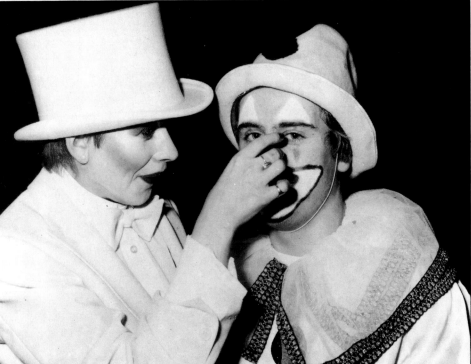

If you use flash to light a portrait subject, you may find that the subject's eyes appear bright red in your pictures. This is known as "red eye", and it is caused by light from the flash reflecting off the back of the subject's eyes and into the camera lens.

Some modern cameras with built-in flash units have a special pre-flash mode (also known as red eye reduction control). When pre-flash mode is activated, the flash fires several low strength bursts of light at the subject just before it fires. This makes the subject's pupils contract, which lessens the red eye effect.

Using simple filters

Sometimes you can improve your pictures by using filters to change, control, or partially block light entering the lens. Although this may sound complicated, filters are just thin sheets of glass, gelatin or plastic that either screw onto the lens front or slip into special holders in the same position.

The filters that are used most often are those that clean up the light from the subject. Skylight or ultra-violet (UV) filters absorb ultraviolet radiation, which can make distant objects appear hazy, particularly when conditions are very bright. Use them in conjunction with a lens hood, which will help to exclude the stray light that sometimes reaches the lens, causing flare and softening the image.

In some circumstances, a polarizing filter can produce even more useful effects. This filter can cut down glare from the sky, from water, from glass or other non-metallic reflective surfaces. Light traveling from these surfaces often becomes polarized, which means that it vibrates mainly in one plane instead of at all angles perpendicular to its line of direction. By blocking the polarized plane, the filter gives a more clearly defined image, and will attractively darken a blue sky.

Another important group of filters absorbs specific colors. A pale yellow filter, for example, passes red and green light but blocks blue. Because this leaves the blue areas underexposed, yellow filters can be used in black-and-white photography to darken the sky and make clouds stand out boldly. With color film, however, every part of the scene will be subtly tinted toward the color of the filter you use. The yellowish series of filters widely known by the Kodak serial number 81, for example, can be used to impart a general warm tint.

You can also buy a great variety of special effects filters. Use them with care as they can all too easily create effects that are garish rather than attractive.

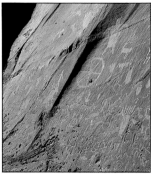
No filter

With polarizing filter

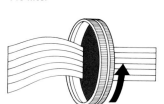
Polarizing filter
This type of filter helps to cut unwanted glare. Rotate the filter's ring until the image in the viewfinder darkens.

The startling difference between the two pictures of prehistoric rock engravings in Utah (above) shows the ability of a polarizing filter to reveal detail that would otherwise be hidden by glare. Polarizing filters also have the effect of darkening blue skies, as in the atmospheric picture of trees (below), and can often enliven landscapes.

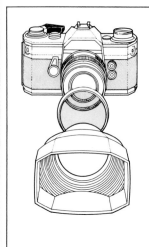
UV filter and lens hood
An ultraviolet filter attached permanently to the lens will improve your outdoor pictures and protect the delicate front of the lens. Lens hoods should frame the picture area closely. Square types such as the one at left with modified corners do this most effectively. They are particularly suited to wide-angle lenses, because circular hoods sometimes cut off the corners of the image at wide apertures.

A soft, misty look can be introduced with a diffusion filter as in the romantic image of the flowers in the picture at far right.

The seascape below has been improved by a graduated filter that darkens part of the image. Without the filter, the sky would have appeared as an empty area of white. The filter contributes the color.

USING COLOR CREATIVELY

Color does more than bring photographs closer to reality. Particular colors often provoke strong responses in the viewer, creating tension or excitement, establishing a soothing feeling of equilibrium or jarring the senses. These powerful reactions may be independent of the subject of the picture, for we react to color emotionally.

Controlling the strength or placement of colors can enable you to produce more effective color pictures. On a few occasions you will have the opportunity to alter the colors of the subject – you could, for example, ask someone to wear a particular color, or change the color of a backdrop. Much more easily, you can manipulate the colors that actually appear in the image by using techniques of composition outlined in this section. For example, you can choose a viewpoint or a lens to include certain areas of color and exclude others. You can fill the viewfinder frame with vivid hues or restrict bright color to just a small area. And you can juxtapose colors for a calming or a vigorous effect.

Understanding the relationship between color and light will further help you to exploit the full potential of the scene you are photographing. This means that time of day and weather strongly influence your pictures, as does whether you are photographing in natural or artificial light.

Colors create mood – that is part of their magic. By using them in a controlled way, you can give pictures just the impact or subtlety you want.

A rainbow in the spray from a fire hose reveals the colors of the sunlight flooding a Pittsburgh intersection. By having the colors arc over the policeman, the photographer infused an ordinary street scene with a sense of wonder.

The richness of color

Strong colors have a more direct impact than those that are muted. Of course, many good photographs have soft colors, for these subtler hues often contribute to the sense of balance or atmosphere in a shot. But when you want colors to contribute drama or have a vigorous effect, you usually want them to appear at their most vivid.

The strongest colors are said to be fully "saturated" – a term borrowed from the dyeing industry. In photography, saturated colors are those that consist of one or two of the primary colors of light – red, green or blue – but not all three, because that introduces an element of grayness. At the same time the saturated colors look most vivid in a certain kind of lighting. For example, a pure red flower will appear more vivid than one that has a brownish tinge, but both will appear most colorful in bright, diffused light. Direct sunlight can make a color

appear less vivid by lightening it – as the left-hand picture of the leaves below demonstrates. Shade, on the other hand, can make the colors appear darker.

When you have identified an area of color that you want to emphasize, the following techniques may help you take full advantage of its richness. First, consider whether you can move around until the angle at which light strikes the subject brings out the strongest color. Unless the subject reflects glare, a position with the sun behind the camera will usually be best. Second, to reproduce the color at maximum saturation, take the exposure reading from the chosen part of the scene rather than the whole view. Although this may underexpose duller parts of the subject, the contrast can enhance the chosen color area. Finally, with some slide films, deliberately underexposing by a half-stop can enrich color, as well as producing good highlight detail.

*1 – **Glare** reflecting from a shiny bush (above) gives the entire photograph a washed-out appearance. The other two pictures were taken in the same light, showing that color saturation in direct sunlight depends on the lighting angle.*

*2 – **Backlighting**, with the bush between camera and sun, gives dramatic contrast in which the leaves are very bright. But because the light shining through the leaves is too harsh, the colors appear somewhat washed-out.*

*3 – **Bright light without glare** shows fully saturated leaves. The photographer took up a position different from the first two, altering the angle between sun, subject and camera. Slight underexposure increases the richly colored effect.*

Color saturation
Pure colors lose intensity if they are either darkened or lightened. The saturated hues at the center of the diagram are progressively desaturated by the addition of white or black. In photography, this means that colors lose strength in shade, or as light glares from a surface. Exposure errors also make colors look less vivid.

Low light *mutes even the pure colors of these flowering trees, an effect that is increased by the haze. The green foliage is so dulled that it is almost gray in color. In conditions such as these, only the strongest colors, perfectly exposed, will preserve any intensity.*

Perfectly lit *by soft window light, a bowl of fruit shows the richness of fully saturated colors. But even here, the effect of light reflecting from the subject can be seen in the highlights on the green apples. With slightly more exposure, these areas would have begun to appear too light and washed-out.*

The dominant color

The ability of modern color film to reproduce all the brilliant colors around us tempts photographers to fill the viewing frame with the richest mixture possible. Sheer profusion of color sometimes works well, but if you are not careful, the picture becomes a jumble of clashing hues.

Often, you can exploit rich, bright color more simply by allowing just one powerful hue to dominate the image. Restricting the color palette in this way can concentrate the impact of the picture – in the startlingly blue seascape shown below, the single block of color seems more emphatic than would several colors jostling for attention.

This way of using color often works best when the dominant color forms a unified background – as does the bright yellow of the umbrella on the right. The more intense the color, the more it will dominate the image, but paler color areas can be used to frame areas of the photograph that are a different hue. For example, in the picture on the right, the lemon of the umbrella makes a lively and vivid backdrop for the girl's shy smile.

To make best use of large, commanding areas of color, try to set them off against other, more neutral, parts of the picture – here the black of the girl's hair, and her white shirt. You may be able to compose the picture so as to exclude discordant, distracting colors in favor of muted hues, such as the soft browns of earth – or of skin itself.

Sea and sky turn deep azure in dawn light. *The dark color, deliberately underexposed, emphasizes the lights of the island temple.*

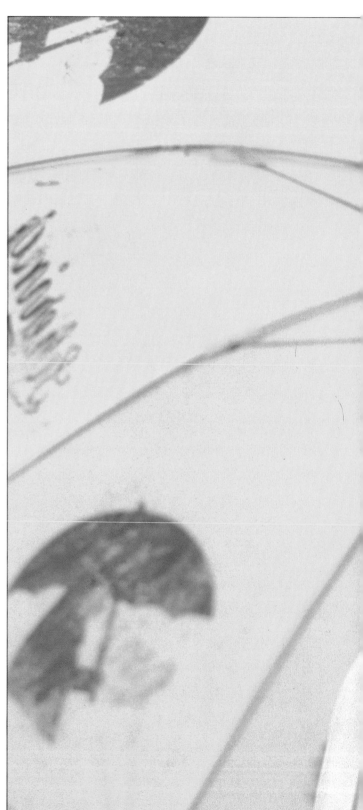

Limited color

Images that have very little color at all can sometimes be extraordinarily evocative. Such nearly monochromatic pictures are expressive in a much more subtle way than are most color photographs, but they often have a compelling simplicity and beauty. Not least, they draw our attention because they are relatively uncommon.

Two main types of monochromatic images are those in which the lighting or the prevailing weather conditions provide an overall draining or blending of colors, and those in which the subject itself has little variety of color. A landscape lit by weak sun early or late in the day, will tend to have a predominant orange glow, especially if there is a haze or dust in the air. Rain, fog, mist, smoke – even pollution in industrial areas – scatter light and mute colors, reducing the color range of the most variegated subjects. You can sometimes use the glow of a fire or the color of artificial light to tint a scene with a single, overall color. One useful tip for enhancing the effect of a colored light source is to shoot toward it without a lens shade, so that light flaring into the lens spreads the color over the whole image, often producing attractive effects.

Subjects that are monochromatic in themselves are usually more difficult to find – unless you can take the picture at close range. As a general rule, the larger your subject, the more likely it is to contain a variety of colors. For this reason, a long lens with its narrow field of view is far more useful than is a wide-angle lens for limiting the color range. Finally, you can always underline the prevailing mood of an existing color range with a pale colored filter.

Soft spray, thrown up by the turbulent waters of Victoria Falls, scatters the light, suppressing true colors and rendering the whole scene in a subdued sepia tone. Only the skeleton of the tree stands out against the mist.

White and black tones can make subtle, effective combinations on color film. You need to develop your powers of observation to find a picture as simple yet expressive as this one.

The golden sunset sky suffuses the Cape of Good Hope with glowing light. A long lens has compressed distance, bringing closer the silhouetted ships on the horizon.

Ice-blue tones of the grass form a soft backdrop to the dark shape of the horse, photographed in failing light. When using a limited color range, look for bold shapes to provide contrast.

Color harmony

Although the way we see colors is highly subjective, most people agree that certain combinations of colors appear more pleasing or harmonious to the eye than others. Moreover, a restricted range of colors makes it easier to create a harmonious composition. A photograph made up of slight variations of a single color, for example, will obviously convey a sense of harmony. So will a mixture of one main color with various neutral shades – grays, browns, white or black. Combining two or more colors requires care. As the color wheel on the right shows, adjacent hues harmonize readily, but opposites contrast strongly. Thus, blues merge well with greens, whereas red and green compete for the viewer's attention setting up an optical impression of vibrancy.

However, there are exceptions to the general rule. Colors that are adjacent on the wheel may clash if they are very bright – a vivid red combined with a bright magenta, for example. Conversely, strongly contrasting colors can harmonize if their tones are either dark and muted or pale and washed out. For example, in the picture of the beach huts on the opposite page, subdued light has blended together a number of different colors. Think of the way the muted red and golden hues of an autumn landscape blend with the subdued greens. In practice, photographing colors harmoniously is a matter of composing your shots carefully to exclude any colors you judge may detract from the mood of the whole. If the hues appear too strident, you can also try waiting for softer lighting from a low or diffused sun to tone everything down.

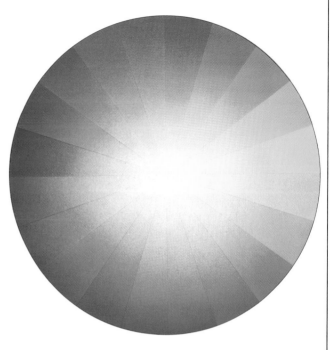

Color wheel
Arrangement of the main color components of light on a wheel makes it easy to see how different hues work together. Here, the wheel is made up of the three primary colors – red, green and blue – and their complementaries – cyan, magenta and yellow. Half the circle has "cool" colors – green, cyan and blue – and half has "warm" colors – magenta, red and yellow. Colors that are close together on the wheel harmonize. But if tones are made paler, even the most contrasting colors blend – as can be seen here toward the center of the wheel.

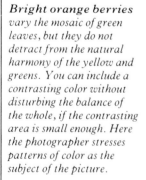

Bright orange berries
vary the mosaic of green leaves, but they do not detract from the natural harmony of the yellow and greens. You can include a contrasting color without disturbing the balance of the whole, if the contrasting area is small enough. Here the photographer stresses patterns of color as the subject of the picture.

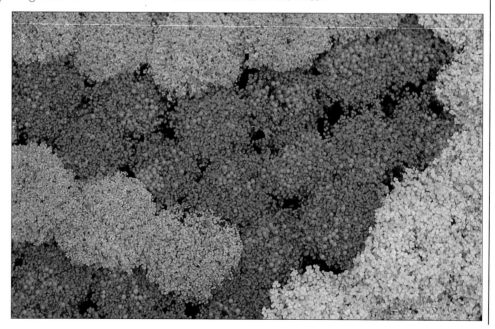

A row of beach huts at dusk creates a darkly harmonious color composition. In spite of the fairly wide range of colors, the tones are all muted and therefore convey a sense of tranquillity. The cool blue sand in the foreground helps to unify the shot.

Half a lemon, dried out by the sun, rests on a translucent painted plate. Although the lighting is bright and direct, all three of the colors blend together, providing a simple, but unusual example of warm color harmony.

Dramatic color

Just as some colors look balanced or harmonious when photographed together, others seem to contrast dramatically, and produce a bold, vibrant effect. You can use such dynamic combinations to inject excitement into a picture, to draw attention to a subject, or purely to create a strong abstract impact. Color contrast is most striking when you restrict your picture to two or three colors — any more than this and the effect will be restless.

The colors likely to produce the most striking contrast are those that lie opposite one another on the color wheel — the warm reds, yellows and oranges against the cool blues and greens, as in the photographs here. But what really determines how much two colors contrast is their relative brightness. Generally the effect is most dramatic if the two hues are equally bright. Pure color contrasts are often easier to find on a relatively small scale — by closing in on a shop window display, for example. When you have complete control over the ingredients of your picture, you can consciously set up bold color contrasts, as the photographer did for the fashion shot on the opposite page.

Ornamental plants *often have colors almost as vivid as the artificial dyes and pigments in fabric and paint. At left, richly colored coleus leaves provide a perfect color contrast – red and green are opposite each other on the color wheel.*

A delicate green sapling *stands out crisply against the bright red fence, below left. The tree's fragility seems underlined by the strength of the red. A powerful yet very simple composition accentuates the dramatic contrast of colors.*

A bright blue door *makes the girl's yellow trousers look all the more vivid. The photographer has used the blue background to both isolate and frame the figure. And the picture shows how contrast increases when two light hues are juxtaposed.*

Abstract color

You can give your pictures a striking abstract quality quite easily by exploiting bold color areas. All you need to do is to frame the subject so that colors rather than recognizable forms are emphasized.

A good way of making color abstract is to exclude part of the subject. We identify things largely by their outlines and the context in which we find them. Isolated by tight or unconventional framing, objects appear as a two-dimensional arrangement in the picture. The effect of the yellow dress opposite was achieved in this way. By cropping out the girl's head with the frame, the photographer has removed the obvious center of attention and concentrated on the composition as an arrangement of colors.

Alternatively, you can tilt the camera so that the subject, seen from an unusual angle, becomes less important than the colors. You can even try taking the picture with the subject deliberately out of focus to make the shapes less distinct and more to be enjoyed as areas of color.

Lighting is an important factor in emphasizing color at the expense of literal representation. Flat light on an overcast day can be used to give a two-dimensional effect because there are no shadows to throw objects into relief. On the other hand, direct sunlight, provided there is no glare, can illuminate colors and bring out strong contrasts between them, producing strikingly vivid effects.

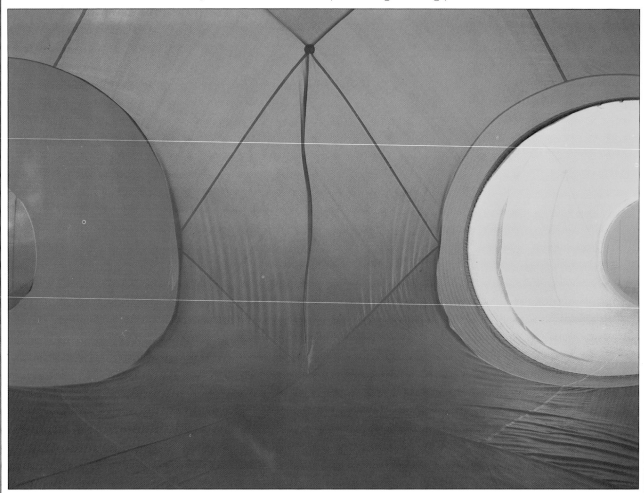

An inflatable play space provides the setting for a boldly abstract composition. The photographer framed the scene to balance the three strong colors of the translucent material and has excluded any details that could act as reference points to help interpret the subject.

Saturated color

You need to expose very carefully to bring out the brilliance of colors in direct sunlight, and to prevent them from becoming dissipated in glare and bouncing reflections. The pictures here show that colors often look richer in more diffused light. This is largely because contrast is reduced, making exposure easier to control. At the same time, the softer light helps to harmonize or balance colors – if that is your aim. And most important of all, diffused sunlight casts softer, less noticeable shadows. In portraiture, particularly, skin tones are thus recorded more accurately, and the whole image is less likely to be confused by the presence of deep, hard-edged shadows.

Light clouds and haze high in the sky diffuse light by redistributing the strongly directional rays of the sun across a larger part of the sky. The result is that shadows become less intense and their edges less sharp. Instead of being bright in the sun or dark in the shade, colors are brought closer together in tone. Provided the cloud cover is light, hues will retain their intensity. And, in the absence of hard shadows or reflected glare, the individual richness of the colors may actually increase. Because the key to showing any color at full saturation is accurate exposure, the reduced contrast between naturally dark and light colors will allow you to choose an exposure that suits both. The varied greens of landscapes can thus be recorded with equal brilliance in the muted light. And in portraits, you can more easily blend and balance flesh tones, clothing and background colors.

A red fish, photographed in Kenya, glows with an almost unnatural brilliance against the equally vivid colors of the fisherman's shorts and T-shirt. The hazy sun reveals the full saturation of all the colors, without the intrusion of dark shadows. And the light keeps to a minimum the glare from the shiny scales.

Soft skin colors gave the key reading for this picture. But the sunlight, diffused by light clouds, restricted the range of tones. Thus reds and greens are correctly exposed also, and appear fully saturated. This light is ideal when you want to bring out the soft modeling of a face.

A sea of tulips vibrates with color, every leaf, stalk and petal standing out in the soft light. Stronger sun might have made the flower heads gleam even more brightly, but the shadows created would have obscured the green parts of the plants, making them dark and underexposed on the film.

Muted color

Photographs in dense haze, mist or fog produce some of the most delicate and subtle color effects. These conditions not only weaken sunlight, but also spread the light around the subject, and themselves become part of the landscape. Haze is made up of microscopic particles suspended in the air – common during long, hot spells and also in polluted areas such as cities. The droplets of water that constitute mist and fog are larger and more often found at higher altitudes, or near rivers, lakes, or the sea.

Haze, mist and fog all thicken the atmosphere, acting as a kind of continuous filter. The result is that intense hues are muted to pastel. At the same time, colors tend to merge into a narrower range, creating images as beautiful and fragile as the harvesting scene below. In extremely dense mist or fog, the colors of a landscape may become almost monochromatic; hence the effects of these weather conditions can be useful if you want to give a soft overall tone to an image or to harmonize colors that would jar with each other in brighter, more direct light. And the absence of distracting detail can help you to appreciate the compositional qualities of a landscape more easily.

The softening of color in haze, mist or fog becomes more pronounced with distance. The farther the subject is from the camera, the more simplified and delicate the image becomes, so that in a misty landscape, the different parts of the scene often appear to be arranged in receding layers of lighter and lighter color, as in the picture of mountain ranges opposite. Sometimes, you can emphasize the sense of depth this produces by choosing a viewpoint that includes strong foreground colors.

Remember that the effect of fog and mist are not always regular and predictable. In a breeze, wisps of mist trail around trees, rocks and hillsides, often linking hues or emphasizing the colors of clear areas. And in dense but localized mist, of the kind that often hangs over wetlands early on a summer morning, trees and other subjects can appear almost in silhouette if the sun is directly behind them. Light itself then supplies the only color, and in low sun, the scene may appear in delicate tones of orange or pink. You should look out for such unusual effects and exploit them by experimenting with viewpoint and camera angle. They open up marvelous opportunities for mood and atmosphere.

Late afternoon haze makes this Burmese agricultural scene almost monochromatic, turning everything a warm golden color. The stubble of the field enhances the feeling of shimmering heat, and the pale rim of light around the group reveals a perfect choice of exposure.

Receding mountains are reduced here into broad washes of color by early morning mist. This creates an imposing sense of depth as the planes of color fade from green to lighter blues. The whole image is given an ethereal quality by the orange light tipping the farthest ridges as the sun penetrates the mist.

135

The balance of color/1

The sun, a candle and a glowing coal all give off light as they release heat. But the color of the light that each produces is not identical, because the heat at which each source burns varies enormously. As a result, each source sends out a different mixture of wavelengths, with substantial effects on the colors of the objects illuminated. These effects are particularly noticeable in color photographs because films are balanced to give accurate colors in light of a particular wavelength mixture.

There is no point in relying on your eyes to detect minor changes in lighting. We see what we expect to see, ignoring subtle variations of color. A white shirt will still look white to us whether we see it in sunlight or indoors under artificial light. However, film records the predominant color of the lighting literally. Ordinary film for daylight use is balanced for average noon light in which the illumination comes mainly from the predominantly white light of the direct sun. Unless you correct it with a filter, lighting of a very different balance will inevitably change the colors in photographs taken with this same film, producing unreal colors – an effect known as a color cast.

The color of a light source does not depend only on its heat. For example, atmospheric factors come into play when we consider the way daylight changes in color. As a result, whereas daylight or noon sun appears neutral, the wavelength mixture reaching us varies as the sun rises or sets. Similarly, clouds or haze filter out some wavelengths by absorption, or scatter others so that they predominate in the light reflected from the sky itself. On a clear day, the sky looks intensely blue because of the scattering of blue wavelengths by atmospheric molecules. And this means that the light is much bluer in shaded areas, where illumination comes only from the sky, than in areas reached by the light of direct sun.

Light sources can be codified according to their so-called color temperature on the kelvin (k) scale. Temperature is the mode of measurement because a heated object, such as an iron bar, will change color from red through yellow and white to dazzling blue as the temperature increases. But remember that the kelvin number assigned to a light source relates to the color of the light produced, not to the physical heat of the source. Thus, the color temperature of daylight may be higher (because bluer) on a cold overcast day when all the light is coming from the sky, than in direct warm sun. At midday, average (photographic) daylight has a color temperature of about 5,500k, and it is for light of this color temperature that most color films are balanced, giving accurate color in normal outdoor scenes.

The color temperature scale

Whether you are photographing in artificial or natural light, all light sources have a certain preponderance of wavelengths that give the lighting a particular color. These different colors are shown below as a band of rising color temperatures, extending from the reddish lighting characteristic of candlelight and sunsets up to the bluer light normally found in pictures taken in the shade or on overcast days. The color effects of natural light in various conditions are illustrated above the color temperature band, those of artificial light sources below the band.

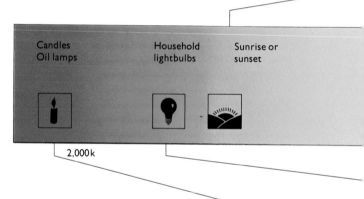

Candles
Oil lamps

Household
lightbulbs

Sunrise or
sunset

2,000k

Candlelight, in the absence of any other light source, produces a strong reddish-yellow cast, because a candle burns at a far lower temperature than the noonday sun. Although the light is usually too dim to show much detail, pictures taken by this source can have strong atmosphere, as in this shot of a Bangkok procession.

At sunrise and sunset, *natural light is at its reddest because the light has to travel farther through the atmosphere. As a result, many short blue wavelengths are absorbed, allowing the longer red wavelengths to predominate. Below, the sunset sky has tinged the gray rocks of the Grand Canyon with red light.*

At noon, *with a few white clouds, daylight is neutral in color. Because this is the light for which most films are balanced, the colors of objects under noon sunlight look correct. The picture of kites on a beach was taken in these conditions – and shows pure whites and reds in the nearest kite.*

In the shade, *photographs often have a strong blue cast, because objects are illuminated only by light reflected from the blue sky, and receive no direct sunlight. Overcast skies also usually produce bluish colors. Here, a cool blue light suffuses both the white ibis and the water.*

| Morning or evening sunlight | Average noon daylight Electronic flash | Hazy sky | Heavily overcast sky | Reflection from clear blue sky (shade) |

5,500 k

16,000 k

Household bulbs *burn hotter than candles, but produce a much yellower light than does the sun. This means that with ordinary daylight film in the camera, pictures taken in room lighting usually have an overall orange cast. The picture of a sleeping child shows that the warm effect of this light can suit skin tones.*

Electronic flash *is balanced to match the color temperature of noon daylight. Thus, you can use it safely indoors or out, without creating color casts. Had this studio flash portrait been taken by the light of tungsten photographic lamps, a special slide film (described overleaf) would have been needed.*

Fluorescent light
This does not belong on the color temperature scale because it is not a burning light source. The color casts it produces vary greatly. Above, the greenish lights of an airport runway give the Concorde a surreal look.

The balance of color/2

Not many situations in photography call for any special measures to cope with the color quality of the light. Most pictures are taken outdoors by the light of the sky or sun, and slight variations in color caused by weather conditions or time of day often add pictorial interest rather than cause problems (see pages 132-35). But sometimes a light source produces a color mixture too far removed from the lighting for which your film is intended. When this happens, unacceptable color casts may appear in the picture – for example, green flesh tones in a portrait. You can avoid this situation either by choosing special film or by using filters to modify the light as it enters the lens. Color print films have a fair tolerance to different kinds of light because corrections can be made in processing, but with slide film the balance is crucial.

A special slide film is available for shooting indoors under tungsten bulbs. However, this film is balanced for powerful lamps used in photography studios, and will not entirely remove the unnatural color cast produced by ordinary, lower-watt bulbs. Alternatively, conversion and light-balancing filters are available in a complete range of colors, including those for fluorescent lighting. Some of the most useful filters are demonstrated on these two pages.

Daylight and film balance
Most color films, print and slide, are designed to work best in daylight, accurately reproducing the colors we see (right). Almost all the film you use will be balanced for daylight. The exception is slide film balanced for tungsten lighting. This film has a bluer quality overall, rendering a scene lit by orange light from tungsten lamps as near white. Used in ordinary daylight, the film produces unnatural blues (far right).

1 – Daylight with daylight film

2 – with tungsten film

Tungsten light and film balance
In tungsten light, whether from ordinary bulbs or special tungsten photographic lamps, film balanced for daylight records an orange or yellow cast (right). Although the warm color can be attractive, this is not how we see the scene. For more accurate results, the light can be partly corrected with a bluish No. 80A filter (far right, above). However, for greater accuracy, use slide film balanced for tungsten light (far right, below).

1 – Tungsten light with daylight film

2 – with No. 80A filter

3 – with tungsten film

Filtering fluorescent light

Although fluorescent lamps look white to the eye, they produce an unpredictable variety of color casts on film – ranging through yellow, blue or green. The scene in an airport control tower at right has a distinctly greenish cast from the fluorescent tubes. A fluorescent filter (far right) does not balance the light perfectly to the daylight film. but does give a warmer, more natural look.

1 – Fluorescent light with daylight film

2 – with fluorescent filter

Filtering overcast daylight

Heavy clouds scatter the shorter blue wavelengths of sunlight, raising the color temperature of the light and producing a blue cast on film (right). This still-life was rephotographed with a No. 81B pink filter to reduce the proportion of blue (far right). Many photographers use this filter as a matter of course on cloudy days.

1 – Overcast daylight with daylight film

2 – with No. 81B filter

Corrective printing: tungsten light

Filtration control in printing may restore accurate colors to print film. The portrait photographed in household tungsten light (right) has a strong orange cast. By asking the printer for a reprint with corrective filtration, (far right), the photographer secured a much more accurate result.

1 – Tungsten light, uncorrected

2 – with corrective printing

Corrective printing: fluorescent light

The green cast from fluorescent light is more obtrusive than the orange from tungsten lamps. This portrait, shot by the light from fluorescent tubes in an office (right), has an unpleasant color if uncorrected. When asked to compensate. the printer produced an improvement (far right), but has not succeeded in imitating the natural colors of a daylit scene.

1 – Fluorescent light, uncorrected

2 – with corrective printing

PICTURES OF OURSELVES

The first pictures any photographer takes are likely to be of people. When they are of family or friends, the most popular subjects, they have a personal meaning that can move us because they record our own lives. But whether the subject is familiar or not, the pictures that we turn to most often do more than simply record what people look like. Instead, they reveal what is individual about the subjects, and perhaps what they are feeling. The portraits on the following pages all exhibit this special quality.

Pictures of people close to us can have a direct emotional impact because the photographer can reveal insights impossible to a casual observer, and catch moments that could never be staged. Yet strong, spontaneous pictures such as the one opposite are relatively rare. Although friends and relatives are convenient subjects, they can also be among the most difficult to photograph well. The first section that follows will suggest ways of avoiding pitfalls, so that your pictures give the impression of having been snatched from life. And it will show you how to capture candid glimpses of people in a variety of settings.

Even more challenging is a formally posed portrait, especially if it is of someone you hardly know. You must quickly establish a basic understanding of character and a mutual confidence. You must decide what surroundings and lighting will suit your subject. And then you must find a pose that is telling, yet lets the subject feel at ease. The same need for consideration and control applies to nude photography. The sections on portraits and nudes show how you can extend your skill and creativity in these areas, both of which require special planning.

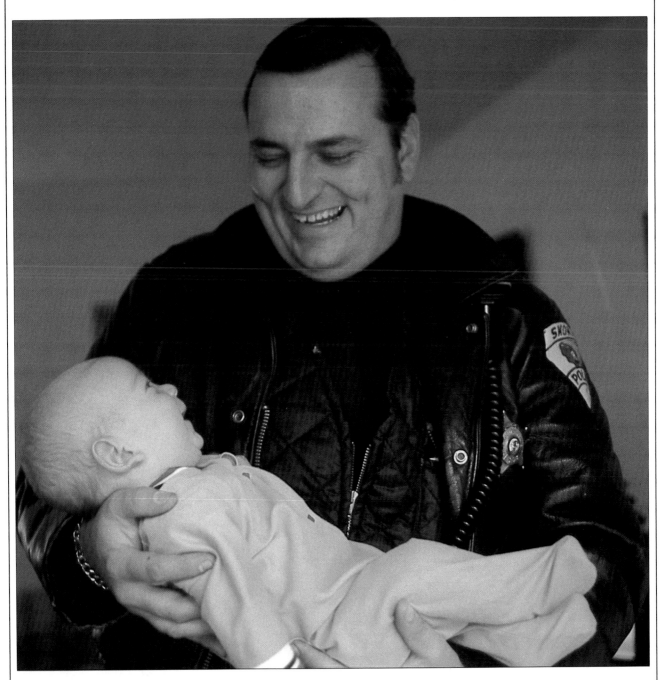

A burly police officer with his baby shows the power of a simple, direct portrait. Their mutual delight is heightened by contrasts – between the father's leather-jacketed toughness and his gentle pride; and between his big hands and the tiny body he is cradling so securely.

The unposed elegance of a fledgling ballerina is captured in this delightful informal picture, taken while the child was lost in thought. A moment later the expression might have changed. Soft light from the window is perfect for the delicate skin tones of her limbs.

The loving glance of a husband at his wife says everything about their amiable relationship. The couple's son took the picture from behind the bench while they were waiting for him to load the camera for a more posed photograph.

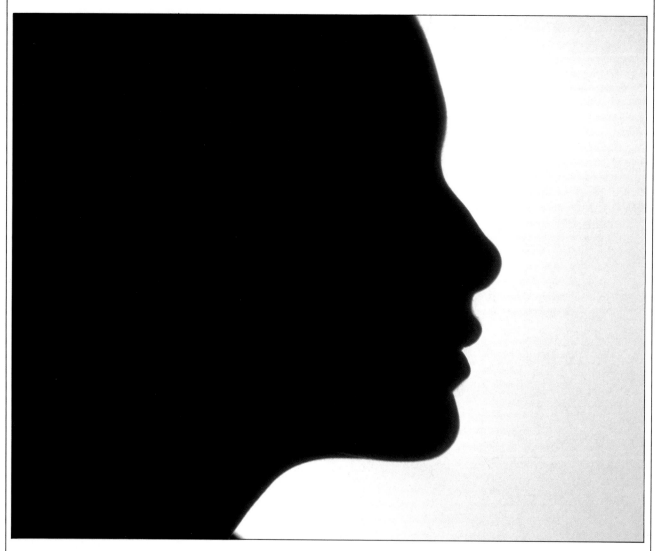

Simplified shape – *the flowing outline of a girl's profile silhouetted against a light background – is the only element in this highly graphic portrait. Backlighting deliberately excludes every surface detail.*

Strong modeling of form
*was needed in this picture to
bring out the expressive force
of a Kickapoo Indian's face.
The photographer used light
from windows on two sides
of a small room to carve
the man's chunky features.*

An old Mexican relaxes in golden
evening sunlight. The photographer
positioned the subject outdoors in
familiar surroundings to achieve this
natural portrait. Yet the warm light
of the low sun is as effective as any
that a studio set-up could provide.

A gaudy red room provides an apt setting for a painter sitting below one of her pictures – a pastiche of Velazquez's celebrated Venus. The photographer posed her to echo the picture, and used a single, large studio flash unit.

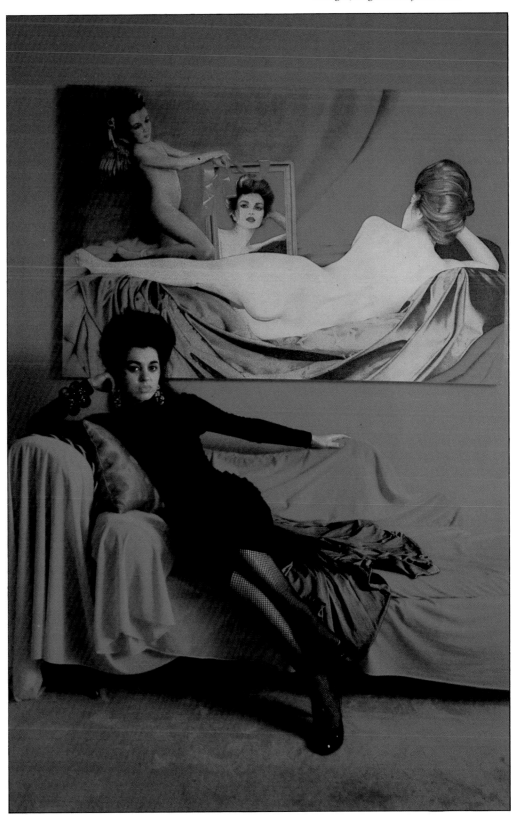

Suspended bird-like above
the swimming pool, a friend of
the photographer's appears in
a spectacular and memorable
head-on view. The picture was
one of several taken as the girl
practiced the dive.

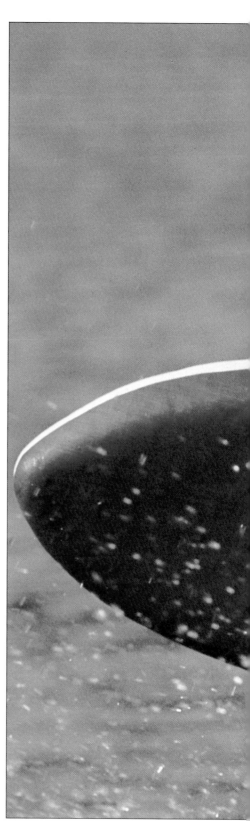

149

A rugged profile (left),
obliquely lit and in close-up,
displays a classic simplicity.
Deliberate underexposure
has increased the dramatic,
high-contrast effect.

A steelworker (above)
stands in the glow of the
furnace he tends. By using
this fiery, unnatural light,
the photographer shows the
hardship of the job and the
stolid toughness of the man.

The romantic mood of this simple nude comes from the use of soft light from a large window, a relaxed pose and an unpretentious setting. The picture's easy naturalness belies its careful planning.

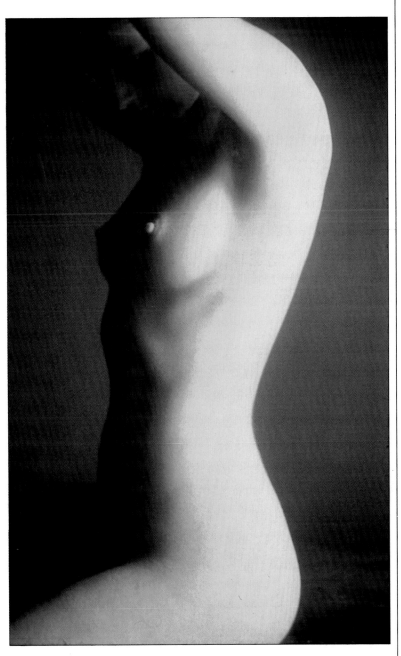

These full forms and classic lines appear almost as a sculpture in light. The photographer used a strong studio photolamp, diffused by a plastic screen and angled to stress the curved outline.

Seated on a rock *above a pool of clear water, a girl becomes part of her setting. The photographer framed the scene to exclude the sky and concentrate on the contrast between her smooth body and the roughness of the rock.*

An athletic black body *(right) lies stretched out in a surreal landscape – in fact Utah's salt flats at sunset. Deliberate underexposure has increased the harsh contrast in a nude of expressive and elemental power.*

PEOPLE AT THEIR BEST

Taking good pictures of people in their daily lives requires some forethought – it is surprisingly easy to end up with a muddled image, or one in which the subject looks bored, listless or wooden. What people really want is a picture that brings out their individuality and shows that they are alive. Whether you are taking the most informal snapshot or carefully recording a family occasion such as a wedding, your aim should be to capture the essence of a subject's personality as reflected in a particular situation. Such clarity comes from knowing in advance what you want an image to portray, and then achieving this in the simplest and most direct way.

The following pages explore techniques for obtaining the best from people – from getting them to appear more natural to placing them in the right light. You can then reach past the barriers that even friends and family put up before the camera, and past the clutter of surroundings, to arrive at whatever is distinctive about the character of your subject.

The halo of light around a girl's tousled red-gold hair seems to embody the warmth of her laughter. By getting the subject to swing round suddenly, the photographer obtained a spontaneous and perfectly relaxed picture. Since the girl's face is out of the sun, there is no squint to mar the effect.

Expressing personality

Faces – especially the faces of people we know – are supremely eloquent guides to personality. Any photographer realizes the advantage of a vivid expression or gesture. Because of this, it is easy to forget that other elements in a picture also provide valuable clues to character.

Everything included in the final image can help in building an impression of the subject, from a person's hairstyle, dress and way of sitting or standing, to pieces of furniture and other objects – indeed the entire setting. Just by placing your subjects in a sympathetic environment, you can reveal something of their personalities. In the two close-ups below on the right, the colors of outdoor settings serve to reinforce the healthy appearance of the subjects. To take such spontaneous pictures, you need to decide in advance what aspect of your subject's character you want to emphasize, and then be on hand with a loaded camera until the moment you are waiting for presents itself.

Photographing people with their favorite possessions will speak volumes about their personalities. You do not need to clutter the picture with objects to get the message across: the best portraits are often those in which the photographer has singled out just a few telling details that seem to encapsulate a person's attitudes and lifestyle. Again, you should plan in advance what you want the picture to say about your subject. The carefully posed portrait on the opposite page is a classic example of how selected details can be strikingly used to express individual personality.

The tanned complexion and windswept hair of this girl, framed by a background of blue sky and water, convey simply but powerfully the independence and vitality of a fresh-air enthusiast.

A style-aware teenager props a shoulder against a boutique window. The girl's defiant attitude, the split image of her reflection, even the eye-catching motif on her shirt, combine to give an image full of character and vitality.

Radiating zest for life, this informal portrait taken at a ski resort acquires additional sparkle from the clean, bright background of the snow. The off-center position of the shot and the angle of the head help to suggest an easy-going, extraverted personality.

Relaxing the subject

Even your closest friends and immediate family – people who are normally quite at ease in your company – can freeze up suddenly when you aim a camera at them. The resulting picture may look stilted and unnatural.

Every photographer has to cope with camera shyness at some time. How you go about relaxing the subject depends partly on what type of person you are dealing with, partly on your relationship with him, and partly on the situation. To a certain extent, you will have to extemporize – but there are some advance preparations you can make. Get the technicalities out of the way well before the portrait session: decide which exposure, lighting angle and camera viewpoint you want – using a stand-in for the subject if necessary – and prefocus whenever this is possible. Unless you are confident of your technique, you are likely to seem nervous, and this will make your subject feel uncomfortable.

Think about props, too. One of the best ways of putting people at ease is to divert their attention from the camera. Giving your subject something to do will help, as in the pictures below of the boy playing with his father's pipe. Adolescents, particularly, tend to appear self-conscious and uncomfortable in portraits. Try to find a situation or setting that will give the subjects confidence.

If you are photographing a couple who enjoy a close relationship, such as the father and son shown here, you may find them becoming so absorbed in each other that they forget the camera completely. Such happy situations are more likely to develop if you remain as unobtrusive as possible. A telephoto lens allows you to distance yourself from your subjects, but still close in on any aspect of their image that catches your eye.

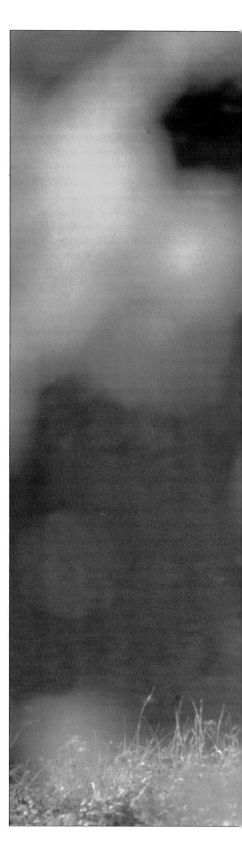

Engrossed in a game with a pipe, the father and son in the two pictures above are completely oblivious to the camera. The use of a 135mm telephoto lens has allowed the photographer to stay back and focus only on the smiling profiles, closely linked, and delicately rimmed by the sunlight.

With the boy relaxed (right), the photographer moved back farther to get a picture that showed more of the setting. The out-of-focus foliage adds to the soft, mellow mood of each of the photographs, and helps to create the sense that the father and son are occupying a private world.

At work and play

We define people as much by what they do as by the way they look, and friends or relatives engaged in activities, whether at work or play, make excellent subjects for informal photographs. Such pictures can reveal fresh facets of personality in someone we know well – and they often succeed in bringing a person to life when a more orthodox and straight-forward portrait would fail to do so.

This is true particularly if your subject tends to be ill at ease before a camera, or has a reserved personality that is difficult to draw out in a posed picture. The great advantage of photographing people intent on what they are doing is that they are unselfconscious. In addition, shared absorption in a hobby, task or game makes it easier to capture a relationship between people. The pictures here of friends tussling over a basketball, of a young fisher-man with his grandfather, and of a camera-shy farmer shearing a sheep, are all examples of people who are completely in their element, and therefore at their most natural and authentic.

Remember that the activity itself will provide more than enough visual interest – so keep the background simple and concentrate on a few selected details. Pictures of children playing are particularly difficult to organize coherently, and you may find that a high viewpoint helps to separate the figures, as in the picture below.

An overhead view of three friends playing basketball has brought clarity to what might have been a confusing picture. The triangular shape of the figures with the colored ball at the apex, is well placed in the frame, and emphasized by the plain, square tiles. Yet the outstretched fingers and straining expressions of the boys still capture the feeling of movement.

The art of shrimp netting *absorbs a boy and his grandfather at the seaside. The intent concentration of the pair excludes the camera's presence – an effect the photographer helped by the use of a telephoto lens. A shallow depth of field has kept the subjects and the reflections in the wet sand sharp while blurring the breakwater and the pier in the background of the picture.*

A shaft of light *focuses attention on the balanced shapes of two faces, one bent down over his task, the other tilting upward. The photographer respected the shearer's reluctance to have a formal portrait taken, and by waiting quietly, captured this telling picture of strength, experience and care. The simple stone wall contrasts well with the sheep's woolly coat.*

163

The right lens

Catching a telling expression or pose is the key to many successful pictures of people. But choice of lens may play an important part in determining the composition and impact of the picture. A standard 50mm or 55mm lens — excellent for half- or full-length portraits — has the outstanding merit of showing people in a natural scale with one another and with their surroundings. Yet you can expand your creative range when photographing people by trying lenses with longer or shorter focal lengths, especially for certain subjects.

A telephoto lens has two distinct qualities that make it useful. First, its magnifying effect allows you to stay well back so that you can fill the frame with a head-and-shoulders portrait without crowding the subject. And second, the shallow depth of field of this lens becomes a particular asset in portraiture, when often you want to blur a confusing background so as to provide a plain frame for the main subject. A lens with a focal length of 200mm or larger can be used, but those of 85mm to 135mm give a more pleasing perspective — and are certainly easier to handle.

Wide-angle lenses come into their own when, conversely, you want to include background or foreground details in the picture — either because the setting is interesting or because it supplies a kind of commentary on the character or interests of the subject. Moderately wide-angle lenses are the most useful, particularly those with focal lengths of 28mm or 35mm. Their broad angles of view and great depth of field mean that you can show sharp details of a subject's environment, whether these details are close to the lens or distant.

A wide-angle lens has special advantages when you are photographing large groups. You can fit everybody into the frame without going so far back that the faces and expressions become lost. Sometimes, too, the tendency of wide-angle lenses to distort perspective at close range can be used creatively, as in the picture of the boy on the right, who is challenging all comers to invade his private territory in a tree house.

An old man's head looks as grand and imposing as a biblical prophet's, an effect helped by the close framing and shallow depth of field of a 200mm telephoto lens. The distance from which you can get close-ups with this lens allows the subject to remain relaxed.

A huge mural dominates the boy's solitary ball game in this unusual picture, taken with a standard lens. The sense of scale would have been less impressive with another focal length: a wide-angle lens would have made the wall appear smaller, and a telephoto lens would have included only part of the scene.

The ideal light

Bright sun and blue sky may seem ideal conditions for photography, but they are seldom good for photographing people. Strong sunlight is too intense to show subtleties of skin tones and texture, and from some angles the harsh light can turn fine lines of character into deep wrinkles. The high sun of noon has particularly unattractive effects, putting deep shadows under a subject's nose and chin and making the eyes sink into dark hollows. In these conditions, look for an area of open shade with enough soft, reflected illumination to light your subject adequately.

The weaker sunlight of morning and evening is much better. Even so, people will find difficulty in facing the sun with their eyes relaxed and open, and you should try to place them so that the light falls on their faces at an angle of about 45 . The soft reddish light of evening warming a tanned face and glinting in the subject's eyes can convey the glow of a summer's day more effectively than the harsh light of noonday, as the amusing and inventive group photograph below shows.

If you want to use oblique directional daylight to bring out the strength of a face, thin clouds or haze will help to diffuse the sunlight and reveal some form. Thicker clouds go farther in diffusing the light, and provide gentle modeling of a face, as is evident in the picture of the old lady opposite with a sheaf of wheat. In addition, overcast weather eases the technical problem of choosing an exposure to suit both highlight and shadow areas without losing detail in either. The ideal illumination is the broad, even light of an overcast day, which is muted but not dull – this kind of light reveals detail clearly but does not create the hard shadows that can ruin a picture. Less-intense light also enables you to open up the aperture so as to reduce depth of field if you need to blur out a background.

Fishing nets on the beach frame an unusual group portrait in which the low evening sun tinges the faces with warm orange light. Harsher noon sunlight would have shown less texture in the nets, and cast obscuring shadows.

Harvest home, and proud of her ability to help, this elderly farmer's wife stands in light diffused by heavy clouds, so that only soft shadows play over her lined face. The fine detail shows what effective pictures can be taken in this light. To offset the blue color tinge that overcast weather often produces on slide film, the photographer used a No. 81A pale yellow conversion filter.

A lazy day by the sea comes to an end for a beach sitter as hazy clouds reduce the intensity of the afternoon sun. The pale, even light and muted colors helped the photographer to capture a picture that evokes the atmosphere perfectly.

167

Backlight and silhouettes

Backlighting, with the light coming from behind the subject, changes our view of a person dramatically by emphasizing the outlines, rather than the detailed forms, of faces and figures. Because people can be identified by outlines alone, when you know them well the results of backlighting can be distinctive and intriguing – a combination of familiarity and mystery.

Depending on the strength and source of light, and the exposure, you can create very different effects with backlighting. Intense light produces dark, almost two-dimensional silhouettes, like those of the children in the photograph below, if you take the meter reading for the bright background. When there is also some frontal lighting – either direct or reflected – you can retain some of the details in silhouetted shapes. For example, in the picture on the opposite page, the photographer chose an exposure that allowed strong sunlight reflected through the window to reveal the delicate tone of the girls' skin. If the sun is not directly behind the subject, the result may be a silhouette ringed with light. Rim lighting, as it is known, imparts a radiant warmth, particularly suited to romantic portraits such as the one on the right.

The aura of light around an embracing couple adds to the romantic intensity of this close-up photograph, while the silhouetting of the figures conveys the impression of a private moment.

Children playing on a jetty (left) are transformed into almost hieroglyphic figures by strong backlighting. The photographer set an exposure for the lighter background, underexposing the figures to obtain the black silhouettes and monochromatic setting.

The willowy profiles of two sisters are backlit by sunlight delicately filtering through curtains. Reflected light from the window gently dapples the girls' soft skin and picks out details in the silhouettes, while the shape of the alcove accentuates the subjects' long, slender limbs.

169

Modifying the light

For photographing people indoors, no source of lighting is as natural and convenient as the daylight coming through a window or an open door. Usually the light is reasonably bright, with none of the color-balance problems of household lighting.

However, unless the room has large windows on more than one wall, window light tends to be strongly directional. If you do not take steps to modify the light, half of your subject's face may come out bright and the other half in deep shadow. Occasionally, this can be an advantage. For the picture below, the photographer deliberately restricted the light from a sunlit window to a narrow beam. As a result, the contrast of light and shade draws attention to the strong lines of her friend's face and chin.

More often, you will want to avoid stark differences between highlight and shadow areas. Strong contrast makes it difficult to select the best exposure for showing natural skin tones or for revealing the subtleties of facial form. One way of reducing contrast is to reflect some of the light streaming through the window back toward the shaded side of your subject's face. For example, the book the child is reading in the picture at the top of this page not only makes a natural prop but also serves the very practical function of lightening shadows on her face. Alternatively, you may be able to place your subject closer to a light-colored internal wall that will reflect back some light.

Softening the light from the window can also help to mute the brighter part of a scene, so that you can increase the exposure and show more detail in the shadows. Lace curtains or translucent blinds will help to diffuse the daylight entering the room. An equally effective diffusion technique is to pin a bed-sheet or tracing paper across the window frame.

A young reader sits by a window, and bright sunlight flooding into the room gives her hair a halo of light. Unmodified, the strong back-lighting would have thrown her face into deep shadow. However, the photographer used her book to bounce back some sunlight and soften the harsh contrast.

Peering from shadows, the young woman at left leans into a pool of light. The photographer needed some way of excluding from this picture the over-cluttered surroundings of the room. She pulled heavy curtains and moved in close for a strong picture that uses just a chink of light.

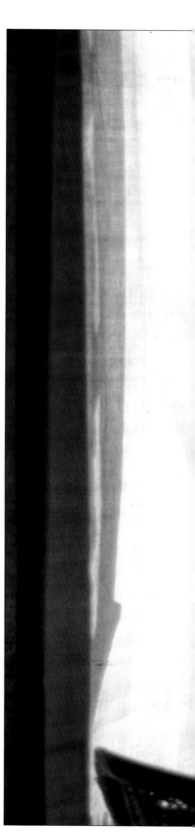

Using flash

An electronic flash unit is a highly useful source of light, but perched on top of the camera, pointing directly forward, much of its potential may be wasted. Pictures taken with the flash in the accessory shoe can look harsh and unnatural – portraits may appear unflattering, because flash, when it is aimed directly in line with the camera, seems to flatten the subject's features.

There are two solutions to this problem. The simplest is to move the flash off the accessory shoe and hold it above or to one side of the camera. To do this, you need a flash cord. Basic types plug into a socket on the camera body and synchronize the flash with the shutter. More advanced types – for use with modern, computer-controlled cameras – have an attachment that slots onto the camera's accessory shoe. Electrical contacts on the attachment link up with those on the accessory shoe and allow exposure information to pass between the camera and the flash.

To provide modeling illumination, point the flash straight toward the subject, but at an angle from the camera. It is easier to do this if you use a long cord and get someone to hold the flash for you.

The other way to improve flash pictures is to use a flash unit with a tilting head, and bounce the light off a reflective surface, such as a white-painted wall or ceiling. This method produces very soft lighting.

For correct exposure with bounce flash using a manual flash unit, calculate the total distance from the tilted flash head to the ceiling and from the ceiling to the subject. Use the exposure table on the flash to find the "correct" aperture for this distance, then set an aperture two stops wider than this – the wider aperture setting compensates for the light that's absorbed by the ceiling.

Self-regulating and dedicated flash units set the correct exposure automatically. With a self-regulating flash, set the largest automatic aperture option and ensure that the sensor cell is pointed directly at your subject when you make an exposure.

If your flash unit has a second head, turn it on for bounce flash exposures. The low strength flash from this head fills-in shadows cast by the main flash and puts an attractive catchlight in your subject's eyes. You can achieve the same effect if you fix a piece of white card to the top of the main flash head. When the flash fires, most of the light bounces off the ceiling, but some of it bounces off the card and directly onto your subject.

Bounce flash has certain limitations – in rooms with high or dark ceilings there is a danger of underexposure. Similarly, it cannot be used in rooms with colored walls or ceilings, as the reflected light takes on the color of the reflective surface. In such cases, try bouncing the flash off a large, white board.

Sparkling highlights give this impromptu portrait a party atmosphere. By taking the flash unit off the camera, the photographer was able to move the shadows to one side, and avoid the flat lighting that flash can produce when mounted on the camera.

Flash off the camera
Hold the flash at arm's length, and point it toward the subject. You need a long flash cord, and it helps if you have someone to hold the flash for you at an appropriate angle.

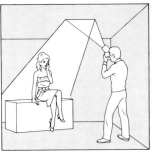

*The **natural look** of the portrait above comes not from daylight, but from bounce flash. With the flash unit pointed at the ceiling, the light reaching the subject is diffused, soft, and even — perfect for portraits.*

Bouncing flash
Choose a wide aperture setting and tilt the flash unit's head upward. This technique works best when the subject is close, and the ceiling or reflective surface is low and white.

Fill-in flash
Bright sunlight casts deep shadows, which can be particularly unflattering for portraits. A flash unit can "lift" the shadows, as the pictures below show. But for a natural look, the flash power needs to be reduced to about half its normal strength.

With dedicated units, the flash uses exposure information from the camera's meter to set the fill-in flash level automatically. On some units, a flash exposure compensation control allows you to alter the brightness of the fill-in illumination.

On self-regulating units you have to "trick" the flash into acting as though your film is faster than it really is. For a half strength burst of flash, set the film speed on the unit to double the speed of the film in the camera. Then, set the smallest automatic aperture option on the lens and take a meter reading. Check that the recommended shutter speed is the same as, or slower than, the camera's flash synchronization speed. Finally, reduce the aperture by a half-stop to adjust for the extra light from the flash.

Without flash

With fill-in flash

Toddlers

Toddlers have none of the inhibitions that often make it difficult to photograph adults. In fact, the main problem is keeping them at arm's length for a photograph. Like any glittering, shiny object, a camera appeals to a child's curiosity, and if you are not careful you may find your lens covered with small sticky fingerprints.

You can get around this problem in several ways. The simplest is to use the element of surprise. Because young children become totally absorbed in activity, you should find it easy to sneak up unobserved. Before you get anywhere near, set the camera to programmed or semi-automatic exposure mode. If you haven't got an autofocus camera, pre-focus the lens for a distance of about three feet and move in quietly until the viewfinder image is sharp. Then, attract the child's attention before releasing the shutter. The wide-eyed expression of surprise on the face of the child in the small picture below is typical of the spontaneous reactions you can capture.

Another technique is to use a telephoto lens and compose the picture farther away from the toddler. This has the added advantage that the increased distance between you and your subject results in a more accurate perspective. Children's heads are bigger in relation to their bodies than are adults' heads, and a standard or wide-angle lens can sometimes exaggerate this. A telephoto lens restores the balance and gives a more natural effect.

The camera position also affects perspective and proportion. Seen from above, children's heads are closer than their feet to the camera – and therefore look bigger on film. Rather than standing up to take the picture, try kneeling or lying on the ground to produce a more intimate and revealing child's-eye view of your small subjects.

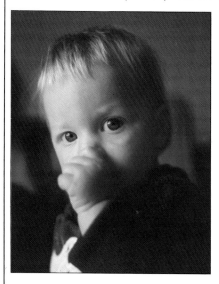

Sucking her thumb, a little girl stares with surprise at her father's camera. For taking pictures such as this by available light indoors, a medium-speed film such as ISO 100 is not sensitive enough. Instead, use an ISO 400 film so that you can freeze the child's movement with a fast shutter speed, instead of having to resort to a flash, which can be alarming if the burst of light is unexpected (1/125 at f/2).

A sunlit deck chair seems as big as a hammock to a two-year-old boy (right). The photographer successfully conveys this sense of scale by composing the picture in such a way that the top of the chair hides half of the child's face, and the striped fabric envelopes his body.

On the seashore, *this little girl is relaxed for the camera. By getting down to her level, instead of standing up, the photographer has made a more intimate, natural picture, and included the surf and horizon in the background.*

Brothers, sisters and friends

Most children are naturally gregarious. Surrounded by their brothers and sisters, or among their friends, their confidence blossoms. Whereas a child alone may be painfully awkward in front of the camera, several together may delight in performing for you.

Often, getting a good picture of children together means finding a midpoint between an overly formal pose and the disjointed effect of allowing the subjects total freedom. With a large group, a useful technique is to arrange them in a fairly structured way, and then wait for them to break the pose. Enough of the original formation will survive to give shape to the image, but the effect will be lively and spontaneous. Another approach is to encourage a boisterous game, joining in at first but then slipping away to take some pictures when the fun becomes unstoppable. Usually you will not need to contrive the action; children playing together will soon present you with a lively composition.

The developing relationships between children are a rewarding aspect of childhood that you will want to include in the family album. If you have more than one child, the emotional closeness, the shared joys and the little dramas of brothers and sisters will have a special meaning to you. To capture these moments on film, a telephoto lens can prove particularly useful – perhaps a 135mm or 200mm telephoto, or a 80-200mm zoom lens. With these, you will be able to close in on the children's private world from a distance and catch intimate expressions, as in the picture of a sister and brother at the bottom of the opposite page. Try to set them against a plain background, or else wait until the children are close together to frame them tightly.

Friends at ballet class rest before practice. The careful composition focuses on one particular girl, but the angle of her gaze directs the viewer to the others in the group.

Boys show off their daring at an adventure playground. By panning the camera at 1/30, the photographer kept the main subject's features sharp and conveyed the action.

In mock aggression, a girl responds to her brother's teasing grab at her mirror. The closeness of the two smiling profiles points up the family resemblance.

Parent and child

The emotional ties between parent and child are profound, but not always obvious. As a result, you may find pictures that clearly express the closeness of a relationship more difficult to take than you might have expected.

A straightforward way to translate the parent-child relationship into visual terms is to choose a moment of physical contact and then close in for a head-and-shoulders shot. You could either use a telephoto lens to frame the picture tightly, or exclude the surroundings by moving in with the camera. This approach will certainly be suitable with smaller children, who are often carried or cuddled in the arms of a parent and who will be at ease in this familiar pose. However, older children who are less demonstrative may not enjoy being forced into such a situation. You may get a more natural picture by simply waiting for a moment when parent and child are looking at each other. Often, eye contact expresses closeness as powerfully as does physical contact – for example, in the picture below, where a father and his daughter are so wrapped up in conversation that they are unaware of the camera.

A parent and child playing together or sharing some other activity often become similarly absorbed, again enabling you to take pictures that are completely spontaneous. To avoid interrupting them, use a telephoto or zoom lens. A fairly fast shutter speed will also help, allowing you to capture the best moments in the action.

Father and daughter communicate interest in each other unmistakably by their close and loving smiles. The photographer used a 135mm lens to crop in and concentrate on the faces.

A first hockey lesson makes a revealing study of parental care, even though the figures are seen only in silhouette. With the light from a low sun glinting on the ice behind the subjects, the photographer gave two stops less exposure than that indicated by the camera's meter. This achieved correct exposure for the ice but showed the hockey players as dark shapes.

The family resemblance is so strong between the mother and daughter above that their two faces, superimposed, seem to express their whole relationship. Even lighting from several flash units gives a flatteringly soft effect.

In her mother's arms, a girl (left) smiles prettily away from the camera – although still a little anxious at being photographed. Close framing helped to exclude bright light from the exposure.

Parents and grandparents

Stereotyping is a special pitfall to avoid when taking photographs of the senior members of the family. Without thinking, we tend to portray the father as the head of the household, cast the mother in the caring role, and accord grandparents a sedate setting that befits the dignity or frailty of their years. You will produce more interesting pictures – and please the subjects too – if you regard older relatives not in terms of their family positions or as representatives of a type-cast generation, but as individuals, each offering different photographic possibilities.

Remember that your family has a life outside the home. The most expressive pictures of parents and grandparents are often taken when they escape their domestic surroundings. Pictures of a grandfather striding across the golf course or, as here, a grandmother riding her bicycle remind us not to equate age with staidness. Emotions, too, can be portrayed eloquently. The picture on the opposite page expresses love as powerfully as any image of a young honeymoon couple could. The close cropping of the image wastes nothing; and yet the color of the man's lined face – sharply revealed by the strong sun – finds an echo in a blur of autumn leaves in the background. Such pictures are effective because they challenge our preconceptions about older people.

Parents tend to relax in the familiar surroundings of their home, and to react delightedly to the picture-taking efforts of their own children. This couple's son caught them perfectly.

An affectionate hug (left) and the man's response seem to encapsulate a lifetime of love in this study of a weatherbeaten couple. The picture's strength lies in its spontaneity and its absolute economy.

A sense of unabated fun shines from this picture of a trim grandmother. The soft, diffused light that filters through the leaves flatters the subject's silver-gray hair and rosy skin tones.

Wedding day/1

At a wedding, a photographer has few second chances – often there is just one opportunity to get everything right. However, there are some simple ways to reduce the risk of disappointment. One of these is the choice of film. Fast color print film (ISO 400) has exceptional tolerance to errors of overexposure, and its great sensitivity gives you the maximum chance of taking pictures indoors by available light, as in the beautiful example below.

In case the light in the church is too dim for a picture even with fast film, a small flash unit is advisable. Also, for portraits, extra light from a flash can help to reduce the tonal contrast between the groom's dark clothes and the bride's white dress: move the groom slightly closer to the camera than the bride, so the flash lights him more brilliantly.

If the weather is good, you will want to take some pictures outdoors. But try to photograph groups in the shade rather than making them face the harshness of direct sunlight. Alternatively, position them with the light behind, and take a close reading. If you have to take pictures in direct sun, be careful of shadows caused by hats. Either move the group so that some light falls on the faces or use a flash at reduced power to fill in the shadows.

Choose a moderately wide-angle lens rather than a standard lens. A 35mm lens, such as the one used for the picture of the bride at right, lets you get closer to the subject in a tight space, and also reduces the chance of a guest walking in front of the camera just at the moment of exposure and thereby ruining your photograph.

A sunlit church calls for careful metering. Here, the large windows and reflective white walls provided plenty of natural light, but the photographer gave one stop more exposure than indicated to compensate for the bright windows in the background.

A nervous bride waits in the church entrance. Even in some large churches, certain areas tend to be relatively cramped. For this picture, the photographer had to use a wide-angle lens in order to encompass all of the flowing lines of the wedding dress.

A wedding cake sometimes appears as a featureless white shape if the picture is taken with direct flash on the camera. To avoid this, the photographer pointed the flash at a white wall on the left, to soften the light, and opened up two stops.

Wedding day/2

Whether or not you are the official photographer, you are likely to use up more rolls of film at a wedding than on any other family occasion. One way to deal with the sheer volume of subject matter is to treat the event as a photographic essay. Instead of ending up with a heap of disparate images, you will have a clear, sequential record of the big day, which will look impressive either in an album or when presented as a slide show.

Because most weddings progress in a similar way, you can readily plot out the main events – the high-points of your essay – well in advance. Use the prearranged length of the ceremony itself and the time at which the reception is due to start as fixed points, and calculate the other timings around them. Dividing the day into stages – the preparations at the bride's home, her arrival at the church, the service, the reception and so on – will also help.

The photo-essay will obviously center around the bride and groom, and you might construct a mini-sequence based just on them. But the full story should include the peripheral characters too. At every stage of the proceedings, try to vary the style and content of your pictures. For example, as well as the traditional view of the bride putting on her finery, photograph her anxious father pacing the hall and looking at his watch. A useful tip is to make sure you take some photographs to link the different stages of your essay. Location shots can serve this purpose. A simple photograph of the church exterior could provide a smooth transition between a picture of the bride's family setting off in their cars, and an interior view looking down the aisle past the ranks of waiting guests.

A variety of backgrounds and groupings will sustain the freshness of a picture-essay. The photographs here, selected from a longer sequence, start with nervous preparations at the bride's home (left and top left) and end with the couple's laughing departure from the church in an open carriage. Natural daylight, flooding softly through net curtains into pale-colored rooms, was perfect for the informal picture of the bride with her hairdresser and for the splendid study of the bridesmaids with a nervous page boy. The photographer sought advance permission to use a flash for the picture as the couple signed the register. To achieve the relaxed sense of fun in the picture above, he asked the best man and the ushers to throw their hats in the air as the ceremony ended.

The snapshot style

Candid pictures do not need the polished technique and perfect composition of more considered types of photography. On the contrary, the imperfections of the hastily taken snapshot – figures awkwardly cut off by the frame, elements out of focus, inaccuracies in exposure – can actually add to the sense of reality and authenticity. They stress the picture's immediacy as a spontaneous image – the record of a passing moment in real life.

The impact of the pictures on these two pages comes from their content rather than their purely photographic qualities. They show how the photographer's alert eye and quick reactions to an action or expression can capture a little slice of life. Even if you do not adopt this approach as a permanent style, you can use it occasionally. When you see something interesting that you know will last for only a second, do not hesitate. Take the picture fast, without even thinking of the technical considerations. You will be surprised at the number of worthwhile photographs you get – images that otherwise would have been missed altogether.

An inflated tire tube provides a youngster with a makeshift sled. A shutter speed of 1/1000 stopped the boy's motion, the excitement of the image more than compensating for the very close framing.

A spontaneous gesture as the groom lifts up the bride conveys the warmth of the moment. The liveliness of the photograph outweighs its technical flaws – the crooked verticals, the figure intruding from the right and the background that is neither very sharp nor wholly blurred.

A bathing beauty *(above) makes a call from a phone-booth near the shore. A quick snapshot caught the incongruity of the moment.*

A traffic cop *(above) calls a halt. Using a standard lens, the photographer simply crouched down quickly and recorded the expression.*

Two friends *(left) leap over a row of wooden posts in spontaneous play. The photographer, relying on fast reactions rather than technical skill, snapped the scene before it passed.*

187

Dealing with strangers

The most completely candid photographs are taken without the subject's knowledge. But there is a limit to the kind of pictures you can take this way. More often, you will need some degree of cooperation from people to obtain a satisfying result.

In most circumstances, a friendly manner and a smile will do the trick. If you look solemn, people may start to wonder just why you are photographing them, whereas a smile can disarm their anxieties and help to put them at ease. How close you move in with your camera is another important factor. People may well object to a photograph if they feel you are becoming too intrusive. By keeping his distance, the photographer who took the picture at right relied on the subjects' passive acceptance and did not need to seek their active cooperation. People with something they are proud to display are more likely to respond to a direct approach. For example, a friendly interest in the garlic seller's work resulted in the sparkling picture below.

Legally, you do not need to seek permission from people you want to photograph in public places if the pictures are for personal, editorial or exhibition use rather than for a commercial purpose such as advertising (when written permission is required). However, judge the situation carefully, do not invade people's privacy, and be ready to defuse things with charm and tact. Sometimes, even mildly hostile reactions can be turned to good effect, as the picture at left below shows.

Taunting the photographer, a young woman tries to spoil his candid picture. The pink tongue toned in perfectly with the subject's carefully color-matched outfit and hair, making an unwittingly humorous and unexpected picture.

The grinning, weathered face of a French garlic seller peers out from among his wares. Chatting to the man about his work encouraged him to show off the skillfully strung bulbs — resulting in a posed but delightfully personal shot.

A couple relax on a park bench in
the evening sun. By keeping his distance,
the photographer avoided the risk of
making the subjects self-conscious. He
underexposed to bring out the strong tonal
contrasts of sunlit and shaded areas.

Faces in the crowd

Turning your camera on the spectators can provide pictures as lively and fascinating as those of the event itself. Make a habit of scanning the crowds every so often, looking out for interesting faces. People cheering on their favorite team, or anxious about the outcome of a feat of daring, or simply waiting for the action to begin, make marvelous subjects for candid photography.

If you are some distance away – perhaps facing a crowd on the other side of a street or stadium – a telephoto lens is very useful. The shallow depth of field and narrow view enable you to pick an individual out of a group or mass of people and to throw surrounding or background details out of focus, as in the two pictures on this page. A long lens is also handy because the compressed perspective can encompass a whole range of facial expressions, as at bottom right, where reactions vary from mild involvement to intense emotion.

If you are in the midst of a crowd, take advantage of your position by looking for interesting subjects close to you, but remember that you will probably have to aim and focus much more swiftly. A wide-angle lens is best for this purpose and lets you frame to include some elements of the surroundings, as in the carnival picture at right.

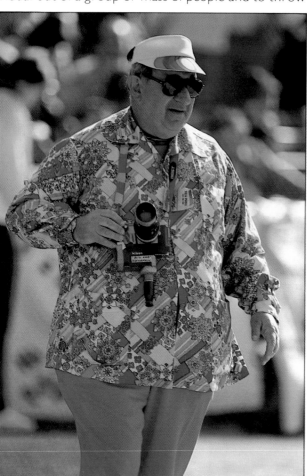

A flower girl seems disgruntled by a long wait in line during a Welsh music festival. The photographer noticed her frown and used the shallow depth of field of a long lens to pick out the face in sharp focus.

The flamboyant attire of a rotund photographer at the 1980 Superbowl in Pasadena provides a lively, colorful image. A 105mm lens isolated the figure and left the busy background unfocused.

A Brazilian woman's vivacious grin seems to draw the viewer right into a carnival scene. The photographer spotted her when he was moving backward through the crowd, and used a 35mm lens to include the glittering hats behind.

The mixed reactions of spectators at a horserace in Calcutta, India (below), produced a fascinating study of human nature. The photographer closed in with a 200mm lens to compress the rows of excited faces.

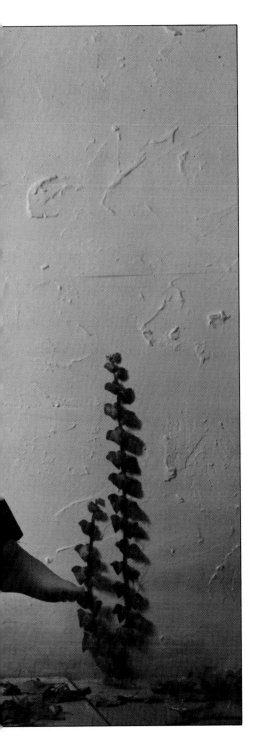

THE ART OF PORTRAITS

Portrait photography relies on a process of cooperation. If someone consents to pose for a portrait, try to establish from the outset that you are working together to achieve a good result. Most people secretly like the idea of a competent photographer taking pictures of them, and you can build on their underlying willingness. But to achieve a simple and natural likeness you will have to overcome initial difficulties, because few people can pose formally for the camera without some tension.

Getting people to relax in front of the camera is largely a matter of communication. Try to bolster your subject's self-confidence. Keep a conversation going and be free with compliments. And make positive suggestions instead of criticisms. For example, if your sitter is frowning, take a few pictures and then encourage a change of pose. Once a subject gets involved and feels things are going well, the frown will disappear naturally.

To inspire confidence in your own ability, plan ahead so that you do not appear undecided about lighting or about backgrounds during the session. Have your equipment set up as you intend to use it. In particular, test any special lighting before the subject arrives. By clearly establishing that you know what you are doing, you will help the subject to feel comfortable and relax.

A little girl's dignity and *poise are emphasized in a superbly composed portrait. Despite the formal pose, the photographer elicited a candid, direct gaze from his subject. A single powerful photolamp on one side provided strongly directional lighting that was ideal for this child's special presence.*

Choosing a pose

Whether the aim of a portrait is to glamorize beauty or to bring out character, the way you pose your subject is crucial. Age, sex and demeanor are all important factors when choosing a pose. To see the truth of this, look at the photographs shown here and then imagine the effect if the subjects exchanged positions with one another. However, several useful guidelines for posing apply to any type of portrait.

First, try to avoid full-face views unless there is a special reason. This approach flatters only some faces. Second, make sure your subject is comfortable. This is particularly important with an older person. Placed in a favorite chair, he or she will automatically settle back into a relaxed position. A chair also provides support for a sitter's arms and

helps to solve a key problem: how to pose the hands.

Hands in a portrait need almost as much attention as the face. They immediately betray whether someone is tense or at ease, and they add considerably to a sense of personality. For example, in the close-up at left below, the clasped hands suggest a contained yet dynamic character. A hand supporting the chin, as in the portrait at right below, will help lead the eye to the face.

With a younger person, you can move away from the more sedate and conventional poses. In the picture at far right, the subject twisted round in her chair for a delightfully informal shot. The classic yet casual pose at the bottom of the same page perfectly suits the woman's elegant composure.

An interlocked position of the hands, with an index finger pointing toward the camera lens, reinforces the impression of a determined character of powerful intellect. The photographer posed the subject resting his elbows on a table and leaning into a pool of light to accentuate the firmly set features.

The bookish personality of an old lady is captured in a pose at her study desk. Seated in her customary chair, she is able to adopt a comfortable, natural position, with both her arms supported. An open book and her scattered papers reflect the gentle, flattering light.

__To convey a kindly authority__ (left), the photographer chose a conventional seated pose and a restrained setting in which muted gray tones blend with the subject's formal dress. The folded hands dominate the lower half of the portrait, balancing a formidable, penetrating stare.

__The spontaneity and sparkle__ in the portrait above resulted from asking the sitter to swivel her body round to meet the camera. Natural light from the window illuminates her clear profile and gives modeling to the arms and hands.

__The confident reclining pose__ and direct, assured gaze of actress Barbara Carrera suggest an extrovert personality who is completely at ease in front of the camera. An unbroken curve leading from the pointed toe of the boot to the hand accentuates the subject's svelte glamor.

195

Full-face or profile?

A full-face view can communicate with a viewer in a very direct way – perhaps through laughter or through the kind of challenging stare seen in the picture at left below. This approach can suit people with good eyes and regular features. But unless a sitter is confident and assertive, you risk the dullness of a passport photograph.

Profile views sometimes look excessively staged, and subjects may be wary of them because most people are not familiar with their own profiles. However, if you liven up the picture, as at right below, profile portraits can be unconventional and striking. This approach shows beautiful hair to advantage, especially with the head thrown back slightly to show the subject's long and graceful neck. In order to emphasize a profile, place the light ahead of the face and slightly farther back than the subject from the camera.

Three-quarter views, as shown in the picture on the opposite page, are in fact much more common in portraiture. They allow eye-contact with the camera, lost in a profile, and give a more relaxed impression than does a full-face portrait. Usually one side of a face looks better than the other, as models are well aware. If you are in doubt, take pictures from both sides and make a choice later. To achieve a natural pose, have your subject face slightly to one side and then look back toward the camera without any head movement. This contributes a hint of spontaneity, as if you have caught a personal glance. Keeping a conversation going will help subjects to relax, and a joke or smile may encourage similar responses. If not, suggest that the subjects stretch, shake their shoulders or even screw up their eyes. A smile may then appear quite naturally when you tell them to relax again.

A gray-eyed beauty fixes the camera with a cool stare. Careful makeup and wet hair simplify her face so that the eyes and mouth stand out.

A splash of water, frozen by an electronic flash, brings this simple profile to life. The girl's tilted head makes her neck seem longer.

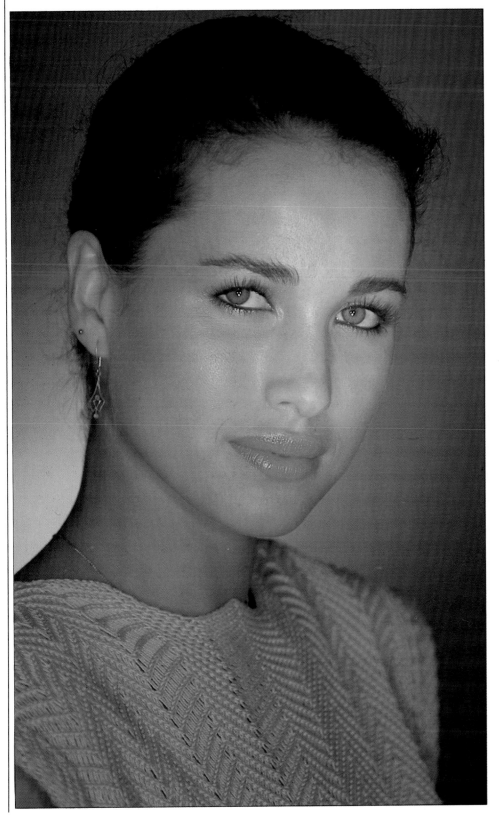

A warm glance, backed up by a hint of a smile, gives this classic three-quarter portrait a relaxed and engaging intimacy. The photographer covered the lights with orange acetate for a bronze glow.

Full-length portraits

Watch two people engrossed in an animated conversation and you will quickly see what an important role the body plays in expressing mood and character. By including the whole body in a picture, you can show the tension or composure in the subject's posture, together with the gestures that add emphasis to a facial expression.

However, a full-length portrait is more complicated than one that shows only the head and shoulders. "What do I do with my hands?" is likely to be your subject's first question. Sometimes, a good way to overcome tension is to seat people on the ground. They will tend to use their hands natur-

ally for balance, as the girl below is doing. Subjects relax more easily when they are sitting down. They also make more compact forms that fit a viewfinder frame better than do the tall thin targets presented by people standing upright. If a seated subject still has difficulty relaxing, suggest the use of a prop such as a book or newspaper.

The most natural full-length portraits are those in which the subjects are absorbed in activity, as is the little girl on the opposite page. Failing this, you can make standing subjects feel less awkward by giving them something to lean or prop an elbow against, as in the series of photographs below opposite.

On the ground, subjects usually take up informal poses and create strong, triangular compositions with their arms and legs.

Seated on a chair, most people relax. If they stretch their legs toward the camera, their feet may look too big. To avoid this, turn the chair sideways or move back.

A young musician intently
practices scales. Choosing
a full-length composition
allowed the photographer
to capture the awkwardness
of this small girl trying
to master an instrument
almost as big as herself.

An easy upright pose
in front of a camera can be
difficult for some people
to sustain without feeling
uncomfortably self-conscious.
The model here shows how
a shift of weight mainly to
one leg makes this kind of
pose look more natural and
spontaneous. It helps to have
something to lean against,
such as this bookcase.

Closing in

Tightly cropped portraits convey limited information about a person but have a compensating impact and intimacy. This is particularly true when such portraits are displayed as large prints showing the subject's features life-size.

To take striking close-ups, it is not enough simply to move the camera to within a few inches of a sitter's face. If you do, very likely the picture will look distorted and even bizarre. At short range, a perfectly normal nose may appear grossly enlarged because of its relative closeness to the lens compared with other parts of the face. In a high-angle view, the brow may seem deformed for the same reason. To restore a subject's features to their correct proportions and still fill the viewfinder frame, you must move back a few feet and use a lens that has a longer focal length. The series of pictures at far right on the opposite page shows how backing away and changing lenses progressively corrects the distortion of the top photograph, which was taken with a wide-angle lens held only 18 inches away.

Lenses with focal lengths between 85mm and 135mm — or medium telephoto zoom lenses — are best for close-ups, allowing you to stand about three to five feet away. But whether you are standing fairly near a subject or farther away with a longer lens, close-ups require extra care because the depth of field is very shallow. Focus on the eyes — or on the nearest eye if the head is turned. Check carefully by using the camera's preview control to see how much of the face is sharp. You can maximize depth of field by taking pictures in bright light and stopping the lens down to a small aperture. However, remember that a sharply focused close-up will expose a face to intense scrutiny, and that you may want to diffuse a strong light to soften the effect.

A penetrating look gains impact from severe framing. By cropping at the hand and forehead, the photographer draws our eyes to the subject's gaze.

A child's softy rounded face (right) emerges from a white towel. To stress the wide-eyed look, the photographer closed in with a 135mm telephoto lens.

*A **profile portrait*** *reduces the risk of awkward distortion because the most important elements – eyes, nose, mouth and chin – are on nearly the same plane. Here, strong sidelighting gives a stark, high-contrast study of character.*

28mm

*1 – **A wide-angle lens*** *fills the frame with a face only at very close range – just over one foot. This makes the subject's nose and the nearer side of the face appear misshapen.*

50mm

*2 – **A standard lens*** *from a distance of about two feet produces a more pleasing image, but some distortion is still evident.*

105mm

*3 – **A moderate telephoto lens*** *lets the photographer stand back about four feet. This shows natural proportions and also avoids crowding the subject with the camera.*

Candid portraits

In a formal portrait, the sitter's eyes are usually the most important feature, expressing character and providing a dominant point of interest. But unplanned portraits can also reveal this expressive quality, without losing the freshness and immediacy of truly candid pictures. In each of the portraits on these pages, the subject is looking directly at the camera, yet the effect is natural and unposed.

The secret of taking such photographs is, above all, to work quickly. A stranger owes you no obligation to cooperate while you set the camera's controls and find your viewpoint. Once your subject is aware of your intentions, any delay will result in unwanted posing, or else in awkwardness and perhaps resentment. Sometimes the best approach is to attract the subject's attention at the last moment – as in the picture at left below.

With a group of people, you can be more open. The man dominating the picture opposite, above, knew he was being photographed but not that he had been singled out from the crowd for a portrait. This image also shows how figures cropped by the edge of the frame strengthen the feeling of a grabbed photograph. In the large picture below, the foreground figure at one side seems included in the frame almost accidentally.

A French farmer looks up from his work with good-natured curiosity as he notices the camera. The photographer used a 28mm lens to include the neat rows of crops, and was all ready to press the shutter release as soon as the subject realized he was being photographed.

A strong face confronts the camera with an unflinching stare. Spotting the subject's cool, enigmatic expression in the midst of a crowd, the photographer closed in with a 105mm lens at a wide aperture to throw the foreground out of focus. The frame edges cutting into the two out-of-focus faces give the picture movement, depth and immediacy.

A sidelong glance gives candid impact to this unusual portrait. The photographer chose a wide-angled lens and focused on the immediate foreground, using fill-in flash for good definition of the subject on an overcast day. The off-balanced framing suggests that the man has just appeared on the scene.

Faces and features

Each face is unique. A good portraitist trades on this individuality by scrutinizing the sitter's features and then considering how best to present them. Often, successful portraits are not conventionally flattering; but an image that stresses bad features and conceals good ones does no service to a subject.

Two essential things to bear in mind when photographing faces are the structure of the features, and the sitter's expression. The comparative portraits below illustrate how a change of lens, lighting, viewpoint, or pose can enhance a subject (bottom row) by making the most of attractive features and minimizing other aspects. For example, a round face (far left) can be slimmed by concentrating light on the center of the face and asking the sitter to lower the head slightly. Conversely, a broader light on a tilted-up head will widen a thin face. Often the length of

a nose is a problem in portraits. Whereas a standard lens used for a close-up may emphasize or even seem to distort noses, a telephoto lens minimizes this effect. Framing a head to leave some space at the top of the image also helps to make the nose less prominent. To play down a receding hairline (far right), avoid lighting the face from above and behind, which will emphasize the bald area and make the face look out of proportion.

Any of these techniques will be wasted if your subject is not relaxed. When someone is nervous in front of the camera lens, the tension often shows in the eyes or mouth. The result may be a strained, tight smile or a mesmerized stare, both of which kill the most carefully composed portrait. The two picture sequences opposite demonstrate simple ways to obtain a natural expression.

A round face (top) viewed head on and fully lit looks too wide. Tilting the head down slightly and reducing the light to a single source (above) shadowed the girl's cheeks and jawline to slim down her attractive face.

Leaning back (top) with his head to one side made this subject look heavy-jowled. The photographer asked him to sit forward and smile at the camera; the result was the much livelier and more flattering portrait above.

The girl's nose (top) is unpleasantly lengthened by a three-quarter close-up with a standard lens. A full face view with a 135mm lens (above) has the effect of shortening the girl's nose and widening her slim face.

A balding head (top) lit from above catches unwanted highlights. By lowering the light source and lens height and getting the subject to raise his head (above), the photographer made the forehead less pronounced.

1

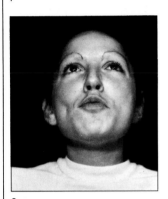

2

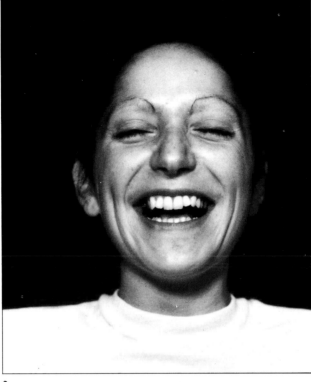

3

Spontaneous laughter
is difficult to capture in a
portrait. *To help this woman
to relax her tense smile (1)
the photographer asked her
to fill her cheeks with air (2),
then blow it out again. The
action is so ridiculous that
it invariably provokes an
outburst of laughter (3).*

1

2

3

*A change of glance breaks
the trance that portrait
subjects sometimes fall into.
To soften this man's fixed
gaze (1), the photographer
asked him to shut his eyes
and look down (2). The final
portrait captures the alert
expression that the subject
wore when he looked up (3).*

The outdoor portrait

Outdoor portraits have an appeal that is hard to match in a studio, particularly when you can use spontaneous incidents, as in the picture below, where a pigeon provided a natural prop. But you need to choose the right time of day. Early or late in the day, when the light falls obliquely on the subject, is a better time than at midday because the light is less harsh. If possible, plan your session for between one and three hours after sunrise or before sunset, although any time when the sun is below an angle of 45 degrees to the horizon will do. Next, decide how to place the subject in relation to the sun. Be prepared to move around to achieve the best balance of lighting and to include in the viewfinder the least distracting background you can find. The diagrams on this page show some of the most effective positions.

The face, of course, is the most important part of a portrait. Make sure that you base your exposure on this, not on the background. To expose the face correctly, close right in and see what combination of aperture and shutter speed is indicated before moving back to your chosen camera position. Handheld meters are particularly useful for portraits. With some, you can take incident light readings by holding the meter just in front of the subject's face and pointing it back toward the camera. Measuring the light falling onto the subject by this method helps to ensure accurate recording of skin tones and color, whatever the brightness of the background or the tones of the subject's clothes. You may find that the light is insufficient for a handheld picture at an adequately fast shutter speed, in which case load up with a faster film or mount your camera on a tripod and ask your subject to adopt a pose that is comfortable and easy to maintain.

A young mother feeding a pigeon shows how spontaneous outdoor portraits can look, even though this one was posed.

Controlling natural light

For portraits, you should take an active approach to sunlight, not just use it as you find it. Some of the examples below suggest advantageous times of day or how to move your subject into the best light. Others show how to modify the light falling onto the subject with reflectors of white cardboard or crumpled foil.

1 – With the sun diffused by haze or light clouds, you have near-ideal conditions for a soft and flattering portrait.

2 – With low, diffused sun, position your subject so that sidelighting creates strong modeling on the face.

3 – With harsh sunlight, place your subject in the shade, where the light will be more even and the shadows softer.

4 – With direct sunlight, place the subject near a large reflective surface to direct light back into the shadows.

5 – With strong, low sidelight, use a special curved reflector opposite the light to fill in areas of unwanted shadow.

6 – With the sun behind the subject, use a reflector to provide the main source of light falling onto the face.

Falling snow (right) is captured with a slow shutter speed of 1/30. In the example here the snow acted as a giant reflector, brightening the light even though the picture was taken late in the afternoon.

On the beach (right), harsh sunlight and reflected glare give an unpromising light. By turning the subject away from the sun and using a small hand mirror to reflect light back onto the girl's face, the photographer found an effective solution.

Bleak conditions (below) provided good shadowless light for a simple and direct portrait of an outdoor man. A wide aperture blurred out the background.

Natural light indoors

As a light source for portraiture, windows give a photographer a double advantage. Light from a window avoids any need for the studio apparatus that can make sitters anxious, and at the same time has a soft, natural quality that is very flattering. Using this simple light source, you can light a subject in countless different ways. The pictures below, with accompanying diagrams, show four main techniques, but there are many more. In each of the two large pictures at right, a window provided strong directional lighting. With the camera to one side of a window and the subject to the other side turned slightly toward the light, you can achieve excellent three-quarter portraits of this kind.

The crucial thing to remember about window lighting is that although the shadows are soft-edged, they can become deep and inky on the side of the head away from the light. In small or pale-colored rooms, the resulting contrast between light and dark may not be extreme because of light reflected off walls and ceiling onto the subject. But in a large room, or one with dark-colored carpets and furnishings, you may have to use a reflector to put some light back into the shadows. You can improvise a reflector from almost anything pale in color. Sheets of polystyrene are excellent, but even a book or sheet of newspaper will do. Shadows become softer as you move the reflector closer to the subject.

When the sun shines directly in through a window, the contrast increases dramatically, and you may need to soften the shadows by diffusing the light itself. You can do this by pinning a white bed sheet or a couple of thicknesses of artist's tracing paper across the window frame.

1 – Silhouette
The pictures with matching diagrams here show some of the ways you can use the light from a single window. With the camera facing the window and exposure based on the highlight, the subject is silhouetted (ISO 64: 1/125 at f/8).

2 – Backlighting
The arrangement was similar for this picture except that the photographer used a reflector to put light into the shadows. Exposure for the face bleached out the window highlight (ISO 64: 1 60 at f/4).

Looking back at a window, the poet Sacheverell Sitwell presents a strong character study. The soft, oblique light shows more form than would a frontal light.

Facing the camera, this young woman sits close to a window so that the light flows around her features, giving even tones. Tracing paper diffused the light.

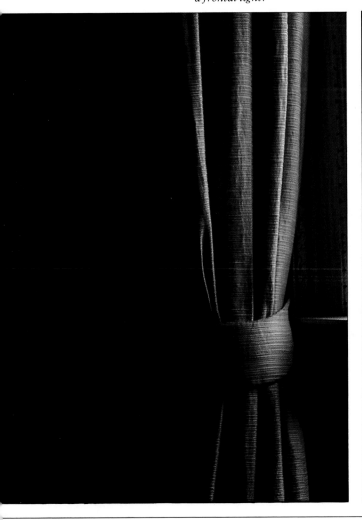

3 – Rimlighting

Moving the subject's chair a little to the left makes a dramatic change. Whereas reflected backlighting was soft and flattering, this arrangement begins to reveal the real texture of the face (ISO 64: 1/60 at f/5.6).

4 – Frontal lighting

Moving the camera around to point into the room places the subject in more even, frontal light. The thin curtains were drawn to act as diffusers, softening the light on the subject's face (ISO 64: 1/60 at f/8).

Lighting faces/1

As a way of lighting faces, special photographic light is far easier to control than natural daylight. Even the simplest of the three types of photographic lamps shown at right gives the photographer considerable flexibility in choosing the direction and intensity of the illumination. Each lamp operates in a slightly different way, but for portrait lighting, similar principles apply to all.

To begin with, place the light source slightly above and to one side of your subject's face. If you do not have a proper support stand, fix the light to a door, a chair-back or a stepladder, using a spring clamp or heavy adhesive tape.

Unless you are aiming for a particularly harsh effect, you should diffuse the beam of a single lamp. You can do this by bouncing the light from a reflective surface, such as a white umbrella, or by passing it through a translucent screen. Tracing paper or muslin stretched on a wooden frame makes an adequate diffuser. Place the screen a few feet in front of the lamp to keep the diffuser clear of the hot surface of the bulb.

To avoid casting dark shadows on parts of the subject's face, place a reflector on the side that is most distant from the lamp. The larger and closer the reflector is to the subject, the softer and paler the shadows will be.

With tungsten lighting, you can measure exposure by using your camera meter in the normal way, but flash exposures are not so simple to judge. The automatic sensor of a portable flash unit will be misled by the brilliant white surface of a diffuser or reflector, so you must set the unit to manual. Work out a standard setting for your lighting arrangement by running bracketed exposure tests in advance, using wider apertures than for normal flash photographs. An accurate alternative to this procedure is to use a special flash exposure meter.

Sidelighting
For this moody image, the photographer pointed a flash into an umbrella reflector at the side of the subject. A cardboard reflector placed opposite softened shadows on the other side of the face.

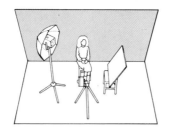

Normal lighting
Here the photographer placed the light at a 45° angle to the subject's face to show more of her features, adjusting the reflector slightly. This is a good arrangement for most portrait photography.

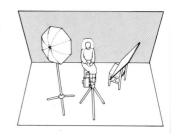

Lighting equipment

A tungsten photolamp (near right) with heatproof reflector is the simplest form of special indoor light. This provides far more light than ordinary bulbs, but you need tungsten-balanced slide film to achieve accurate colors. With a portable flash (center) or powerful studio flash units (far right), you can use film balanced for daylight.

Tungsten photolamp

This gives continuous light so that you can see how the illumination falls on the subject. The type shown is fitted with a reflector dish and a clamp for mounting onto convenient bases.

Portable electronic flash

The strong light from these battery-powered units should be diffused through a screen or bounced off a reflective surface. To preview the effect of the lighting angle, light the scene first with a desk lamp in the position of the flash.

Studio flash

This studio flash unit is fitted with a polished reflector. A built-in tungsten lamp gives continuous light for previewing the lighting effect.

Frontal lighting

Placing the light very close to the camera produces a flatter portrait with greater brilliance. The sitter's eyes reflect the light, and the shadows are small.

Lighting faces/2

With two lamps instead of one, the scope of portrait lighting expands dramatically. You can use the second lamp to control more precisely the relative brightness of highlights and shadows, or for effects such as illuminating a background or casting a golden halo of light around a subject's head.

Dark-haired people often appear in portraits with black, featureless hair. To prevent this and put detail back into the hair, place a second light above your subject. Make sure that no light falls on the face by restricting the beam with a snoot – a conical attachment that fits over the light.

Another way to make hair look more interesting is through backlighting. Place a second lamp down low behind the subject, out of sight and aimed toward the camera. This puts a ring of light around a sitter's head. Because hidden backlighting or top-lighting makes no significant contribution to the overall level of light, there is no need to take either into account when setting the exposure controls.

By turning the backlight around, you can illuminate the background. If placed close to the back-drop, the lamp will cast a small pool of light, as in the picture at top right. Moving the background and lamp apart makes the illumination more even. You can also use a second light in place of a reflector to fill in shadows on a face. However, if you do this, make sure the second light is sufficiently far from the face that it does not create a second set of shadows.

Positioning a fill-in light is simple. Switch on the main light first, and direct it as if you were using only one light source. Then switch on the fill-in light, and place this close to the camera – not in the position where you would normally put a reflector. Any subsidiary fill-in light should be dimmer than the main light. If both lamps are of a similar power, place the fill-in light about twice as far from the subject as is the main light.

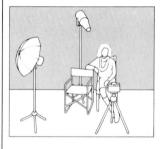

Hair light
A narrowed beam behind and above a portrait sitter puts extra light into the hair, adding brilliance and detail without affecting the main lighting on the face.

Background light (right)
Throwing light on a printed background such as this will bring out its texture and pattern. You can also use a background light to add color to a plain white wall by fitting a piece of colored acetate over the lamp.

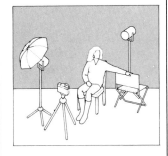

Backlighting (below)
By placing a light behind the sitter, shining through her hair, the photographer encircled her head with a ring of light. This technique can be useful to distinguish a sitter's dark hair from a background of similar color.

Group portraits

The aim of a group portrait is to show everybody looking alert and attentive and at the same time to convey the sense of a common bond. The secret is first to get the general arrangement of the group right and then to work on the pose and appearance of each individual. Encourage the members of the group to relax by talking to one another, but keep sufficient control to command their undivided attention when you are ready to take the picture.

The photographer built the picture at near right around a common theme by arranging a restaurant's staff around a table laden with food, then positioned each one according to his individual role. Because figures in front can obscure those behind, posing large, informal groups presents a special challenge. One natural solution is to move the group to a flight of steps or a slope, as in the picture below. Failing this, get higher with the camera. Even standing on a chair will give you a better view of each individual.

When you are photographing a group indoors, you may have to set a wide aperture to take maximum advantage of restricted light. Unless you can retain adequate depth of field by using a wide-angle lens, you will need to arrange your subjects at roughly equal distances from the camera so that all come within the narrow zone of focus. And if you are using flash or tungsten photolamps, maintaining an equal distance is also important to avoid uneven lighting. With a group close-up, as on the opposite page, you can bring people together simply by having them turn their shoulders or put an arm around the next person.

An oak-paneled room provides the setting for this formal portrait of staff at a traditional restaurant. The semi-circular composition draws the viewer's eye to each figure in turn, then back to the table in the foreground that provides the focus of attention.

Eleven mountaineers give the camera their attention right on cue. By posing the figures a pace apart, the photographer allowed them to express some individuality without losing a feeling of the comradeship that exists within a climbing team.

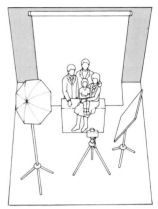

Three generations *appear in this family group, yet the photographer succeeded in uniting all four of the figures in a powerful composition. Meticulous lighting and a seamless paper background helped (see above), but the picture owes its strength mainly to the curving line of faces and arms that sweeps down, and round to the foreground.*

215

Self-portraits

The simplest way to take your own portrait is to photograph your reflection in a mirror. Of course, if you hold the viewfinder to your eye, the camera will appear in the picture and obscure part of your face. The diagram below at left shows how you can avoid this by first lining up the picture and then raising your head above the camera before releasing the shutter. If you have an autofocus camera, you'll find photography easier with the focus control set to manual, if this is possible. Remember that the focusing distance is actually that from the lens to the mirror and back to your position: it is the reflection, not the mirror, on which you must focus. With a single lens reflex camera, you simply focus on the reflection as it appears in the viewfinder. Alternatively, use a tape measure to find the total distance from you to the mirror and back to the camera, and then set this distance on the focusing scale.

The other main way to take a self-portrait is to use a cable release or the camera's self-timer while posing in front of the lens (as illustrated below middle and right). Set up the camera on a tripod and look through the viewfinder to see where you should stand or sit. Then place something, perhaps a chair, in this position to adjust the framing and focus. To prevent errors in framing, leave space around where your head will be.

When using the self-timer, practice releasing it and taking up your pose a few times before loading film. For more exact control over the moment of exposure, you have to use a special long cable release, as shown in the middle diagram below and used for the picture of a woman looking through a wet window on the opposite page. A mirror placed behind the camera is useful for monitoring your expression in an eerie picture such as the one at top right opposite.

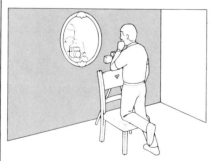

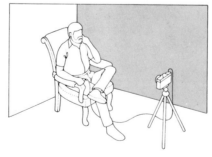

In a mirror, you can see exactly how your expression looks. For the picture above, the photographer gauged the correct viewpoint and focus with the camera steadied on a tripod, then lifted his head clear. Alternatively, stand in front of the mirror with the camera at waist level and tilt the lens upward until the camera's reflection appears to point directly toward you.

A long cable release permits you to sit in a chair while you take your picture. However, because you must press a plunger at the end of the cable to release the shutter, you may need to disguise the cable in the picture. The photographer above is holding the cable unobtrusively along the arm of the chair on which his hand rests, and the pose seems completely natural.

A self-timer leaves your hands free, but the camera can catch you unawares – in the picture at top the photographer's eyes are closed. The white-striped lever next to the lens in the picture above sets the camera's self-timer mechanism. Usually the delay is eight to ten seconds, and you should practice to get the timing right. Self-timers on some cameras may incorporate bleepers or flashing lights.

A glowing lamp illuminates a man's features from below, giving this unusual self-portrait an eerie, supernatural aura. Outlandish ideas such as this often work better if the photographer is alone with the camera, unobserved and uninhibited.

Tripod and cable release
A tripod makes self-portraiture easier – an adjustable head directs the camera where you choose. A long cable release screws into the camera's shutter release knob, and enables you to trip the shutter from a distance after posing yourself.

An outdoor self-portrait shows not just the photographer, but his home and garden as well. The twisted reflection in the plastic mirror is disquieting – an effect the photographer heightened by averting his face as he took the picture.

Through a wet window, this self-portrait looks like the face of a wax doll. In order to get the composition right, the photographer first framed and focused a single pane in a leaded window, then walked outside with a cable release to pose behind the pane and take the picture.

217

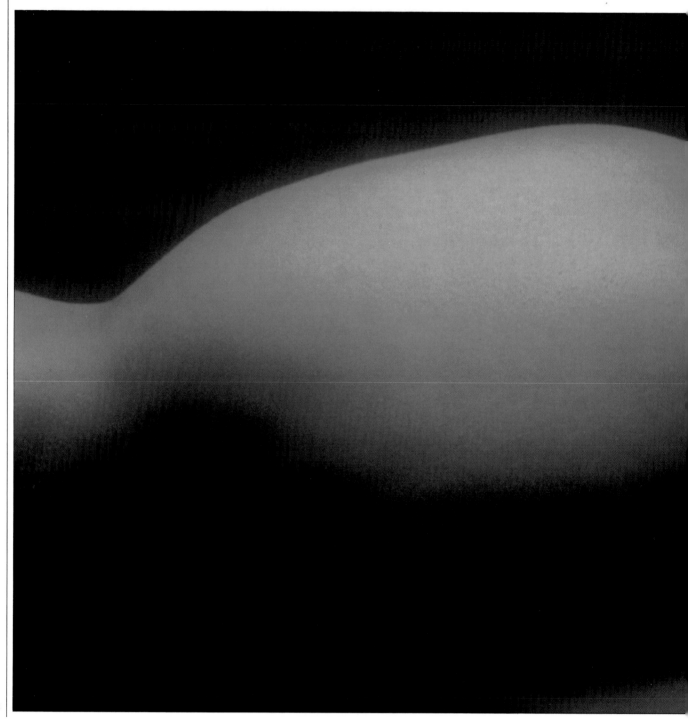

PHOTOGRAPHING THE NUDE

Photography can make of a naked body pictures ranging from high art to cheesecake vulgarity. Few images have more power to evoke strong feelings. And few subjects need more skill, tact and judgment of what will produce a successful image. The aim of this final section is to look at nude photography as a classic way of studying shape, form, texture and the strength or grace of the human body when in motion and at rest.

If you are exploring this subject for the first time, a good starting point is to form a precise idea of the picture you are going to take and then try to control all the elements toward that end. This does not rule out improvisation; an unexpected lighting effect or a blowing drapery may initiate a wholly different idea. But in nude photography an unplanned approach is likely to produce only a graceless picture. To reveal the visual richness of the human form, and to do so without blatancy, you must exercise the maximum care and selectivity. This is true whether you are showing a full figure or closing in on the kind of elemental form abstracted in the picture opposite. Only by learning to control the pose, the setting and the lighting can you produce photographs that reveal an inherent beauty rather than a clinical truth.

Like a smooth stone softened by river water, a woman's hip becomes a pure sculptured form in this study. The photographer used diffused toplighting to create subtle gradations of tone that suggest the bone beneath the skin.

The simple approach

Nude photography requires mutual confidence between you and your subject. No one – not even the most experienced model – feels completely at ease unclothed before a camera. Dancers, who are used to controlling their bodies and regarding them objectively, often make good subjects, as do gymnasts. But if you live in or near a large city, you might consider hiring a professional model. Even then, much will depend on your ability to make your subject feel at ease.

An indoor setting is best unless you can find a completely secluded garden or beach. Your subject will be more relaxed if assured of this kind of privacy, and indoors you will have more control of lighting and background. In addition, you can set up your equipment well in advance and make sure the room is warm: mottled skin and goose bumps are not conducive to good pictures.

The subject should always wear loose clothing for several hours before a session: underwear elastic or tight waistbands leave marks on skin that do not fade quickly. Conduct the session as a two-way process in which the subject is involved in what you are trying to achieve. You will get better results if you

explain why you want a different pose and if you encourage the subject to suggest ideas.

Simple, classical poses are frequently the most effective, certainly for a start. A pose that appeals to your sense of the dramatic will not work if it makes your subject feel physically uncomfortable or embarrassed. Few bodies are perfect, and most people are self-conscious about defects, real or imagined. The two photographs here show how comfortable poses, and the use of lighting to conceal as well as to reveal, can produce images that owe their beauty to simplicity. The pictures also show how black-and-white film, emphasizes light and line, and helps to make the images objective.

One way to accentuate lovely lines, such as the curve of breast and hip opposite, is to use a pose that gently stretches and tautens the body. Here, the model raised her arms to create a graceful, fluid line from elbow to thigh. Partly concealing the face helps to focus attention on the figure, and will help to give a shy subject more confidence. Finally, encourage your model to take deep breaths. This will help to release any tension, and also gives a more flattering line to the stomach and waist.

The rounded purity of a
female form is outlined by
strong sidelighting from a
window. The woman's pose,
with her arms raised above
her head and with her weight
resting on one side, gives
movement and attractively
lengthens the body's line.

The natural seated pose
at left accentuates the clean
supple lines of a youthful
body. To put the subject at
ease, the photographer simply
used light from a flash unit
bounced off the ceiling for
a gentle, flattering effect.

Human geometry

One approach to nude photography is to consider the body mainly in terms of contours and shapes. Reduced to a series of curving outlines, nudes make strong, graphic images.

To emphasize shape, you need to simplify the figure, using shadow to suppress surface detail and to limit the tonal range that provides modeling and the sense of rounded form. Lighting is the key. A hard light from above and behind the subject will highlight structural outlines and create dense shadows to block in shapes. Strong backlighting will reduce the figure to a silhouette, or make limbs seem almost translucent in a blaze of light, as in the image below. Softer backlighting combined with toplighting, at far right, displays a torso's symmetry and suggests its rounded form.

Try to pose the subject in ways that stress the body's natural lines. An arched back, arms at full stretch or limbs bent at acute angles will all create dramatic shapes that lighting angles can further exaggerate. Sometimes you can use the strange shapes cast by shadows as key elements, prompting a viewer to see familiar outlines in a new way. The undulating shadow of the girl's stretched body in the middle picture is a striking example.

However carefully you pose and light a figure, you can easily ruin the desired effect with a confusing background. Plain backgrounds that provide some tonal or color contrast with the subject are best. If the surroundings include distracting elements, change your viewpoint to omit them. Alternatively, frame the figure so that the background becomes part of a calculated pattern of shapes.

Intense backlighting from several photoflood lamps gives a refined, translucent quality to the lines of a profiled, reclining woman resting one hand on her hip.

The generous curves of
a seated female nude (above)
are framed to display their
perfect symmetry. Soft light
above and behind the figure
emphasizes the fluid outline.

The athletic tautness of
the girl's body at left is
accentuated by hard, direct
sunlight. A curving shadow
on the sand echoes and
exaggerates the shapes.

223

Form and figure

The human figure, with its complex, subtle and shifting masses, has always preoccupied sculptors and challenged their basic ability to translate living forms into stone or wood. For photographers, using light and shade to give a realistic impression of a figure in the round has a similar fascination.

Lighting for form must be angled in relation to the camera viewpoint so that it skates across the body to show a deepening of tone as surfaces turn away from the light. The photographer who took the picture below placed a flash unit to one side of the woman, at an oblique angle. He then positioned the tripod-mounted camera above, and pointing down at, the body – as shown in the diagram. To soften the lighting and create a romantic mood, the flash was fired through a large sheet of diffusing material and a reflector was placed opposite the light on the other side of the body. The diffused lighting is flattering, bringing out form and refining the body's lines. A harder light used without a reflector will produce a more contrasty effect – emphasizing shape, but obscuring form.

Natural daylight is more difficult to control than is studio lighting, but its broad, even quality often provides the best illumination for modeling a figure. The sequence at near right shows how moving a subject and changing the camera viewpoint can convert a shape into a fully rounded form as the light on the boy becomes more oblique. And in the picture opposite, sunlight striking a sunbather produces a strong impression of the girl's rounded limbs and torso curving away into shadow.

2

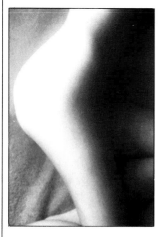
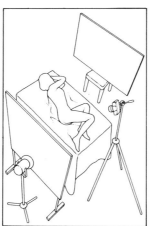

3

A soft sidelight, as diagrammed at the right, shows the gentle curves of a slender woman. A lamp directed through diffusing material lit her from one side, and a reflector placed opposite lightened the shadows.

Near a window (1) the man at top dissolves in an intense, overexposed highlight. Facing the window (2), he appears simply as a dark shape. But farther back (3), sidelight from another window reveals his form.

Strong sun and shadows model the body of a girl as she turns to smile at the camera. Sun lotion glistening on her skin intensifies the highlights and adds to the tonal gradations that convey the sense of roundnesss.

Texture and the body

Glamor photographs tend to portray bodies as uniformly even and smooth – and therefore unreal. But human skin – the basis of our whole sense of touch – has textural qualities, and photographs that use light to explore these qualities communicate strongly because they add a new, tactile dimension that moves the image closer to real life.

To show skin texture in sharp detail, strong side-lighting is best. Indoors, the simplest approach is to position the subject so that natural light from a window falls on one side. Alternatively, angle a tungsten photolamp to cast an oblique light on the figure. Often you can reveal interesting textural contrasts by closing in on a selected part of the body. For example, in the picture below, the fuzzy texture of a man's leg and forearm contrasts with the smoothness of his shoulder and torso.

Another way to emphasize texture is to oil or wet the body so that the surface reflects light. Oil has a dramatic, sculptural effect; for this reason, it is more suitable for abstract images. But water gives a delightfully fresh, natural look. And cold water has an invigorating effect, tautening the skin and making it glow alive.

A plain dark background, as in the two pictures on this page, will throw textures into relief. On the other hand, textured surroundings can accentuate the softness and delicacy of skin and hair. You could experiment with thick toweling or a gauzy material indoors. And outdoors the natural textures of sand, wood or rocks, as in the picture opposite, all provide effective contrasts.

A play of water gives movement and light to the supple body above. Gleaming highlights on the ribs contrast with the rounded, shadowed areas of the thigh and hip. Droplets of water accentuate the slightly granular texture of the skin. The model stood under a shower for a picture taken with flash to freeze the drops.

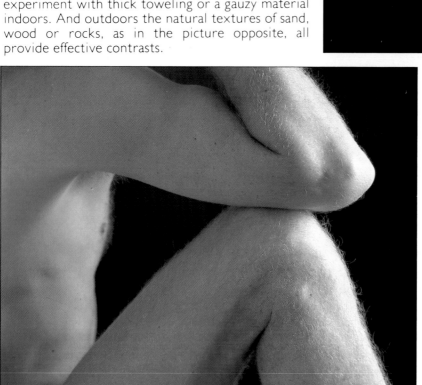

Strong, oblique light picks out the downy hairs covering a man's arm and leg. Softer light on the rest of the body heightens the contrast between smooth, hairless areas and the coarser texture of the skin on the prominent knee and elbow.

A crouching figure within a secluded bowl of rock seems to fit naturally into her surroundings. Rounded contours of weathered sandstone echo the subject's soft curves and set up a subtle contrast between rough and smooth surfaces.

The minimal approach

Some of the most expressive studies of nudes show only a small part of the body. One practical advantage of this is that you can avoid a subject's weaker features and concentrate instead on his or her strongest attribute – perhaps the beautiful line of a back or the shape of a muscular leg. More positively, you can focus on detail to create arresting semi-abstract images. A picture' that includes the whole body inevitably lessens the impact of individual parts, and also involves the viewer in a subjective way with the model. Cropping the head out of the frame immediately focuses attention on the contours, shapes or forms of the body and limbs and makes us consider their objective qualities.

Considered in this anonymous way, sections of the body make compelling compositional features. For example, the pictures on these two pages all take what may be called a minimal approach to the nude – using parts of the body as relatively small areas in the picture frame. Because sections of the body, even when isolated in this way, still retain human connotations, such images often have a surprising power, as in the picture below.

Sometimes outdoor settings enable you to frame the subject so that a detail of the body appears to become part of the surroundings. At near right there are similarities in tone, texture and form between the midriff and the indented sand. And the boulderlike shape in the foreground of the seascape opposite is only just recognizable as the nape of a neck and a curved back.

The navel in a tanned, taut stomach (above) echoes the pattern of an oval dip in the sand. Sharp focusing on the body, while allowing the background to blur, has made the different textures appear remarkably similar.

An upright torso (left) etched against a spacious beach and sky establishes a commanding stillness. Bold framing, with the legs and arms cropped out, suggests solidity and permanence, a more-than-human presence.

The smooth curve *(below)*
lined up precisely with the
edge of the sea, puzzles the
eye. To make this striking
composition, the subject bent
her neck beneath the lens.

Nudes in landscapes

In outdoor settings, nude figures can seem to blend in as natural forms in natural surroundings. A landscape context can have many different meanings depending largely on the viewpoint. For example, in the picture at left below, the photographer has suggested a harmonious relationship between the woman and the earth by placing her in the foreground to emphasize similarities of scale and shape with the rocks she embraces. Conversely, a small, distant figure overwhelmed by a stormy landscape might have suggested helplessness.

The ability of landscape elements to give nudes a poetic power appears even in a picture such as that at right below, in which the loneliness of an abandoned house is conveyed simply by the foreground weeds and the reflection of a hillside and sky in the right-hand window. The large picture opposite links nature and humankind more deliberately by using the side of a shadowed tree to suggest that the figure is half-flesh, half-bark.

Finding a private outdoor location is not easy; it is usually a good idea to look for one in advance and then return with your model and equipment. Even at popular places, you can often work uninterrupted just after dawn on a summer morning, when the soft, oblique light is also ideal for showing form. Take blankets or a warm cape so that your model can keep warm during and after a photo session.

Crouched on the sand, this woman seems to draw warmth from the rocks. A graduated filter over the lens made the distant landscape dark and stormlike, but left the foreground unchanged.

Tall weeds, and torn paper pasted over the windows of a derelict house set up the eerie mood of this picture. A few visual clues – the reflected sky and hillside – establish the location.

Merging with a tree, a body half-hidden in shadow seems smooth on one side, gnarled on the other. The light and dark bands echo the vertical lines of the surrounding woodland.

231

The studio nude

Photographing the nude in the studio has more in common with still-life work than with portraiture. The conventions that govern portrait lighting become less important when the subject is nude, and the photographer is freer to use the face and body as elements in an abstract composition.

By carefully positioning the studio lamps, you can reveal as much, or as little, as you choose of a model's body. Backlighting, or lighting just the background rather than the figure, allows you to create a mysterious silhouette, as below at right. By progressively introducing lights or reflectors, you can gradually restore form and roundness to the body.

Hard lighting rarely suits the nude; it emphasizes even a slight lack of muscle tone. However, if you are photographing someone in fine physical shape, such as the figure on the opposite page, using an undiffused light source to form brilliant highlights on the skin can create dramatic effects.

Diffuse lighting is flattering to the rounded curves of the female form, producing gentle shadows when the light source is on one side. By diffusing a large, front light source, you can produce near-shadowless lighting that works well when you want to focus on shape rather than contours, as in the stylized image below at left.

Shining eyes (above) gaze intently at the viewer in this unusual nude study. To create the tightly framed rectangle of light on the model's face, the photographer masked the front of a tungsten spotlight with barndoors.

White makeup and a highly stylized pose evoke the traditions of mime and theater. Soft lighting and cardboard reflectors prevented harsh shadows from breaking up the blanched perfection of the model's body.

A black figure (opposite) seems to have turned to gold in hard toplighting that strikes the tensed musculature of his shoulders and buttocks. Body oil helped to create the glossy highlights that emphasize the statuesque effect.

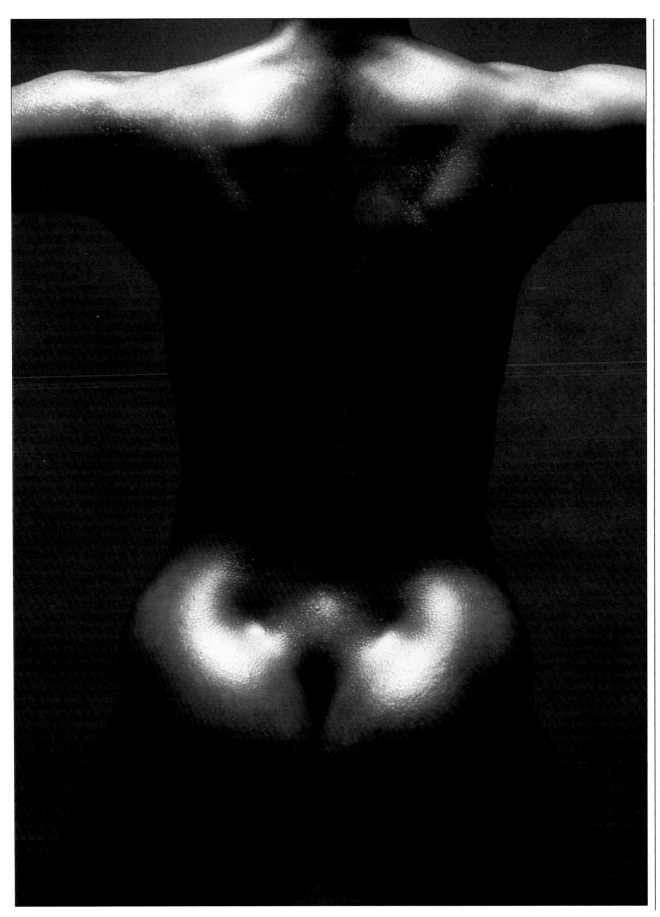

THE WORLD AROUND US

For the photographer, travel and nature — which often go hand in hand — are creative adventures. Outside of your daily environment, you can record the unfamiliar with a fresh eye. And the sheer range of subject matter offers unique opportunities to go exploring with a camera. This can be as true of a family outing or vacation as of special trips to out-of-the-way or exotic places, such as those pictured in the portfolio that follows.

Purely as a record of experience, travel photos are often irreplaceable – you cannot go back. This means that to find, take, and bring home an accurate record you need to be well prepared. The first section in this part of the book covers such practical matters as what equipment to carry, how to deal with the challenges of varying locations, and tips on composing images that capture the atmosphere and spirit of people and places.

Nature is full of marvels and surprises. They may be on the awesome scale of a mountain peak or as small and quick as a hummingbird. The other two sections in this part look at both the landscape and the creatures that inhabit it, showing how to find rewarding subjects and compose pictures that capture the beauty, strangeness or grandeur of the natural world in all its forms.

The Taj Mahal, framed in a view from the Agra fort, appears as a hazy outline against the setting sun. The pair of monkeys playing on the parapet adds lively foreground interest to this unusual view of a much-photographed landmark. By just masking the sun with the top of the alcove frame, the photographer was able to follow the ordinary exposure reading.

A yacht lies moored on a tranquil sea at Antigua. The photographer chose his viewpoint carefully, off-centering the main subject and including the small island and the low-lying clouds to break up the smooth expanse of water and sky. A polarizing filter helped to deepen the brilliant blues.

An Israeli elder blows the shofar – a ram's-horn trumpet – to herald the beginning of the Jewish New Year. The photographer closed in with a telephoto lens to fill the frame with selected details of the subject: the hands holding the ornate horn inscribed with Hebrew characters, the bearded face and ceremonial headdress.

A junk crossing Hong Kong
harbor picks up the soft
light of dawn on its fan-
shaped sails. Against the
background of the modern
city, the traditional craft
provides a contrast between
old and new, and at once
identifies the scene.

A Household Cavalryman stands motionless on parade in Whitehall, London. The unusual viewpoint and the imaginative cropping of the image focuses attention on the ornate burnished helmet and braided collar – details that convey a ritual splendor.

A Bedouin confronts the
camera with eloquent dark
eyes. The beautiful silver
jewelry, the colorful veil
and the mingled candor and
mystery in the woman's gaze
give this portrait magnetic
charm. A wide aperture threw
the background out of focus
to make a soft-hued setting.

Passengers on a Chilean
train read their newspapers
to while away the journey.
Observing the crowded train
draw into the station, the
photographer tightly framed
one car so as to include the
identifying lettering. The
result was this fascinating
vignette of everyday life.

Waves pound the rocky promontory of Point Lobos, California – one of the most photographed of America's scenic coasts. To emphasize the inexorable force of the sea in its timeless assault on the land, the photographer used a 200mm telephoto lens to close in on the breakers and blurred their motion with a slow shutter speed of 1/8.

The calm of evening descends on the Grand Canyon, bathed in the soft and warm light of the setting sun. Careful choice of this as the best time of day to express the character of the famous landscape gave the picture its mood and its originality. A half-stop less exposure than indicated by the camera's meter brought out the subtle colors of stone and sky (ISO 64 film: 1/60 at f/4).

Storm clouds *gather over a remote*
Canadian farmstead. The bold approach to
composition, with the leaden sky taking
up almost the entire frame, makes the
most of the strange lighting effect. The
long red barn, centered in the frame, is
a strong visual element that helps to
break up the straight line of the horizon.

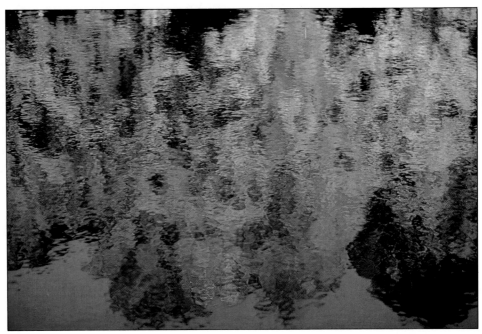

The shimmering reflection of leaves changing color in the fall gives this image the quality of an Impressionist painting. The movement of the sunlit water conveys the rich, glowing colors more effectively than would a more conventional view of the landscape.

An Alaskan brown bear *scoops up a fine fish in icy waters. Preoccupied with finding a meal, the animal was not aware of the well-hidden camera. The photographer had waited with a 200mm lens and set a shutter speed of 1/250 to record the peak moment of the catch.*

A flock of egrets is disturbed into sudden light. The photographer used a 300mm lens to make the subjects stand out against an unfocused background. A shutter speed of 1/125 has frozen some movement but blurred the rapidly beating wings to suggest the graceful rhythm of the birds in flight.

Wild poppies *flourish on a patch of rough ground. The photographer moved in close with a short telephoto lens to fill the frame with the small subjects and used backlighting to intensify the brilliant, clear colors of the flowers.*

A fallen leaf, coated with frost,
lies caught in a mesh of stiff grass.
The photographer carefully composed the
picture to reveal the intricate patterns
of the tangled grass and the leaf's
structure, traced with silver. He used a
standard lens at its closest focus – $1\frac{1}{2}$ feet.

THE TRAVELING CAMERA

Anticipation is one of the pleasures of travel. And with some advance knowledge of where you are going, you will waste less time and come back with a more interesting photographic record. Also, you will take better pictures if you have packed the right equipment. So before you leave, research the places you will visit, using guides, travel books, brochures and magazines. Such visual material will provide a starting point for your own pictures. You should also find out what kind of weather to expect and the starting times of any special events to be held during your stay. All this research will also help you decide what equipment to take along.

Once you arrive, keep in mind that the best travel photographs convey strongly the character of a place. This is not simply a matter of including some recognizable feature in the viewfinder. An important ingredient is your awareness of being a traveler, of experiencing different light and air, unfamiliar sights, smells and sounds. For a travel picture really to work, it has to capture some of this heightened awareness. Be receptive to the mood of a place and to your own feelings about it. Then look for a telling image or an evocative effect of light, as in the view of Rio de Janeiro opposite, that may express how you feel. Only by finding an individual point of view can you communicate a sense of being in a place.

Rio's famed skyline *challenges the visitor wanting an original view. To get this enchanted cityscape, the photographer waited until twilight, when colorful shimmering lights dramatically set off the city's mountains against the rose-hued sky.*

What to take

A full moon rises over a Mexican bay, silhouetting a rocky island against a silvery reflection in the water. Beyond, lights suspended over the stern of a fishing boat illuminate the nets. The idyllic scene seems perfect for a photograph, a special vacation moment. Yet it never reaches the film, for the photographer has forgotten to pack a tripod, and there is no suitable support nearby for the long exposure required. Such a missed opportunity shows the importance of care and forethought in selecting the equipment to take with you.

Ideally, you would have a full range of accessories when traveling. In reality, bulk and weight limit what you can take, no matter how extensive the equipment you have at home. Trying to carry more than is comfortable merely discourages you from taking pictures – a strong argument for keeping the

selection simple. The items shown on these two pages comprise a limited selection from a standard range of 35mm equipment; they are chosen to be light and to fit into a small shoulder bag. The 28-200mm superzoom lens can cope with most common situations, but you may wish to substitute another zoom or supplement it with other lenses that extend the focal length range upwards or downwards. For example, if you shoot a lot of interiors or scenic views, you may prefer to add a 24mm wide-angle lens. Or photographers who frequently use longer lenses might find the maximum focal length of 200mm too limiting, and instead choose a 75-300mm zoom. A 50mm standard lens is also a popular choice as it has a wide maximum aperture. This makes it possible to shoot in dim light without the need for a flashgun or ultra fast film.

A basic travel kit
A single camera and zoom lens, along with a few other accessories shown here, can cover many travel situations. By adding a good tripod, as illustrated on the opposite page, you will also be able to take pictures in extremely low light.

A lens shade is helpful, and essential in bright sun.

A lens cap should be fitted on each lens not in use.

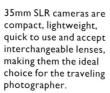

35mm SLR cameras are compact, lightweight, quick to use and accept interchangeable lenses, making them the ideal choice for the traveling photographer.

Replacement batteries are essential – without battery power the camera is useless.

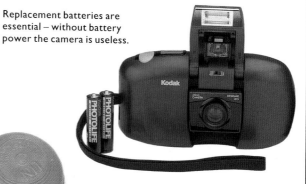

A mini compact camera is useful for snapshots and candid photos, and takes up only a small amount of room in the equipment bag.

Basic filters for color film are a polarizer (above left) to darken blue skies and a No. 81B to warm hues on dull days.

Minimum cleaning equipment consists of a blower brush (left) to remove dust, plus lens tissues to wipe glass surfaces.

The equipment bag

A sturdy canvas bag such as that shown below will carry the full outfit illustrated on these pages, plus all the film you will need. Choose a bag that will take a small tripod tucked under the flap (as at left) or attached to the front by straps. A medium-size bag such as this can be taken on aircraft as hand baggage and safely stowed under your seat to minimize risks of damage or loss.

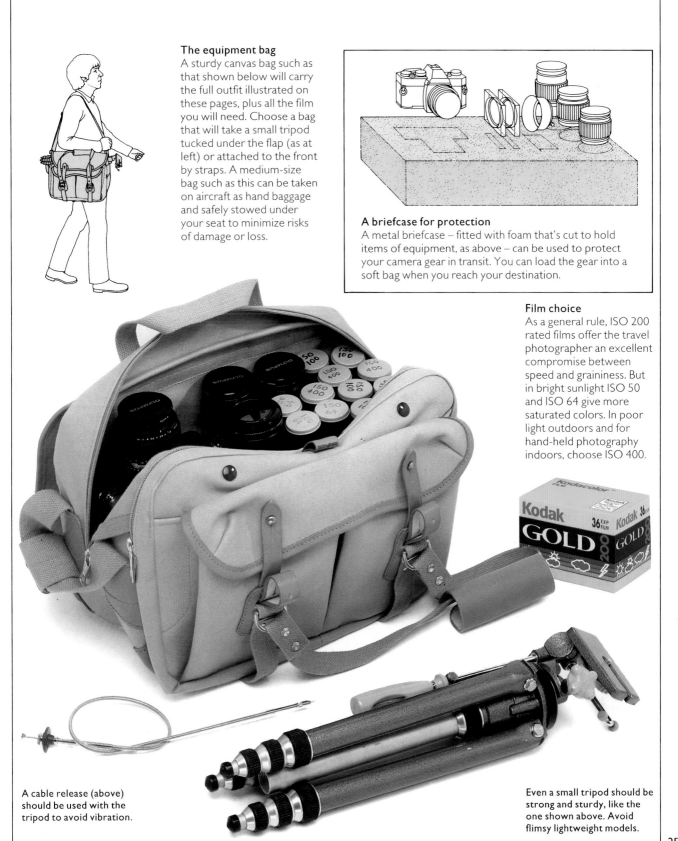

A briefcase for protection

A metal briefcase – fitted with foam that's cut to hold items of equipment, as above – can be used to protect your camera gear in transit. You can load the gear into a soft bag when you reach your destination.

Film choice

As a general rule, ISO 200 rated films offer the travel photographer an excellent compromise between speed and graininess. But in bright sunlight ISO 50 and ISO 64 give more saturated colors. In poor light outdoors and for hand-held photography indoors, choose ISO 400.

A cable release (above) should be used with the tripod to avoid vibration.

Even a small tripod should be strong and sturdy, like the one shown above. Avoid flimsy lightweight models.

Judging a location

Once you have researched a locale and have a clear idea of the subjects you want to photograph, you should consider the best conditions for taking your pictures. Of course if you are recording an event, timing, and to a certain extent camera position, will be predetermined. But for more stable subjects – scenic views and interesting landmarks or buildings – the time of day and the viewpoint you choose are all-important, as illustrated here.

The first step at any site is to make a reconnaissance visit. If time and the site permit, walk around the subject to assess every possible angle. Make running notes of the advantages and disadvantages of various approaches, and try to imagine how changing lighting conditions will affect each view. Again, postcards of the subject will provide useful comparisons. Deciding when and how to take the picture will depend on what you want to convey about the

Cinderella's Castle in *Disneyworld, Florida, forms a backdrop for a colorful parade (above). The photographer chose to concentrate on the holiday atmosphere of the scene, taking the picture in bright light and using a 105mm telephoto lens to make the castle a prominent subject.*

Outlined against the sky at sunset (right), the castle takes on a fittingly fairytale appearance. This picture evokes a romantic mood largely by means of backlighting from a low sun, which has cast warm reflections onto the walls of the castle and the still water beneath.

place, and whether or not you want to include other elements in the composition. For example, the photographer of the picture at left on the opposite page made the castle the setting for a vibrant street parade in brilliant sunshine. The second picture shows a quite different approach: the photographer used the sunset to create a mood of fantasy.

To help you to choose the most effective lighting conditions, find out both the time and the direction of sunrise and sunset; these will depend on the season as well as the place. Remember that the angle and quality of early light change very quickly; arriving at the site even ten minutes late may mean missing the best picture. You may also need to take the weather into account. Where the climate is consistent, you can plan your pictures precisely. Otherwise, be prepared to visit a site several times until conditions are right.

A nighttime view of the floodlit castle (above) produced a contrasty image with a strong theatrical quality. The photographer set a slow shutter speed of 1/60 at f/4 and used the light patterns made by globed streetlights to balance the uniform darkness of the foreground.

In late afternoon, lengthening shadows and oblique, raking light reveal the texture and form of the castle. The selection of a fairly distant camera position encompasses the whole tranquil setting, with the meandering course of the water leading the eye to the subject.

Classic sites

To visit a world-famous site of great beauty and importance, and yet to be so familiar with pictures of it that it seems commonplace, is a frustrating experience. The Coliseum in Rome, the Parthenon in Athens, the Eiffel Tower in Paris – such sites are photographed by so many tourists that picturing them in a fresh way is a real challenge.

One point to remember is that these places have an equally stultifying effect on most photographers. Look at a dozen pictures of a famous landmark and you will see that the same viewpoint – often at the same time of day – has been used. So take the obvious pictures if you feel inclined, but then explore other possibilities.

A number of historical buildings are on such a grand scale that they dominate not only the immediate vicinity but a large surrounding area as well. The Eiffel Tower is a case in point: the familiar outline can be seen from many different parts of the city, and because the tower is instantly recognizable, you can afford to be adventurous in your approach to framing and viewpoint. The pictures on these pages show just a few of the possibilities. In the photograph below, the Eiffel Tower is a background element in a view across the city rooftops. On the opposite page, a wide-angle view from the base emphasizes the shape and structure of the tower. And in the picture at right, the tower itself provides an aerial view that includes its familiar shadow. By adopting similar approaches to other classic subjects, you can obtain images that convey all their imposing character – but in unexpected ways.

The shadow of the Eiffel Tower breaks up the symmetry of a bird's-eye view across the Seine to the Palais de Chaillot. The photographer took the picture from midway up the tower, choosing a time when the sun cast long shadows.

Montmartre rooftops make an unusual foreground frame for the tower, softly outlined against the dawn sky. The photographer used a 300mm telephoto lens to compress the distance.

A floodlit view from
the foot of the Eiffel Tower
emphasizes the massive scale
of the construction. A 16mm
wide-angle lens exaggerated
the span of the arches, and
a starburst filter produced
the radiating points of light
at each of the corners.

The looming shape of
the tower dwarfs a church
spire in the foreground. To
stress the architectural
contrasts, the photographer
centered the subjects in the
frame and used a 400mm lens.

Everyday living

Some of the most fascinating contrasts between one place and another occur at the level of daily life. What is unremarkable to the local people – their work, domestic life and customs – provides a wealth of insights for the visitor, whether traveling in his own country or to more exotic places.

Photographs of people at work reveal much about their culture, as does the picture of Sri Lankan tea-pickers opposite. You must bear in mind that many communities begin the day very early, and you may have to rise at dawn to get the most lively pictures. Photographing the local form of transportation is another good way to convey the flavor of everyday life. Railways have a distinctive character in different countries, and you might frame a traveler in a car window, as in the picture below at left. Religion plays a major and visible role in many countries. The photographer of the Muslim at prayer, below, saw the opportunity for an unusual composition typifying the Islamic way of life.

You do not need any special techniques to obtain such intriguing vignettes: just an acute eye, a willingness to venture off the tourist track, and some discretion. For example, find out if photography is permitted before intruding into a place of prayer and always try to be unobtrusive.

A railway passenger in Kowloon, Hong Kong, gazes pensively from his window seat. The unusual framing produced an image combining the everyday and the exotic.

A Muslim at the Blue Mosque, Istanbul, prostrates himself in prayer. Standing on a step, the photographer pointed downward with a 35mm lens at full aperture.

A string of worry beads casually looped over a man's sun-darkened fingers conveys a ubiquitous facet of life in Greece. The photographer spotted the subject in a café in Corfu and closed in with a 80-200 mm zoom lens to frame the hand and the silver beads against the dark background.

Sri Lankan women pick tea on a hill plantation. To emphasize the patterns made by the colorful figures moving along the rows of tea plants with their large back baskets, the photographer chose a vertical format and used a 400 mm telephoto lens to compress the perspective.

The original approach

The most fascinating images in a travel portfolio will reveal the photographer's individual interests. What attracts one person may go unnoticed by the next. Wherever you are, make a habit of carefully looking for the distinctive and original aspects of what you see around you.

A detailed approach, isolating just a small part of a scene, is the most effective means of putting your personal stamp on a picture. Frequently, you can frame and dramatize a detail more effectively by using a telephoto or zoom lens than by getting close with a standard lens. You might select a slightly incongruous element, such as the traditional-style clock in modern surroundings, below. Or you could frame a classic subject in a fresh way, as in the picture of the Statue of Liberty, opposite. Finally, remember that you can often make a more interesting picture by enlarging and cropping an image at the printing stage – as demonstrated by the photograph of the woman's capped head below at left.

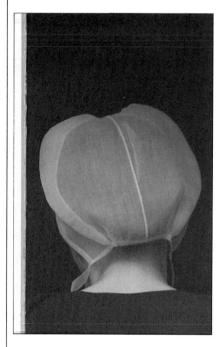

An Amish woman (above) attends Sunday prayer in Lancaster, Pennsylvania. The photographer carefully cropped the detail from a larger image, taken on ISO 400 film – for a soft-toned grainy effect – with a 400mm telephoto lens.

An ornate clock (right) hanging over an insurance building in the City of London bears the company's motto. The photographer used a 300mm lens to throw the geometric lines of modern buildings behind out of focus, obtaining a contrast between old and new, but without clutter.

The head of the Statue of Liberty
is tightly framed to make a semi-abstract
image. Standing on Liberty Island, the
photographer used a 500mm mirror lens
to achieve this unusual view.

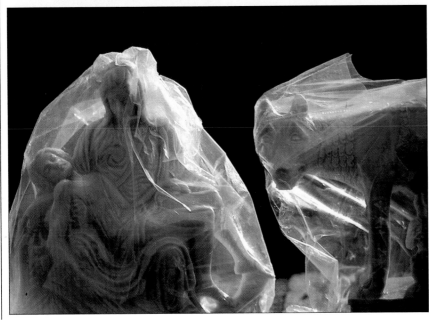

A cowboy's gun in its worn holster
caught the photographer's eye in a
reconstructed Wild West town in
Tombstone, Arizona. A 105mm macro
lens filled the frame with the detail.

Replicas on sale in a souvenir booth
in Rome (left) invite comparison with
their famous originals. The morning light
behind the statuettes revealed their
details through the transparent plastic.

Developing a theme

The pictures on these two pages were all taken in Venice, the city of canals. They show how a single idea or visual element, in this case reflections in water, can lend continuity to travel photographs. By developing such a theme you can also introduce an element of personal interpretation.

Try to decide first what you feel is unique or most significant about a location. Take a little time to explore and get to know your subject. You can combine this process with researching the best views to photograph, but the aim should be to form a general impression. Then look for a way to translate your idea into pictures with a simple visual element that

you can repeat and develop – not in every single photograph but in a proportion of them. If your choice of a theme is apt, you will be surprised at the number of visual opportunities it opens up.

Thematic ideas are best kept simple. For example, the coexistence of old and new in a place famous only for its archaeological remains might suggest as a theme pictures of ruins with modern advertising signs deliberately included in the foreground. Other ideas could be the variety of crafts practiced in a location, or the village-like pockets of individuality that survive in some of the biggest and most anonymous cities.

A woman at her housework (above) *seems to waver in the summer heat. In fact, the photograph shows a reflection in the mirror-like surface of a canal on a bright day, with the picture printed upside down. The photographer focused on the reflection with a 105 mm telephoto lens.*

Pedestrians cross a cat-walk (right), *placed over the flooded pavement of St. Mark's Square. A 200 mm lens emphasized the walkers and their reflection, with the bold architecture of the arcade of the Doge's Palace as a backdrop.*

Gondolas stand idle (left), their distinctive shapes repeated in the misty reflection. The photographer used a 135 mm lens to concentrate on the graphic qualities of this detail.

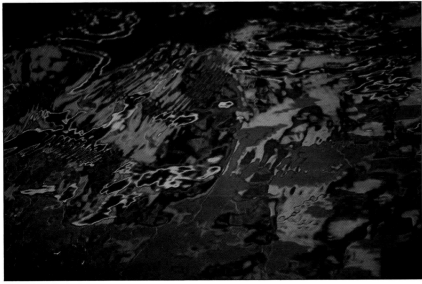

Ripples of color (left) fill the whole picture, with no recognizable element to give a clue to the scene's location. Yet this abstract image makes an expressive addition to a series portraying the moods of Venice. The photographer focused an 85 mm lens on the surface of the water to catch the shimmering details sharply.

The special event

To photograph an organized event comprehensively, you need to prepare thoroughly in advance. The picture essay here shows just how much can be achieved by good planning, and its lessons will apply to many events closer to home.

The Venice Vogalonga is an informal Italian regatta that takes place every May. It is very much a local affair, organized by the Venetian boatmen for the Venetians themselves rather than for visitors to the city. The photographer wanted to convey not only the scale of the occasion and the picturesque setting, but also the lighthearted, popular character of the event. Having found out when and where the boats would start and the route they would follow (diagrammed below), he carried out a reconnaissance to locate the best standpoints for different pictures of the event.

A belltower on the island of San Giorgio Maggiore provided an ideal high-angle viewpoint for the start of the race (right). But on-the-spot research indicated that the liveliest action would take place at the opposite end of the city, in the Cannaregio area, where most of the boatmen live. To take in both aspects, timing was crucial. The photographer calculated that there would just be time to photograph the beginning of the race, take a boat across the Giudecca Canal to the main island, and then run through the city to a camera position on the Cannaregio Canal before the first boats arrived.

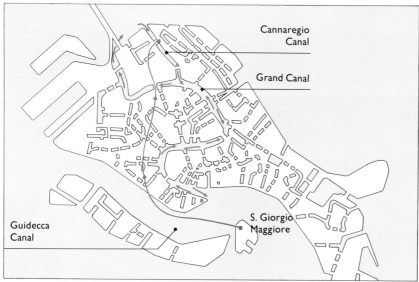

On the map of Venice above, blue arrows mark the route of the Vogalonga boats with the blue dot marking the starting and finishing point. A red line shows the photographer's route.

Spectators view the progress of friends and relatives competing in the boat race from their apartment windows overlooking the Cannaregio canal. The decorative facade strongly establishes the Venetian setting.

Hundreds of boats dot the lagoon leading into the Grand Canal. A position in a belltower on San Giorgio Maggiore gave the photographer this splendid panoramic view with a 35 mm lens of the beginning of the Venice Vogalonga.

A lady gondolier, sporting her chosen colors, sculls gently along with a watchful eye out for other craft. The image conveys the open informality of the race: any Venetian can take part.

An eight-crew boat, its lighted flares spluttering in a drizzle, speeds down the Cannaregio Canal on the homeward run. The flamboyant craft and its wake of smoke made an atmospheric closing image.

265

Exotic glimpses

In the West, we are used to photographs that identify people; faces, expressions and clothing give clues to character. The pictures on these pages, all taken in Morocco by Belgian photographer Harry Gruyaert, offer instead tantalizing glimpses of people who are almost entirely hidden from our gaze. In most of the pictures, not only the faces but also the bodies are shrouded. Yet these anonymous, elusive figures exert a powerful presence.

Gruyaert has visited Morocco several times to study the place and its people. The strength of his images arises from his fascination with the country, its customs and the relationships between its people and their surroundings. With the women, he often found himself involved in a game: they were hiding from the camera and provoking it at the same time. The rich colors, the quality of the light, the shadows, the intricate details of the settings: all these were used to place the subjects firmly within their context and to evoke mood and depth. In most of the pictures, a wall provides the background, emphasizing the security of an enclosed world.

Mysterious veiled heads (above) are crisscrossed by shafts of sunlight, the bars of shadow echoing the narrow eye-slits in the women's hoods. Gruyaert set his 35 mm lens at full aperture for this searching close-up view to register the foreground figure slightly out of focus and lead the eye to the figure behind.

A distant figure (above) blends into the pattern of shadows on a sunlit wall. Strong color, texture and shape give greater weight to the foreground of the composition, emphasizing by contrast the elusive, unattainable quality of the figure. The lines of the palm trunks convey depth and provide a natural frame.

A figure in black (left) stands barefoot in the courtyard of a mosque in Fez. The dynamic pattern of the tiles and the stillness of the worshipper create a tension that gives the image tremendous power. The angled, overhead view, framed to include the steep roof, conveys the sense of privacy of an enclosed space.

Dark eyes *are just discernible behind a heavy veil as a passing woman turns to watch the camera (above). The simple shape of the white robes is echoed in the background figures and in the low parapet behind them. Horizontal bands of soft color create a mood of serenity and help give visual unity to the image.*

Marrakesh women *(left) shield their unveiled faces from the camera. Their different reactions produce an intriguing image in which the arrangement of patterns and colors against the rough textured wall at first confuses the eye. To bring out the richness of color and detail, Gruyaert underexposed by one stop.*

The picture essay/1

While single subjects such as local celebrations or styles of dress suit the mini-essay treatment, broader subjects – the life of a region you are exploring, or a city – merit a longer, in-depth approach. And to do justice to the wealth of subject matter, you may need to spend several days working on a theme and finding the best images to express it.

The picture at left and those on the next two pages show how British photographer Michael Freeman approached a detailed photo-essay. His subject is the city of Cartagena, on Colombia's Caribbean seaboard. Freeman wanted to convey something of the city's fascinating history – it was one of the first colonial settlements of the Americas, and the capital of the Spanish Main – as well as its vibrant Latin culture and the tropical setting. Pulling these strands together required a clearly devised plan of action.

The first step was to make a list of topics: views of the setting; architecture old and new; portraits; street life; and activities and events unique to and typical of the place. From this list, Freeman chose subjects that most effectively conveyed the different aspects, taking viewpoints and time of day into account. Because Cartagena is built on several islands, surrounded by marshes and the sea, finding a good vantage point for a clear overview of the city was difficult. To take the scene-setting opener at left, Freeman went to the roof of a modern building in the early evening, used a wide-angle lens and waited until the street lights came on. The next three pictures in the essay, on the following page, provide a contrast between old and new, with different lighting conditions emphasizing the shape or detail of the buildings. Next, two lively images of street life – a Cartagenero playing in a lunchtime band, and examples of local transportation – present a more detailed approach. The essay ends with a very un-citylike picture. But in fact, the fishing scene is strongly typical of the place: such marshy waterways infiltrate Cartagena on all sides.

At twilight, Cartagena's city center twinkles with colored lights. Standing on a prominent rooftop, the photographer waited until just after sunset to get a mixture of natural and artificial light, and took the picture with a wide-angle 20 mm lens for a broad panoramic view.

The picture essay/2

The late afternoon sun brings out the rich colors of the Spanish colonial-style cathedral (right). The photographer used ISO 64 film for good, strong detail, and closed in with a 400mm telephoto lens to record the subject large in the frame.

Modern high-rise buildings on one of Cartagena's islands (below) are softly outlined by the setting sun. From the vantage point of a hill overlooking the island and the bay, the photographer was able to include the shimmering wash of gold on the water and the fringed shapes of palms suggesting a tropical setting.

Tiled roofs and jutting balconies (above) overhang a narrow street in an old quarter of the city. The crosslight from a low sun revealed the textures of the bleached stone walls and rough tiles.

A band musician plays his saxhorn during a lunchtime performance. Using a 180mm lens, the photographer closed in for a head-and-shoulders portrait of the player, centering the subject in the frame and throwing the surroundings out of focus.

Gaily decorated local buses crowd a main street. The photographer chose a high camera position and a diagonal view to convey lively movement in this typical scene, and used a medium telephoto lens to fill the frame with the subjects.

Fishermen paddle their boat on a still lagoon at sunrise. Both the subject and time of day form an effective contrast, in mood and color, with preceding images. The photographer used a 400mm telephoto lens at an exposure of 1/125 at f/5.6.

THE NATURAL LANDSCAPE

For photographers, as for painters, landscape holds a lasting appeal. No other subject is so accessible; what we see can be photographed today or tomorrow, in natural light and usually without special equipment. Moreover, the subject seems almost inexhaustible, ranging from the tranquil beauty of fertile woodlands to the stark grandeur of open mountains and deserts.

Yet good landscape photographs are rare. Partly because there are no obvious technical problems, the tendency is to assume that our strong impressions of the scenery will translate themselves onto film effortlessly. The skill of taking landscape pictures lies in understanding how a scene will work photographically instead of just being overwhelmed by the beauty of it all. To compress the sheer scope of a landscape into one image, you need to isolate the visual qualities that will re-create the panoramic view you see or suggest its depth and distance. This section explains some simple techniques that can help you to convey scope, capture natural drama and reveal patterns and textures in ways that will give fresh, original expression to the classic landscape themes.

A still lake mirrors a distant snow-capped peak in the Kluane Game Sanctuary, Yukon, Canada. Framing to show a broad expanse of sky and using a wide-angle lens emphasized a panoramic view.

The spirit of the place

The appeal of a particular place is evident when you are actually there, because you use all your senses to appreciate the surroundings. But this strong impression can be difficult to convey on film. The play of light, the feel of the wind and the sounds and smells of the sea or the countryside all contribute as much to your experience as the view itself.

To have any hope of conveying this overall impression in a photograph, you need to give time and thought to selecting an image. Try first to decide exactly why the scene attracted you photographically. Perhaps you were drawn to permanent features – the shape of a mountain or the fault lines in a rock. Or perhaps the visual quality that attracted you is more transient – the patterns of shadows or the deep-red color of sandstone cliffs at sunset.

The feeling of a particular season, accentuated by lighting conditions, can play a powerful part in creating atmosphere. For example, in the picture below, a low sun emphasizes the cold crispness of a winter landscape. The photographer has distilled his own experience of the scene largely by the choice of his camera angle in relation to the light.

An even clearer example of how technique can serve a personal interpretation is the seascape opposite. The photographer has responded to the shapes of trees growing tenaciously on an islet and accentuated this by selecting an exposure that shows them in silhouette. And in the picture at the bottom of the same page, a choice of lens and a viewpoint that fills the frame with trees convey the lonely vastness of forested hills in fall.

A low morning mist hangs over the frosted ground in Montana's Paradise Valley. The photographer made use of the backlighting from a low sun to highlight a furring of frost along the ridges and the lacy pattern of the rime-covered branches.

Wind-beaten trees *cling to a tiny island. To obtain the silhouetted shapes of the stunted branches and the groups of rocks studding a glittering sea, the photographer deliberately underexposed by two stops, setting 1/250 at f/16.*

Tall evergreens *rise above a yellow mass of woodland turning its leaves in fall. The photographer chose a high viewpoint on a ridge, used a 200mm lens and set a small aperture of f/16 to ensure maximum crispness.*

Viewpoint and scope

Seen from an open viewpoint, the whole landscape appears to spread out in a sweeping panorama. A good photograph of such a scene can re-create for the viewer the same feelings of freedom and exhilaration that originally inspired the photographer.

To evoke these feelings, concentrate attention on the distant horizon and try to strike a harmonious equilibrium between land and sky. This is easiest if you use a wide-angle lens – which naturally takes in a broader view – and compose the image so as to eliminate the foreground, as in the picture at right.

A broken canopy of clouds can help to draw the eye forward across the landscape, as the picture below shows. Point the camera slightly upward so that the horizon does not divide the image into two exactly equal parts.

Even with a standard lens, you can often suggest the openness of landscape by ordering or making a big print and cropping the image at top and bottom, as shown at the bottom of these pages. The use of slow film will help make sure that the enlarged part of the picture does not look too grainy.

Fluffy clouds cast a pattern of shadows on a spread of green fields. A 28mm lens slightly distorted the shape of the clouds, which appear to be moving rapidly toward the distant horizon.

A thicket of silhouetted trees is an interesting composition as it appears in the original picture (above). But by cropping to a horizontal shape, the photographer further strengthened the image. The cropped version, with much of the foreground eliminated, allows the viewer to scan the horizon – as if standing right behind the camera on the side of the darkening hill.

A valley and rolling hills form a prelude to snow-capped mountains in this Bolivian landscape. The photographer's choice of a wide-angle lens and a high viewpoint has enabled him to convey powerfully the grandeur of the vast plain.

Viewpoint and depth

Depth and distance are important elements in most landscape pictures. One useful way to suggest depth is to use a wide-angle lens and choose a viewpoint close to the ground. This will create an image that emphasizes the expanse of land stretching away into the distance, as shown at the bottom of this page. Because such a photograph relies for its effect on sharply focused detail from the foreground through to the horizon, you should set the lens to a small aperture to maximize depth of field.

An alternative approach is to use atmospheric haze to give an impression of distance. To exagger- ate the effects of haze and mist, use a telephoto lens – which compresses distance – and compose the image to include both near and far features, as in the picture below.

Even on a clear day, careful composition can help to give a sensation of depth and scale. The picture on the opposite page illustrates how this can be done successfully. The photographer framed this scene so that a nearby, shadowed pillar of stone dominated the view. Without this point of interest in the foreground, the image would have looked more two-dimensional.

Mountain crags recede into a swirling mist in the Italian Dolomites. The photographer left his UV filter off the lens to make the mist seem thicker and thus increase the apparent distance between the peaks.

Windswept dunes lead the eye back to the horizon in Utah's stark Monument Valley. Using a 28mm lens, the photographer crouched down on the ground so that the snaking lines in the sand dominate the image.

A natural pinnacle towers over the landscape. in Bryce Canyon, Utah. By taking the exposure meter reading from the far hills and sky, the photographer rendered the rock as a stark silhouette. This black shape in the foreground helps to create a sense of distance.

The marks of man

Many landscape photographers attempt to exclude signs of human habitation or at least play them down. But the pictures here show a more positive response. In all three the landscape is largely natural, but some human element forms a key part of the image: a rough track cuts through an immense wilderness, stone walls thread a hillside with pattern, and a red and white deck chair adds a splash of color in a somber park. The photographers could all have changed viewpoints or lenses to minimize or exclude the human elements, but chose instead to make them cornerstones of the compositions.

Such signs of human activity need to be included with care. You can easily mar landscape pictures by allowing power lines, advertisements, parked cars, roads, or even people to clutter an otherwise unspoiled and natural scene. Keep these elements out of the frame unless you can see a way to use them effectively.

First, carefully study the scene to see if anything at all intrusive appears in the viewfinder. If you spot an unwanted detail, try adjusting the composition. For example, by using a wide-angle lens and moving a foot or two to one side, you may be able to hide the offending detail behind a rock, a tree or the crest of a slope. Narrowing the view with a lens of a longer focal length can also be useful. But if you really want to show untouched landscapes, the best tip is to take pictures early in the morning when there will be fewer cars or people.

A dirt road stretches into the distance across an African plain. By centering on this ribbon of color, the photographer found a bold composition in an almost featureless landscape.

Walled fields surround a lonely English farm. These human creations, framed from a distant slope with a 200mm telephoto lens, made a more interesting picture than the barren hillsides higher up.

A backlit chair stands
out brightly amid the dark
trees of a city park in the
evening. The photographer
used a 105 mm lens for a
selective view that included
the chair as a focal point
of the composition.

Exploiting drama

Many landscapes suit a restrained, straightforward style of photography that allows the view to speak for itself without introducing any feeling of camera trickery. But some spectacular landforms or seascapes demand special photographic treatment to convey their full drama. Often, the solution is to take the boldest possible approach in lighting, lens choice and viewpoint, as in the pictures here.

With unusual rock shapes, try to show the outline more strongly than anything else. For example, use a telephoto lens to close in and frame the subject tightly, as in the picture at right. Then you could look for a way to silhouette the shapes against the sun, perhaps returning at the right time of day to make this possible. The two pictures on this page show how you can do this either by masking the sun or with the sun very low in the sky.

You can also use the special visual characteristics of lenses with focal lengths of less than 24mm or telephoto lenses with focal lengths of at least 200mm. Very wide-angle lenses distort the appearance of the subject, especially if you tilt the camera. Telephoto lenses compress perspective so dramatically that mountain peaks can be made to loom over foreground crags, as at the top of the opposite page.

Long telephoto lenses also let you take pictures from a greater distance, increasing the number of viewpoints available. For the picture at the bottom of the opposite page, the photographer found that the most dramatic view of the reef islet was from nearby cliffs rather than the much closer beach.

A stone pillar (above), silhouetted against the setting sun, illustrates the value of returning to a spot at different times of day. At noon the colors were insipid and the column looked dull, but the photographer came back and positioned himself to catch the silhouetted rock just as the sun sank between the pillars.

A rock arch (left) stands starkly against the sky in a view with an 18mm lens. To intensify the color to a deep indigo, the photographer used a polarizing filter and cut the exposure by two stops, thus creating an unusually dark and graphic image.

A distant mountain
(above) rises through mist.
A 200mm lens brought the
mountain closer and gave a
sense of scale, while an aperture
of f/16 kept the sheer rock
and perched bird in focus as
a powerful framing device.

White waves (left) wash
against a tiny island in this
unusual cliff-top view, while
the surrounding sea appears
almost black. The deliberate
underexposure enhanced the
feeling of bleakness, and a
200mm lens closed in to
accentuate the dizzy feeling
of looking down from a height.

Patterns in nature

One way to give visual order to landscape pictures is to concentrate on images that have a strong element of pattern. The repetition inherent in the processes of nature provides a rich source of pattern, but you need to use close observations and appropriate angles of view to exploit this. For example, from many viewpoints pine trees present a visual jumble; it needed an alert eye and careful framing to achieve the rhythmic image of parallel trunks below.

Often a high viewpoint will reveal patterns invisible from ground level. The winding course of the river in the picture at the bottom of this page made a graphic image only when the photographer climbed to a vantage point above the valley.

Patterns will sometimes become more evident through a telephoto lens, as in the pictures on the opposite page. The lens both restricts the scene and flattens the perspective, thus helping to create juxtapositions of colors, shapes or lines that establish a sense of regularity.

Pine trees form a barred pattern of trunks and twigs in soft browns and greens. The photographer carefully leveled the camera to ensure the perfect parallels.

A Sussex river catches the last of the afternoon light and glistens like quicksilver. Earlier in the day, when the sun was higher, the colors of water and land would have blended, masking the striking S shape.

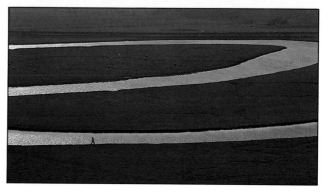

Melting snow on a steep canyon wall accentuates a pattern of rock outcrops and eroded channels. To isolate this powerful image from a broader, less orderly view, the photographer used a 300mm telephoto lens.

Ranks of tall, green rice on an Indonesian hillside show the influence of man in patterning the landscape. The photographer included the brightly dressed figure to vary the monochromatic color scheme and contrast with the horizontal lines.

Trees and forests

Woods and forests form distinctive landscapes in their own right and create complex environments. that need different compositional approaches than those required to photograph a single tree.

First, look for a dominant point of interest. In a forest, a view that includes a tangle of branches, a mass of foliage and a variety of vegetation on the ground can easily appear as a disordered jumble. You may have to move around to find a unified image. The photographers who took the pictures shown here all chose different angles of view to convey specific impressions of woodland. The compositions are effective partly because of what they exclude. For example, in the picture below, a close viewpoint crops out the tops of the trees and

details at ground level to concentrate on the trunks and bright patches of sunlit leaves. This is a good approach where the trees grow closely together. For a more distant view, look for a clearing in the trees – a natural glade, a forest creek, or perhaps a firebreak. The photograph at top right captures the mood of a woodland scene even though the trees themselves are secondary to the path that leads the viewer into the frame.

If you cannot find a satisfying view at eye level, one alternative is to point the camera upward and frame the tops of trees. The patterns and colors of leafy branches will stand out strongly against a clear blue sky, particularly the glowing shades of autumn, as in the image at far right.

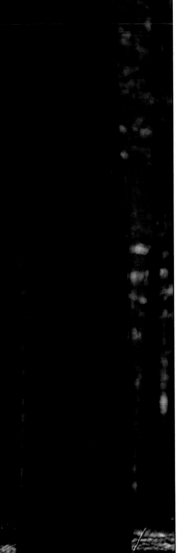

Sunlight filtering down to the forest floor (below) throws brilliant highlights on low, leafy branches. The photographer moved round the subject until the light was directly behind, and set a wide aperture to throw the surroundings out of focus.

Dappled shade on a path winding through a carpet of bluebells creates an idyllic woodland scene. Trees leaning inward help to draw the eye to the center and beyond into the inviting distance. To retain detail in the shady areas, the photographer took an exposure reading from the foreground left-hand corner.

Autumn leaves blaze with color against a brilliant blue sky. To intensify the contrast and give good color saturation, the photographer used a polarizing filter, which darkened the sky and reduced the flare caused by light reflecting off the shiny leaf surfaces.

Sea and shore

On a calm, overcast day, the sea and wet sand reflect the sky's soft shades of gray and hint at colors that are muted, never brash and brilliant. Often, such cloudy weather seems unpromising for photography. But color film has a remarkable ability to record subtle differences of color. Sometimes this produces scenes tinted with exquisitely delicate hues, particularly at dawn and dusk when sky and sea or sand change through shades of pink and blue, as they do in the picture below. Avoid underexposure in cloudy conditions, or the sea will look dull and leaden. If anything, a little extra exposure is best, to capture the pastel hues.

Sunlight shows the sea in another mood, picking out deeper, richer colors and touching the breakers with brilliant white crests. On a sunny day, pay special attention to the movement of clouds. When they cross the sun, clouds can throw deep shadows on the sea, producing dark horizons that form a dramatic contrast with the color of sunlit water closer to the shore, as in the image at right. To prevent errors of exposure in such a high-contrast scene, take a meter reading from a midtone – the area between the horizon and the breaking waves in the example shown here.

In blustery weather, you can get good pictures near rocks, where the sea throws up jets of spray, especially if you stand so that the waves are backlit, as in the picture at the bottom of this page. If you can get close enough, a wide-angle lens makes the scene look even more dramatic, but take care that spray does not splash your camera. Wipe away the corrosive salt-water before it dries, and always keep the lens covered with a skylight filter.

A cloudy seascape (left) turns pink and turquoise as the sun rises. The receding waves left the beach wet, and the photographer used the sheen of the water to mirror the colors of the early-morning sky.

A wide sea (right) threatened to soak the photographer when he took this picture, so he moved back from the shore and used a 135mm telephoto lens to frame the waves against the orange light of dusk.

A white breaker
crashes onto the beach,
adding a froth of white to
the blues of sea and sky.
A polarizing filter helped
make the colors deeper.

Mountain landscapes

Every mountain region has its own distinctive character, and you can make interesting pictures by taking a broad, encompassing viewpoint that shows a whole environment or relates a zone of vegetation to the bleaker ground above. Often the scenery will alter dramatically from one zone to the next as you climb higher. In tropical regions, there may be many scenic zones, from rain forests upward. In harsh northern climates, even the lower slopes may be too cold and wet for forest, so there is an abrupt transition from brushwood to bare rock.

The picture below, taken in New Zealand, shows how a close foreground view of even a plain expanse of scrub can add scale and contrast to a range of hills. In the similar New Zealand scene at the bottom of the opposite page, the same photographer was able to exploit the strange lighting effect before a storm to accentuate the colors and patterns of the landscape. If lighting conditions are less spectacular, try to find some element in the foreground to provide a focus of interest – perhaps a twisted, stunted tree or a small lake.

In higher mountain country, distant views of the peaks help to convey the dramatic shifts from one level of vegetation to the next. In the picture at far right, for example, overhanging branches provide a frame for the broken ridge behind and a contrast to its bleached, barren structure. Among the high peaks, it is often the sheer expanse of featureless snow and ice that conveys the bleak mood of the environment, and if the sun is overhead pictures can lack contrast and scale. To counter this, take your pictures early or late in the day when the sun creates shadows and highlights on the ice.

The flaring rays of a low sun (above) reveal the clarity of an alpine summit near Tignes in France. The photographer removed his protective UV filter to avoid the double image that could otherwise result from pointing the camera into the sun.

Spiky brushwood gives way to somber slopes dusted with snow. A close view of the bare twigs and poor soil emphasized the rugged high-country setting.

A fallen tree and leafy branches (above) give greater dimension to a view of the Andes. The contrast between the shady foreground, with its patchy vegetation, and the stark white crags against a clear sky conveys the rapid scenery changes typical of high mountain regions.

Sunlight breaking through a stormy sky (left) deepens the dull gold of tussock grass and gently undulating hills. Long shadows on the slopes and a splash of green help to break up the uniform tones of the landscape.

291

Natural forces

Natural wonders such as hot springs, waterfalls and – most sensationally – erupting volcanoes have such visual drama that even a casual snapshot may result in an impressive picture. Yet you still need to apply the same thought and effort that you would give to less spectacular scenery. The pictures on these two pages show how much the use of color, pattern and good composition can intensify the impact of an already interesting subject.

In the picture below, the photographer used a 28mm lens to focus sharply on the colored algae of a hot spring in Yellowstone National Park, and to get so close that he could show the eerie darkness of the lower depths. By contrast, the picture alongside, of spurting lava, gains much of its power from the choice of a nighttime view, giving a strong pattern of red against black. The same photographer, Ernst Haas, also took the view of a dormant volcano on the opposite page, artfully timing his inclusion of a wispy cloud in the composition to suggest the fierce inner life that produced the stark black of the rough cinder slope. Color is again a key element in the waterfall picture at the bottom of the opposite page. Cover the red flower with your finger to see how much drama is lost without this carefully placed color accent.

A lava jet (above) *throws molten rock into the air. Using a 400mm lens on a tripod, the photographer set a shutter speed of 1/15, so that the lava left glowing traces across the frame.*

A thermal spring (left) *harbors a surprise – rings of colored algae. A polarizing filter over the camera's lens eliminated the sun's reflection on the water, so that the colors in the pool appeared more saturated on film.*

A snow-patterned volcano (above) seems to puff steam as a passing cloud brushes its dormant summit. To record the high contrast between snow and cinder, the photographer took a meter reading from each area and averaged the results.

The enormous power of Victoria Falls, Zimbabwe, sends up a haze of drifting spray. A view through the lush vegetation on the cliffside gives scale and color to the image.

Sky and wind

In blustery weather the clouds sweep quickly across the sky and their shadows cast a moving pattern of light and dark over the landscape, so that the scene changes minute by minute. A viewpoint high enough to enable you to look out over the shapes of hills and valleys helps to reveal the patches of light in the most graphic way, as in the picture below.

As a general rule, set the exposure to suit the sunlit portion of these scenes. To do this, wait until a patch of light passes over your camera position, then take a meter reading from the ground nearby. This should give you the correct reading for the overall view.

Grass, water or trees in front of the camera will all show the effects of wind. A fast shutter speed, such as 1/250, freezes movement if you want an absolutely sharp image, but often slight blurring gives a more vivid impression of a windy day, as does the tree in the image below. If the light is very strong, you may need to use a neutral density (gray) filter to reduce the brightness so that you can select a shutter speed slow enough to produce the degree of blurring you want.

Often, windy weather breaks up heavy clouds into distinctive patterns, such as those shown on the opposite page. Broken clouds also offer good chances to take dramatic pictures of the sun, which is usually too bright to be photographed directly, especially with a telephoto lens, unless it is low in the sky veiled by clouds.

A swaying tree conveys expressively the violence of the wind. To blur the tree's outline, the photographer set a minimum aperture of f/22, which allowed the use of a shutter speed of 1/15 – slow enough to show considerable movement.

The sun (left), enlarged by a 400mm lens, shines through scudding clouds. At this degree of magnification, and without the clouds to moderate the rays, the sun would have been much too bright to photograph without a filter.

Golden clouds, blown by the wind, create a pattern of whorled lines that sweep the eye into the distance. The photographer waited until just after sunset before taking the picture, so that the clouds are lit from below – but the sun itself is hidden.

ANIMALS AND PLANTS

Animals and plants are the living components of the landscape. To photograph them successfully, you need a special alertness combined with techniques borrowed from the tracker and the naturalist. It takes knowledge of animal habitats and also stalking skill to approach a wild creature such as the wolf in the picture at left. And it takes quick reflexes to get a creatively framed picture before the animal vanishes. Alternatively, you may need to cultivate the patience to wait in a well-chosen but possibly uncomfortable location until the animal appears – or perhaps does not appear at all.

In compensation for these difficulties, the rewards are tremendous. The thrill of getting close enough to an elusive subject to frame it in your viewfinder is something that few other areas of photography can offer. If you are well prepared, you can usually find the subject you want, and wildlife preserves will offer plenty of practice without your needing to travel to exotic locations. The section that follows deals with techniques and equipment that will help you capture pictures of subjects as different as a herd of a deer, a backyard squirrel or the challenging simplicity of a single flower.

A timber wolf, caught unawares, glances toward the camera. While hiking through the backwoods, the photographer saw the subject and took the picture quickly with a 135mm lens before the wolf turned and fled.

297

Finding animals

None of the pictures on these two pages would have been captured without some knowledge of the habits of the animals in question. Learning a little of the annual, seasonal and daily routines of wild creatures helps you find and photograph them; the most successful wildlife photographers are to some extent naturalists as well.

Most animals share a few behavioral characteristics that can help you to locate them. For example, mammals and birds tend to be particularly active shortly after sunrise and just before sunset, when many move to and from water, nests or dens to look for food. The deer at right have come to drink in a stream in the evening. And a forest clearing that seems desolate by day may come alive with grazing deer and feeding birds at dusk. As another useful pointer, remember that sources of food and water will most likely attract creatures in times of hardship. In the dryness of high summer, waterholes and streambeds provide perfect opportunities for photography of a whole variety of animals.

However, in each location and with each individual species, the details of behavior will vary and you need to use any local knowledge you can find. Pamphlets on sale at National Parks and other wildlife sanctuaries help, but a park ranger will give you even better information if you ask. Having a trained guide accompany you may seem to reduce the sense of adventure but will greatly increase your chances of getting good pictures.

A doe and her fawn come to a stream to drink in the Aransas Wildlife Reserve, Texas. A 300mm lens framed the subjects from the cover of trees, with warm evening light showing their color to best advantage.

An alligator lies in the shallows of the Florida Everglades, mouth open for cooling in the humid heat. Guided to the basking creature, the photographer was able to approach close enough to use a 105mm lens.

Two young raccoons peer out from their den in a pine tree. Knowing where to find them, the photographer waited with a 200mm lens until the two brightly marked faces appeared.

Dress and equipment

When wearing normal clothes and moving about in a normal way, a human being represents one of the most visible, noisy and strongly scented of all potential enemies to a wild animal. So if you want to photograph anything more than the animal's tail vanishing into the distance, be very careful about what you wear and what you carry.

If you are stalking animals on foot, you must do your best to blend into the surroundings. Even if you do not go to the lengths of wearing full camouflage, always try to be aware of how the animal will see you. Most animals, such as the jackrabbit at right, are sharp eyed, highly sensitive to movement and equipped with senses of smell and hearing that far surpass those of humans.

As a first precaution, wear drab clothing, preferably similar in tone and color to the surroundings, and remove anything that might catch the sunlight, such as a wristwatch. If you have fair skin, wear some headgear to darken or shadow your face, as shown below. Empty your pockets of any coins or keys that might jangle as you walk. And avoid wearing artificial scent or deodorant; human body scent is alarming enough to animals without the addition of extra smells. Loose clothing that buttons at the wrists and neck, together with long trousers, will help to conceal your scent.

Carry as few pieces of equipment as possible so that you can walk more quietly. Unless you have established a fixed position in advance, you will never have time to set up a tripod, change lenses or attach filters. The figure illustrated below is well equipped with two cameras, one with a very long lens and the other with a moderate telephoto zoom lens. Carry a few rolls of film and a spare camera battery in your pockets, avoiding a shoulder bag if possible.

Camouflage

The best clothes for stalking animals are military surplus items, which are also cheap and comfortable. But there is no need to overdo it; the basic rule is to avoid garments that are notably lighter or darker than your surroundings.

A hunting vest (left) has useful pouches for equipment, but you must wear a long-sleeved shirt. A hooded jacket (right) will hide your face in shadow.

Streaks of dirt or camouflage makeup on your cheeks (left) will make you less conspicuous at a distance. A dark woolen helmet (right) serves the same purpose.

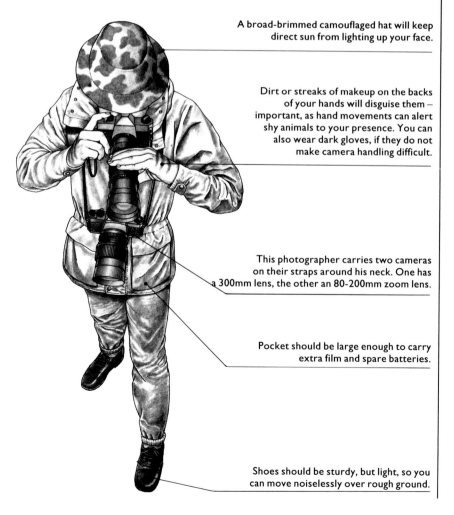

A broad-brimmed camouflaged hat will keep direct sun from lighting up your face.

Dirt or streaks of makeup on the backs of your hands will disguise them — important, as hand movements can alert shy animals to your presence. You can also wear dark gloves, if they do not make camera handling difficult.

This photographer carries two cameras on their straps around his neck. One has a 300mm lens, the other an 80-200mm zoom lens.

Pocket should be large enough to carry extra film and spare batteries.

Shoes should be sturdy, but light, so you can move noiselessly over rough ground.

A blacktail jackrabbit sits alert in tall grass. The photographer came across the animal in the late afternoon and crept closer from the dark cover of trees, using a 300mm lens to close in.

80-200mm

200mm

135mm

300mm

Shoulder stock (above)
This additional support for a telephoto lens helps keep the camera steady and allows you to concentrate on the animals appearing in the viewfinder.

Taping the camera (above)
Black tape on shiny camera surfaces reduces the risk of metal glinting in the sun. Lightly cover the prism head and the front of the top- and base-plates.

Lenses for wildlife (above)
Telephoto lenses are essential, allowing you to fill the frame with animals that you cannot approach closely. Telephoto zooms aid precise composition: those with large, constant maximum apertures are most suitable for wildlife photography. Lenses with a focal length longer than 400mm need the support of a tripod and thus are most suitable for use from blinds. With a steady hand, you may be able to handhold a 300mm lens at a speed of 1/250, making it suitable for stalking if you use fast film. The 135mm and 80-200mm lenses have large maximum apertures, ideal in woods where you may see animals close up.

Telephoto lenses

When looking at a wildlife subject through a long telephoto lens, one of the most striking things about the image is the shallow depth of field, particularly when the lens is set at a wide aperture. Although the narrow zone of sharp focus may seem to present a problem, in practice you may find it often helps you. Lying in wait, you can conceal yourself and your equipment behind vegetation, and the lens will throw the intervening screen of foliage out of focus, as in the picture at bottom right. With a fixed-aperture mirror lens, used for the picture below, out-of-focus highlights appear as bright discs, known as "doughnuts" – an effect created by the mirror elements

within this type of lens, which fold up the light path and thus make the lens more compact.

Shallow depth of field is sometimes also useful to isolate small subjects. For example, in the picture at right, the out-of-focus background draws attention to the birds, despite their relatively small size.

To shift focus with a telephoto lens, you must turn the focusing ring farther than on a standard lens, and an extra second spent focusing can mean a missed picture. With a manual focus telephoto, you can reduce this risk if you keep the lens always set to a point in the middle distance, so that you need to make only small focusing adjustments.

Led by a stag, kudus splash across a flooded African plain. A 500 mm mirror lens picks them out against the light and creates a shimmering wash as highlights in the out-of-focus foreground reproduce as discs – a characteristic effect of this lens. Since the aperture was fixed at f/11 the photographer had to use a fast shutter speed to prevent overexposure.

A pair of seabirds perch on a cliff face. The photographer set up his camera on a tripod at the cliff edge, focused carefully on the ledge at a wide aperture and waited until the puffins landed on one of their favourite perches.

A baby orangutan waits for its mother, and the photographer's 300 mm lens crops tightly in on its anxious expression to make a striking animal portrait taken from a hidden position.

Birds in flight

When on the ground, birds can seem ungainly and awkward; their true grace and beauty emerge only in flight. Try to take pictures when the birds are close enough to fill a good area of the viewfinder frame. If you are using a telephoto lens, large species such as herons, storks and pelicans present good subjects, even at a height. But often the best moments to capture birds are when they are taking off or landing, particularly if you can include a reflection in the frame, as in the picture at top right.

Focusing manually on a speeding subject can present problems even for the most experienced photographer, though most modern autofocus cameras are able to keep up. Many species of birds hover steadily on thermals and updrafts. For example, seagulls tend to follow boats at a fixed distance, so that framing and focusing are easy as the birds spread their wings to catch the rising air.

For a bird flying toward the camera, preset the focus and press the shutter release when the bird begins to look almost sharp. If you are using an autofocus camera, select either continuous focus or predictive focus.

When the direction of flight is past the camera, you should pan to follow the birds, as the photographer did for the picture at right center. Birds usually follow a fixed route when leaving or returning to a nest, so you may get several chances to take the same picture.

A heron takes flight and a 300 mm lens isolates the elegant outline against the surface of the water. Laboring to gain height, the bird was slow enough to allow the photographer to take several pictures.

Soaring seagulls (*below*) present an easy target as they hover above the deck rail of the boat on which the photographer was standing. They were so close that even with a standard lens the birds appear sufficiently big to dominate the picture.

Speeding birds flash past the camera, their outlines blurred by a shutter speed of 1/15. The result is an image that sums up the magic of flight.

A tern (*below*) wheels around a high cliff top. The photographer preset the focusing ring on the 300 mm lens and took a series of pictures as birds from a flock flew into the plane of sharp focus.

Getting closer

Around every wild animal is an invisible boundary – a territory, within which any intrusion or disturbance will trigger alarm.

As soon as you approach too close, the animal will simply leave or make for a safe hiding place. You may get a blurred view of it bolting – or you may never see your potential subject at all. Pictures in which animals seem as unaware of the camera as the red deer on the opposite page require very great care and skill in stalking, even when you are using powerful telephoto lens.

Learn to use the skills of the woodsman. Look for the quietest paths, avoiding dry, crackly undergrowth or mud that will squelch underfoot. Choose routes across the countryside that give natural cover

– for example, the shelter of rocks or trees. And keep below the tops of ridges to avoid showing up on the skyline. Take note of the direction of the wind, and if you have the choice, walk with the wind in your face or to one side so that your scent does not drift ahead, signaling your presence.

When you see a subject in the distance, stop for a moment and take stock. The illustration below shows a sample situation, with some suggestions about how you might approach animals you have sighted. If the animals look at you, stop and remain still until they look away. Above all, be patient, and do not expect to get too close. If you think the animals may move off before you reach your chosen position, try taking one or two pictures on the way.

Crossing open ground
This view of wooded country indicates the kind of first view you may have of animals you want to photograph. There is a considerable distance to cover, and several routes are possible.

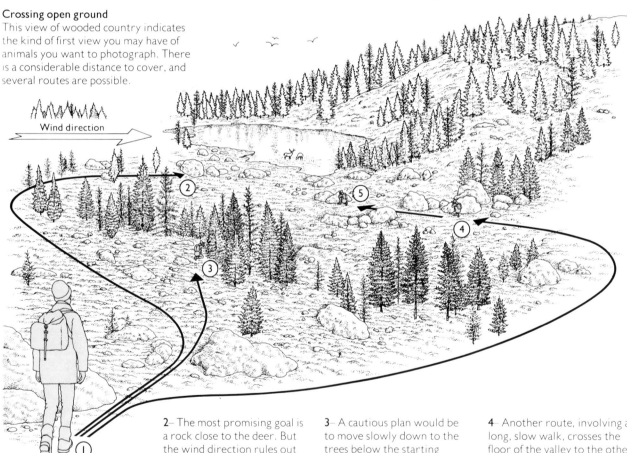

Wind direction

1– At the starting position, the photographer is close to the skyline. Take care to stay low at this stage.

2– The most promising goal is a rock close to the deer. But the wind direction rules out an approach from that side.

3– A cautious plan would be to move slowly down to the trees below the starting position and use them as a protective screen.

4– Another route, involving a long, slow walk, crosses the floor of the valley to the other side and then swings back behind rocks and trees toward where the deer are grazing.

5– Having taken some pictures from a safe position without frightening the deer away, you could move to a much nearer rock – and with luck get a really good close-up.

In a sunlit Bavarian glade, a pair of deer stand silently unaware of the camera in an image that sums up the peace of the woods. The photographer carefully approached them with a telephoto lens to a distance of about 20 yards.

Using vehicles

Stalking on foot may be exciting but it is not always the best way to approach animals in the wild. A car or boat will often leave wildlife relatively undisturbed, because animals do not necessarily associate vehicles with the presence of people inside. This is especially true when vehicles are a regular sight, as they are in many national parks. In these conditions, the animals become accustomed to seeing and hearing cars and learn that they represent no threat.

The picture of the leopard below was taken from a vehicle specially modified to carry visitors through an African game park, but the same advantages apply in less exotic locations; a vehicle both protects you from potentially dangerous animals and allows you to approach them closely. For example, the bear at right was photographed near a roadside in Alaska.

Even if your subject is not dangerous – perhaps a bird of prey you have spotted perching on a branch while you are driving past – you probably have a better chance of getting a picture if you stay inside the vehicle. However, be careful how you stop the car. Coast gradually to a halt and leave the motor running for a while before you switch it off. Try to wind down the window when the animal is looking away and set up the camera as quietly as possible.

Boats can be even more useful vantage points. With the motor off, you can drift with the stream or stay anchored without disturbing aquatic animals, sometimes getting really close, as with the heron at the bottom of the opposite page.

A leopard *(above) rests on a dead bough – a classic picture by a famous wildlife photographer, Eric Hosking, who approached the animal in a safari van and used a 200mm lens from 25 yards. A similar van (left) accompanied the one in which the photographer was traveling, but still did not disturb the impassive beast.*

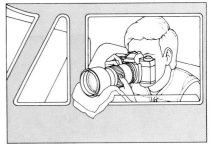

A grizzly bear walks through scrub close to the side of the road. A 400mm lens gave good detail of the subject from a distance of about 40 yards. To use a telephoto lens from a car window for such pictures, a folded jacket makes a good improvised support, as shown above.

A heron fishes among reeds in the Florida Everglades. The photographer switched off his boat engine so that he could drift quietly into the reeds where he had seen the bird, as shown in the illustration above. Covered by a coat and remaining motionless, he was able to float to within 14 feet, sufficient with a 300mm lens for a close-up of the heron in dappled sunlight.

Wildlife with flash

Many animals – mammals in particular – become active only as night falls. Nature pictures taken with flash at night have a special vividness, perhaps because they show us a world of hidden activity.

Nocturnal animals can see in the dark much better than humans. Nevertheless, if you give your eyes 20 minutes or so to adapt to the darkness, you will find that they become more sensitive, particularly to movement at the periphery of your vision. To stalk animals at night, you must be aware of everything around you and not look fixedly ahead.

If the night is black, carry a flashlight with a cardboard snoot that narrows the beam. Far from causing alarm, a bright light often mesmerizes animals and may pick up the telltale twin reflections of their eyes, giving you a useful guide to focusing. However, the best chance of getting pictures such as the one

of the badger on the opposite page is to wait patiently in a suitable camera position and use a remote release if necessary.

Unless the subject is very close to the camera, use the most powerful flash you can. Outdoors, with no reflective surfaces, the light loses intensity quickly, so you should first check what range your unit provides by making some test exposures at different distances. Even with a powerful flash, you may need to use a fast film of ISO 400 or ISO 1000 for subjects more than a few feet away.

Flash is useful during the day also if you want to freeze fast-moving subjects; the picture of a hovering hummingbird below shows just how fast flash can be. However, the unit must be close to the subject so that the burst of light is very short and bright enough to overpower the daylight.

A tiny hummingbird sips nectar from a flower, its wing beats frozen by twin automatic flash units. Despite the very brief flash duration (1/10,000) the bird's wing tips are still slightly blurred. The photographer placed the camera on a tripod, as shown below, and used a 100mm macro lens at f/11.

Flash equipment
For tiny subjects, such as the bird in the picture above, flash units like the one at left provide ample power. In addition, their exposure-regulating circuits provide a useful way to control flash duration, as they curtail the flash quickly when the subject is close to the flash unit. To soften harsh shadows or to create more even lighting, it is possible to link two or more flash units with a cable, as here, or to trigger them with a remote control device.

A badger emerges from hiding, and a flash unit illuminates it brilliantly. The photographer located the den by day, and set up the camera and flash while there was still enough light to focus. He used a tripod to support the motor-driven camera, and attached the flash unit to a stand as diagrammed at right. When the animal appeared, the photographer triggered the camera and flash with a remote release.

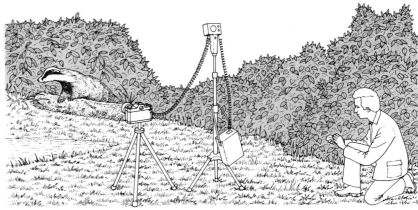

311

Animals in town and garden

Cities, towns and suburbs support a surprising variety of birds and mammals, and you can photograph much of this wildlife without even leaving the house. For example a camera set up in a living room captured the charming picture of the sparrow on the opposite page.

Birds are usually the easiest subjects to photograph at home. Attracting them is simply a matter of providing a nesting box, a water drip or a feeder. To make a water drip, just hand up an old bucket full of water, and prick a tiny hole in the bottom. The dripping water will catch the light and attract a variety of birds.

If you put out food or water regularly for a week or so, you should have enough visitors to make it worth setting up the camera. Nesting boxes require more patience, and may not attract a tenant until the following season.

Mammals are more difficult to photograph because many of them are nocturnal. However, some species, such as the raccoon and squirrel shown here, are up and about by day, and because they are larger than the typical town bird, you do not need to be so close or have such a long lens to photograph them. Mammals will come for bait just as birds do, but bait is not always necessary; most animals are creatures of habit, and often you can locate them by simple, quiet patience and regular observation.

An agile squirrel (left) raids a feed table, giving the photographer a welcome bonus – he had been expecting birds. A 200mm lens filled the frame with the feeder, which had been set up nine yards away from a window.

A young raccoon (left) peeps out over a log before taking the bait – a raw egg – hidden nearby. By leaving an egg in the garden closer each day to a window where he had set up the camera, the photographer gradually over-came the animal's shyness.

A common sparrow (right) swings on a bag of nuts just four feet from the camera. Because the bait was so close, a 135mm lens provided enough magnification to get an excellent picture. But at that range, the photographer had to keep very still to avoid scaring the bird.

Animals at the zoo

The time of day is almost as important in zoo photography as in the wild. To get effective pictures like that of the romping polar bear at the bottom of this page, you need to be on hand at feeding times or else arrive when the zoo opens and the animals tend to be more active.

There are some simple ways to make the animals' surroundings as well as their behavior look as natural as possible. Modern zoos that use moats and ditches rather than bars make it possible to screen out all surroundings except those that suggest the animals' natural habitat. One effective technique is to close in on the subjects as tightly as possible with a telephoto lens. You could even consider showing just a detail – an approach that works well for subjects that have strong color markings, such as the toucan below.

By walking around the subject, you may be able to find a camera angle that allows you to use lighting to hide evidence of an artificial environment. For example, in the polar bear picture, backlighting in bright sunlight has thrown into deep shadow the masonry walls at the back of the pool. And by aiming up high into the light, the photographer of the monkeys at the bottom of the opposite page suggested a jungle setting.

A toucan's bright bib of yellow feathers forms a marked contrast to the deep black of the majority of its plumage. The photographer set his zoom lens to its maximum focal length of 200mm to frame the bird's head, bill and breast. At this focal length, the bars of the bird's enclosure blurred out.

A polar bear splashing in its pool is caught by a fast shutter speed of 1/1000. The photographer took up his position across a moat just before feeding time, when the animal's impatience ensured a lively action picture.

A green snake coiled on a branch makes an effective image. The photographer noticed the snake in a reptile house and chose an angle that would suggest a natural-looking background. A wide aperture helped to throw out of focus a concrete wall behind the branches.

A pair of zoo monkeys chatter on a high branch in the Monkey Jungle near Miami. To avoid recording people and paths in the background, the photographer aimed up at the sky. He allowed an extra stop-and-a-half exposure so that the monkeys would not appear as silhouettes.

Flowers/1

Wildflowers can splash patches of bright, often startling, color across otherwise bare landscapes or form brilliant contrasts with the subdued browns and greens of foliage and trees. To make the most of such contrasts, try to relate the flowers to their surroundings. One way to do this is to select a viewpoint low to the ground and quite close to the plant, as the photographer did when taking the striking picture below.

For maximum depth of field, stop the lens down to a small aperture and use the camera's depth-of-field preview control to check that both flower and background are in sharp focus. If the flowers are sheltered, you may be able to balance a very small aperture by using a slow shutter speed, with the camera on a tripod or other support.

An alternative to this kind of richly detailed image is to throw foreground flowers out of focus so that only their intense colors catch the eye. Use a telephoto lens set at a wide aperture and focus on the background. In the picture at right, a mirror lens has spread the flower heads into blobs of color, almost as if dropped from a full paint brush, creating a picture that has far more impact and immediacy than one designed to record the flowers accurately, as a recognizable species.

Red and yellow flowers (right) contrast with the dull olives of woodland. A 500mm mirror lens produced a shimmering effect in the foreground flowers and in the equally out-of-focus background highlights. Such lenses save weight when you go walking, being much lighter than telephoto lenses of the equivalent focal length.

Claret-cup cacti (left) thrive on a barren crag above a valley in Big Bend National Park, Texas. To keep both parts of the picture in focus, the photographer used an aperture of f/16. The bright sunshine enabled him to set a shutter speed fast enough to stop the wind-blown blossoms from blurring.

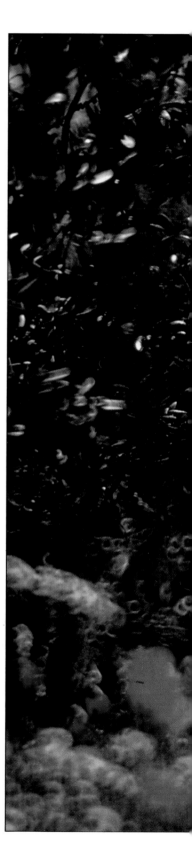

Flowers/2

A single flower isolated from its surroundings can make a strikingly beautiful picture. But to fill the frame with it, you must use careful close-up techniques, if necessary using the specialized equipment illustrated opposite. Begin by finding a good specimen that is not scarred or torn, then concentrate on simplifying the picture. Foreground or background foliage can easily become distracting unless you tidy up the area around the plant. Tie back superfluous flower heads or plants, especially those that are darker or lighter than the rest of the vegetation, as these will show up on film even if you try to blur out the background.

In flower portraiture, lighting is crucial. A good time to take pictures is early morning, when flowers are still fresh with dew. In the picture below, taken just after sunrise, the photographer used backlighting to isolate the flower. Later in the day, to avoid conflicting shadows, photograph flowers in the shade or when clouds diffuse the light.

Because depth of field is so shallow in close-ups, a small aperture is essential – and this may in turn force you to set a slow shutter speed. Secure the camera to a tripod, and in windy conditions wait for a moment of stillness before pressing the shutter release. When a breeze keeps a flower in constant motion, use a windbreak, which can also serve as a plain background. You can also place a length of stiff wire alongside the stem and use a spring clip to support the flower, as diagrammed at right below. Check through the camera's viewfinder to ensure that the clip does not appear in the picture.

Brilliant red flowers *seem to glow when lit from behind. By framing the plant against a shadowed area, the photographer made an image that shows the spiked stem and flower heads with immaculate simplicity. The low sun also creates an effect of rimlighting that clearly reveals the plant's structure.*

Close-up equipment for flowers

Flowers are static subjects and allow a more considered close-up approach than do insects. For precisely adjusted framing and a steady camera, use a tripod. A 50mm or 55mm macro lens will let you close in on single blooms and will retain the autofocus capability of suitably equipped SLR cameras. Extension tubes used with a conventional standard lens offer a cheaper alternative. A bellows unit gives greater flexibility, enabling you to adjust the framing and magnification exactly as desired.

55mm macro lens

Set of extension tubes with standard lens

Bellows unit with standard lens

A caterpillar makes a perfect match with the flower head it feeds on. For this carefully prepared picture, the photographer used black cardboard as a contrasting background and supported the plant stem with a wire as shown in the diagram below. A bellows unit mounted on a tripod allowed perfect framing of the six-inch-high detail with a 50mm lens.

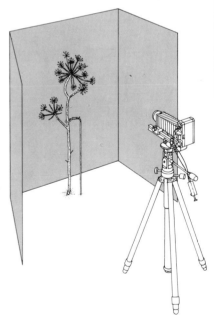

EXTENDING YOUR RANGE

Anyone who has mastered the basic skills of photography and seeks further challenges is in an enviable position. It would take a lifetime to exhaust all the possible ways of creating photographic images. And whatever your special interests, there will inevitably be a way of extending them into the realm of advanced image making. For example, if you want to capture the exuberant vitality of an athlete in motion or of children at play, you are likely to find the split-second timing of action photography highly rewarding. At the other extreme, if your interests run toward taking professionally lit portraits or fashioning carefully composed still-lifes, like the one shown opposite, you will no doubt delight in the enormous control that you gain over a picture's appearance as you learn to use studio techniques.

Action photography and studio techniques are only two of the subjects explored in this last part of the book. There is also a section demonstrating some simple methods you can use to create dramatic special effects. And another section describes how you can use adverse weather and tricky lighting conditions to produce striking imagery. In the two concluding sections, you will see how to develop and print your pictures and how to present the best of them in slide shows and albums or as framed prints. The representative sampling of pictures on the following pages shows the immensely varied results that these advanced techniques can produce with a bit of diligence and imagination.

A wriggle of light twists around a wooden knob and a feather, and rises behind them in a bold crescent to create a cool still-life with a hint of Oriental imagery. Light shining through a cardboard cutout was responsible for the main crescent, while a curved acrylic sheet created the compressed reflections of the crescent and knob at the bottom.

Fencing's elegance *is
captured (above) in a spectral
image. A slow shutter of 1/8
had the effect of dissolving
the figures' swift motions
against the dark backdrop.*

The graceful arc of a
gymnast's legs slicing the
air (right) appears in
consecutive images by means
of a stroboscopic flash unit
firing rapid flashes. The
continuous illumination from
overhead stadium lights
picks up a sweeping amber
trace. The gymnast's iron
stillness and the multiple
images of his legs suggest
both speed and control.

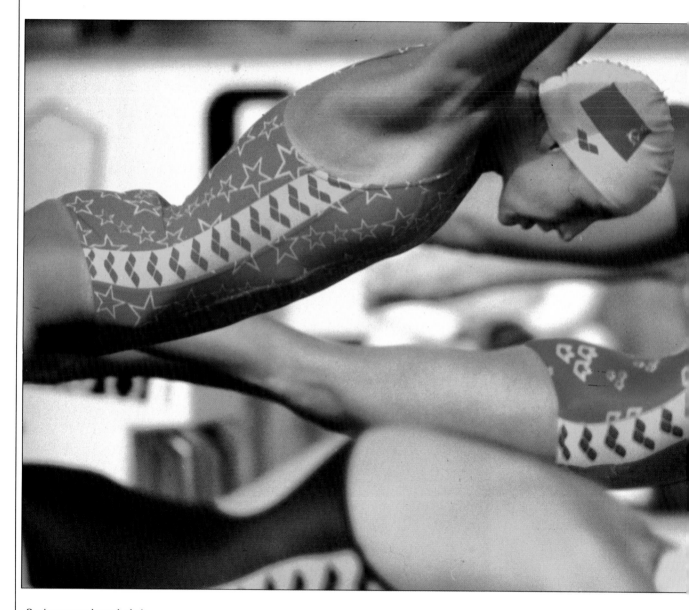

Swimmers *launch their bodies toward the water at the start of a race. Arched backs generate a sense of powerful propulsion, and the eel-like limbs, crammed into the frame by a telephoto lens, are stopped with a shutter speed of 1/1000.*

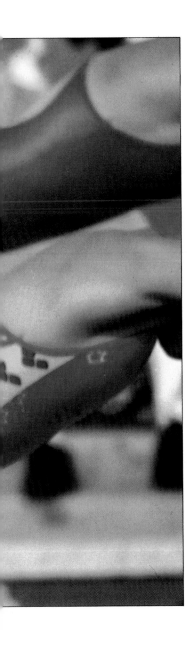

Sweat and water spray
from the contorted face of
Larry Holmes as he ends a
punishing sparring session
in preparation for a world
heavyweight title defense.
The ringside photographer
closed in and used flash
to freeze the droplets.

A motorcycle racer banks over to take a corner, the bright red of the rider's suit standing out against the dark of the track. The photographer used a special prism filter to create the repeated image that gives such a dramatic impression of high speed.

A plastic sandal and a
bulb of garlic (below),
faintly reflected in the
sheet of red acrylic they
stand on, make a memorable
still-life with visually strong
contrasts of color, form and
texture, and of organic and
man-made materials. The
light source was a diffused
photolamp angled onto the
subjects from above. The
lamp produced a reflected
highlight on the toe of the
sandal, the focal point of
the composition.

A glass of carbonated
mineral water (right),
containing an ice cube, a
slice of lemon and a cherry,
fills the frame with an
image of thirst-quenching
refreshment. A portable flash
unit, aimed at a reflector
immediately behind the glass,
was quite adequate to light
this small subject, and the
burst of light was brief
enough to freeze the motion
of the tiny bubbles.

A model in a bathing suit (above)
is rimlit by a pair of studio flash
units, while a reflector above the camera
provides fill-in lighting for her back. Her
hair was gently lifted by an electric
fan. The crossed poles provide balance
in this simple composition.

A young girl (right) delights in her
reflection in a large, free-standing
distorting mirror. The girl was shy at
first in front of the camera and all the
equipment; but, as the photographer
guessed, the novelty of the mirror soon
dispelled her inhibition.

Unearthly blue light and deep shadows (left) impart a macabre air to a portrait. The photograph was taken on tungsten-balanced film, with the subject lit from below by daylight-balanced fluorescent tube lighting. The closeness of the light source washed out part of the image, imparting a sense of the supernatural.

A silhouetted profile (right) blends naturally into a starlit seascape. Four elements in combination make up the image. To obtain the silhouette, the photographer posed the woman against a white background, lit only the background and used a blue filter over the lens. Tiny holes pierced in black cardboard produced an image of twinkling stars. After sandwiching this with the silhouette, the photographer copied the sandwich onto a sheet of film masked off at the bottom. With the top masked in turn, a second exposure recorded the sea. Finally, the photographer copied a slide of the moon onto the same piece of film, exposing the sky area alone.

In warm evening light, a ship under construction in Morocco acquires rich tones, while the cloudless sky takes on a beautiful purple hue. To capture this extraordinary lighting effect accurately on daylight-balanced color film, the photographer used a blue 80C color conversion filter, which prevented the scene from looking too red.

CATCHING THE ACTION

One of photography's greatest pleasures is catching the peak of action – whether it be the headlong charge of a football player, the leap of a marlin from the sea or, as in the picture at left, the joyous dash of children down a sand dune. The opportunities for such shots are unlimited, but good action pictures are more often the result of skill, planning and proper equipment than of sheer luck.

Good action photography demands a honing of a whole range of normal photographic skills. With little time to select the exposure, focus on the subject or frame the image, you must make decisions about the viewpoint and timing of the picture in advance. Some simple basic techniques, such as prefocusing, increase your chances of getting just the picture you want instead of a blurry, half-cropped subject.

Shutter speed is the essential means of control in action photography. In good light, you can make exposures fast enough to freeze almost any rapidly moving subject with a clarity never visible to the eye. And in duller light, you can maintain adequate shutter speed by using fast film and fast lenses. But often you can convey action even more dramatically by deliberately blurring parts of the image, as shown by some of the special techniques in this section.

Playing children stream
down a massive dune. The
photographer waited until
the group formed a diagonal
composition across the slope
before arresting their motion
with a fast shutter at 1/500.

The action around us

The great advantage of ordinary action situations is their accessibility. You can study a scene at your leisure, look for good subjects, try out different viewpoints and return later if the light is poor.

Essentially there are two approaches you can take with everyday action photography. You can go to a promising location, such as a busy street, and snatch the action as it happens, or you can plan a particular photograph. The picture of motorcyclists on the opposite page was set up in advance: the photographer fixed his camera to the back of a car and waited until the bikes were just a few feet away before triggering the shutter.

Anticipation is also important with a more spontaneous approach. Evaluate the setting and decide how you want to portray the subject. The two pictures at right and far right here show figures in motion, and both were taken with a telephoto lens – but the results are very different. For the rollerskaters, the photographer closed in to make the subjects fill the frame and threw the distracting background out of focus. The figure on the beach is more abstract, and the long lens has been used to bring the background closer. In some situations, you can predict what will happen and preset your camera so that you are ready to catch the moment of action. The picture below is an example: two children were playing with a hose, and sooner or later, one was bound to turn the water on his friend.

Rollerskate novices (above) have a go. A 300mm lens at maximum aperture enabled the photographer to close in and catch the mingled excitement and uncertainty, while reducing the color and movement in the background to a soft blur.

A boy's face (left) registers the shock of an unexpected shower. The photographer preset the focus and an exposure of 1/125 at f/5.6 and then just waited for the fun to start.

An early morning bather
(above) prepares to plunge
into the surf. A 300mm lens
has compressed perspective
so that the mountains and
ships seem nearer and form
a backdrop to the figure.

Two motorcycles (right)
seem to bear down on the
viewer at dizzying speed.
The photographer attached
the camera to the tail of a
car – driven ahead of the bikes
by a friend – and operated
the shutter with a cable
release from the back seat.
A 15mm wide-angle lens gave
broad coverage and good
depth of field, while a shutter
speed of 1/125 streaked
the background.

Fast shutter

Action photography calls for a camera with a top shutter speed of at least 1/1000. Some modern cameras are even faster – as quick as 1/8000, or even 1/12,000. But must you use your camera's fastest speed to freeze action, or will a slower speed be sufficient?

The answer obviously depends on how fast your subject is moving, but other factors are important too. For example, the world's fastest sprinter reaches a speed of about 27 miles per hour, and in the course of an exposure lasting 1/1000, his body will have moved forward about half an inch. If you are photographing a whole field of six or eight runners from some distance with a standard lens, then body movement of half an inch is unlikely to be significant, and the picture will look sharp. But if you choose to close in with a powerful telephoto lens and show the strain on the face of the leading runner as he crosses the finishing line, a half-inch movement could make the magnified winner's profile look blurred and indistinct.

In sporting events such as auto racing, in which speeds are many times faster than on a running track, the direction of movement has an even greater bearing on the sharpness. If the subject is moving directly toward or away from the camera, the image in the viewfinder does not move across the frame. Instead, it simply appears to get bigger or smaller, and to arrest this slight change you can use shutter speeds that would be too slow to freeze the same subject passing across the frame, as demonstrated in the sequence below at left.

The chart below at right offers a rough guide to the relative shutter speeds at which you should be able to freeze different kinds of movement. But bear in mind that a host of factors can affect sharpness, including the focal length of your lens and your distance from the subject. You should use these speeds experimentally, and combine them with swinging the camera around to follow the subject – the panning technique explained in detail on pages 346-47.

Movement within the frame
This sequence of photographs of a car traveling at a constant 40 miles per hour was taken at the same shutter speed of 1/125. It shows how you can choose a camera position to stop the subject's movement at relatively slow shutter speed.

1 – With the camera pointing across the road, the passing car appears moderately blurred in the final image.

2 – With the camera on the inside of a bend, the car approaches at a 45° angle and appears much sharper.

3 – With the camera on the outside of a bend, the car comes almost directly toward it, and is entirely sharp.

Speeds to freeze movement
The chart below indicates the slowest shutter speeds that will stop the movement across the frame of some common subjects. A lot depends on the subject's distance from the camera – the speeds given here are for subjects at a distance that makes them fill the frame of a 35mm camera, held horizontally. Subjects farther away will need slightly slower speeds. If the subject is moving toward or away from the camera, you can allow a speed one or two stops slower than is indicated.

Child sprinting	1/250
Adult running	1/250
Adult sprinting	1/500
Car at 40 m.p.h.	1/500
Car at 80 m.p.h.	1/1000
Fast racing car	1/2000
Fast train	1/1000
Tennis serve	1/1000
Tennis stroke	1/500
Skier	1/1000
Water skier	1/500
Skateboarder	1/500
Cyclist	1/500
Swimmer	1/125
Diver	1/1000
Trotting horse	1/250
Galloping horse	1/1000

A girl lunges for the ball in a beach game, recorded in sharp detail by a shutter speed of 1/1000. In spite of the fast shutter, some blur has registered on the ball, because its movement is across the frame, not toward the camera.

Fast film

Shutter speeds fast enough to freeze rapid action dramatically reduce the amount of light that gets to the film. One solution – often the only one – is to use faster film, as outlined in the table at right.

To freeze the action of the circus performer below, the photographer had to use a shutter speed of 1/500. With a medium-speed film, the dim lighting of the big top would have forced him to use an aperture of f/1.8 – impractical because his lens had a maximum aperture of f/4. Loading the camera with ISO 400 film enabled him to capture the scene with the f/4 aperture.

In exceptionally bad light, even the fastest film may not be sufficiently sensitive. But by increasing the development time of color slide or black-and-white film during processing – a technique called pushing the film – you may be able to wring out a little extra speed. To use this technique – illustrated at the bottom of the opposite page – you set the camera's film speed dial at one or two stops above the ISO rating of the film you are using. Then, when you send the film to a laboratory, ask the processor to increase development equivalently.

The availability of fast film

The 35mm format offers the broadest range of fast films, though medium format 120 rollfilm also comes in a wide selection of fast speeds.

Color prints

The fastest color print film has a speed of ISO 3200. This is available in 120 and 35mm formats. However, most film manufacturers limit their fastest color print film to ISO 1600.

Color slides

The fastest 35mm color slide film has a speed of ISO 1600. In the 120 format, the top speed is ISO 1000, though pushing the film increases this to ISO 2000 (see box opposite below).

Black-and-white

Black-and-white film has speeds up to ISO 3200 in the 35mm format, but the limit in the 120 format is ISO 400. Pushing the films can double or even treble their effective speeds.

A human canonball speeds toward the safety net. The photographer used a 200mm lens from a normal seat in the circus tent, with fast ISO 400 film.

At a harness race, rapidly fading sunlight casts a warm glow on a horse and driver. Only by using a film with a speed of ISO 400 was the photographer able to catch a sharp image (1/250 at f/2.8, 135mm lens).

Pushing film

For the sequence below, the photographer progressively uprated the film speed to achieve faster shutter speeds and less blur, thus effectively underexposing. The processor then "pushed" the film's development time to compensate.

Developed normally, ISO 400 film has good color, but dim light forced the photographer to use a speed of 1/60, so movement has blurred the picture.

Uprating the film one stop (to 800), gives a speed of 1/125, which records a sharper image. But longer development boosts grain and dulls color.

Pushing film too far can cut image quality. Here, a three stop push gives a speed of 1/500, but grain size and color are unacceptable.

Prefocusing

The furious pace of much action photography means that maintaining sharp focus at all times is extremely difficult – some subjects move so rapidly that even the most up-to-date autofocus cameras struggle to keep up with the action.

With autofocus cameras, the problem is not the focusing itself, but the short delay while the camera evaluates sharpness, and moves the lens elements to the right position. If you are using an autofocus lens that has a focus-limiting device, you can use this to reduce the delay, as explained below at right. Otherwise, try panning with the subject as it passes.

You may alternatively wish to focus manually, and prefocus the lens. You determine where the best of the action is likely to happen, focus on that spot, wait for the subject to reach it, and then release the shutter.

The most critical judgement is timing. Press the shutter release a fraction too soon or too late, and the subject will be out of focus. The trick is to anticipate the moment at which the subject will reach the point of focus, and shoot a fraction of a second before. For your first attempts, try prefocusing on a fixed, well-defined area. Take the example of a horse clearing a jump at left below. You can prefocus on the top rail in the knowledge that the animal must pass that spot. Having focused, wait until the horse's leading foreleg has just crossed the bar – then shoot. This allows for your reaction time, and for the time taken by the camera's mirror to flip out of the way of the film, giving you a perfectly focused image.

Some autofocus SLRs have a trap focus mode which automatically releases the shutter at the right moment. You prefocus the lens, and the camera fires the shutter the moment a subject enters the autofocus frame at the same distance from the camera as the plane of sharp focus.

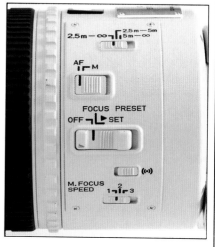

Focus-limiting devices
The newest autofocus lenses adjust focus very rapidly indeed, but there is still a significant time-lag while the lens "hunts" for the subject. The delay is longest when the lens has to make large changes in focus. To solve this problem, some lenses have a switch that limits the travel of the focusing mechanism. For example, the lens shown above can be set to "hunt" only in the range 5m-∞. By switching to this setting when photographing distant subjects, you will greatly reduce the camera's response time.

A horse and rider are stopped in mid-jump. The fence rails provided the photographer with an ideal prefocusing spot. As soon as the forelegs came into focus, he pressed the shutter release.

Jogging companions pound along a quiet sidewalk. The photographer noted the couple approaching and prefocused on a spot ahead, then waited until they were just coming into focus to fire the shutter at a setting of 1/500.

Panning

By following a moving subject across the frame with your camera during exposure, you effectively reduce the rate of movement. Panning, as this technique is called, enables you to use a relatively slow shutter speed to stop action, while creating background blur to help suggest movement.

In some areas of high-speed photography, panning is essential if you want a sharp image of the subject. With a static camera position, even a shutter speed of 1/8000 may not be fast enough to freeze a racing car or motorcycle traveling across the frame close to you. But by panning you can obtain the kind of crisp image illustrated at the bottom of this page. In an absolutely sharp panned picture the speed of the subject relative to the movement of the camera during the exposure is zero. By slowing the shutter speed and the speed of the panning movement, you can blur or streak the subject. Against a colorful background, slight blurring can suggest a whirling velocity, as in the photograph at right.

Whatever the subject and shutter speed, the basic object of panning is to achieve a smooth, continuous movement of the camera. Start by assessing in advance the course that the subject will take, and prefocus on the spot at which you estimate the subject will pass closest to you. Stand facing this spot with your shoulders parallel to the subject's line, and set a shutter speed of around 1/60 or 1/125, depending on the subject's speed. As the subject approaches, without moving your feet, swivel your hips round to pick it up in the viewfinder. Keep the subject in the center of the frame until it is almost directly in front of you and then press the shutter release. Remember to follow through smoothly after the exposure to avoid any image distortion.

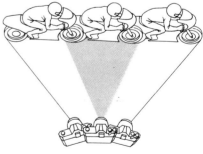

Accurate panning, as diagrammed above, froze the movement of the racing motorcycle at left. The photographer selected a shutter speed of 1/1000 and pressed the shutter release in the middle of the swiveling motion plotted in the diagram. This ensured a sharp image in the exact center of the frame.

Horses racing across a field convey the joy of free movement. Fast panning at 1/60 recorded the main subject's head and shoulders crisply: but the galloping hooves, the other horses and the verdant surroundings have streaked and blurred.

Polo ponies, photographed at two different shutter speeds, show how the effects of panning can be controlled. The photographer set a shutter speed of 1/8 for the picture at left in order to creatively mask all detail. At 1/125, panning has stopped the pony – but has only just blurred the background.

Blurring movement

By setting really slow shutter speeds – 1/8 or slower – movement itself becomes the subject of your pictures, and the shape and detail of the moving object dissolves into an impressionistic blur.

This technique works best in brilliant sunshine, when colors look brightest and contrast is high. Sun reflected on water, as in the picture below, can create beautiful effects. However, in bright sun you may have to use a neutral density filter to prevent overexposure, even at minimum aperture.

At very slow shutter speeds, you will find it increasingly difficult to hold the camera steady. The conventional way to deal with unsteadiness is to mount the camera on a tripod. But if sharp background detail is not a priority, you may be able to turn camera shake to your advantage. For example, in the picture on the opposite page, camera movement has combined with the violent kicks of the horse to convey the excitement of the rodeo.

The viewfinder of an SLR camera goes black during exposure, and at shutter speeds longer than about 1/4, this can be a distraction. Keep both eyes open and follow the subject by looking over the top of the camera while the viewfinder is dark.

Soccer players (left)
swirl against a bright green
Astroturf background as an
attacker escapes a tackle.
An exposure of 1/4 enabled
the photographer to create
a blurred impression of
speed and agility. The slow
shutter speed required an
aperture of f/22 with a
neutral density filter
to avoid overexposure.

Windsurfers (left)
glide across the waves in
brilliant sunshine. Bracing
the camera on the side of
a bouncing motorboat, and
using a slow speed of 1/8 at
f/22, turned the reflected
sunlight into sparkling white
squiggles.

A bucking bronco (right)
kicks furiously, attempting
to dislodge its rider. The
photographer set a shutter
speed of 1/30 and sharply
jerked the camera upward
at the moment of exposure
for the streaked effect.

Track and field

The most important factor in deciding how you should photograph a running race is the length of the course. An approach that produces good pictures of a sprint will not necessarily work well if you apply it to a marathon.

Short track races last just seconds, and you may have time to take only one picture. At such events, decide which part of the race you most want to photograph, and concentrate on capturing this one moment. For example, in the picture at right, the photographer chose to show the runners accelerating just after the starting pistol was fired.

Middle-distance races of course last longer than sprints and, if you can move freely around the track, you may be able to get pictures of both start and finish. However, if you are confined to a single place, perhaps a seat in the stands, try to be close to the finish, or overlooking the final bend where the runners put on a last effort to gain the lead.

Marathons and other long races have rather different action peaks for the photographer. The massed start makes a dramatic contrast with the finish, where the leading runner may cross the line while the rest of the field is out of sight. The miles that separate start and finish give ample opportunity for portraying the isolation and exhaustion of individual runners, although the finish can provide particularly poignant moments – as at right below.

Four sprinters (above) surge forward at the start of a 100 meter race. Looking down the track from an ordinary seat in the stands, the photographer prefocused a 200mm lens on a selected group, with a speed of 1/1000 to fix their burst of energy in motionless symmetry.

A lone runner (left) crosses a hill during a cross-country race. By using a 400mm lens, the photographer isolated him against the backdrop of a distant valley.

An exhausted winner (left) hits the tape at the end of a road race. Free public access to the finish line meant that a 135mm lens was sufficient to fill the frame with a close-cropped image of the victor.

Winter sports

To catch the exhilaration of winter sports, you must first adjust your photographic techniques to compensate for the low temperatures, and for the glare of snow or ice.

Exposure control needs special attention in snow-covered settings. An SLR's through-the-lens meter will indicate a reduced exposure to deal with the large expanse of white, and to retain a brilliant whiteness you should increase the metered exposure by between one and two stops. Remember to revert to normal exposure settings for pictures such as the one at bottom right, in which the sky rather than the snow forms the background.

On a sunny day, the areas of snow in shade reflect the color of the sky, so they look blue on film.

Provided that other parts of the picture are sunlit, these blue shadows look quite natural, as can be seen from the image below. But if the entire scene is in the shade, you should use a No. 85C orange filter.

In cold weather, you need to take extra care of your camera. Keep it warm under your coat between exposures, because the batteries that power the meter, and possibly also the shutter, provide less current when they get cold. When you finish taking pictures, wrap your camera in a plastic bag before taking it indoors. Otherwise, moisture may condense on the cold surfaces, and damage the camera's mechanism. In extremely cold conditions, bare skin sticks to exposed bare-metal parts of camera and lens, so cover these with tape.

Laughing and tumbling, a crowd of friends enjoy the year's first snow. The photographer pointed down from a high bank to provide a uniform background that focused attention on the colors and swirling action.

Flying through the air, a ski hotdogger judges her landing. A polarizing filter darkened the blue sky, and a shutter speed of 1/1000 caught a sharp picture of the flurry of snow.

Speeding downhill, a skier turns to follow the trail. To prevent the snow from looking a featureless white, the photographer waited until late in the afternoon, when a low sun emphasized each hillock and picked out the tracks of earlier skiers.

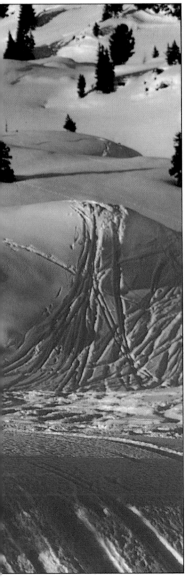

353

On the water

Water is a superb indicator of speed and movement. With activities that take place on the surface – waterskiing, surfing and windsurfing – you can use the flying spray and the foaming wake to convey the invigorating excitement of the action.

Like snow and ice, water reflects a great deal of light, especially spray or a breaking wave. Usually, you will need to open up at least half a stop to avoid underexposing your subject. Surfing, windsurfing and waterskiing usually take place some way from the shore, so you will need a long telephoto lens to close in on the subject if you are standing on the beach. The ideal position for taking waterskiing pictures is from the back of the towing boat. The skier's distance from the boat remains constant, so focusing is easy. A 300mm lens will enable you to frame the skier tightly. But you might instead concentrate on the wall of spray sent up by the skis, and keep the figure itself quite small. This approach is equally effective from the shore, and if you photograph at dusk you can obtain truly dramatic effects, as in the picture opposite.

A vantage point on a rocky headland can bring you close to surfboarders or windsurfers, but these two subjects present spectacular images even from a distance, as the photograph below demonstrates. With windsurfing, the camera angle is particularly important; the best pictures show the subject either backlit or, as here, heading toward the camera so that both the sail and the windsurfer are visible.

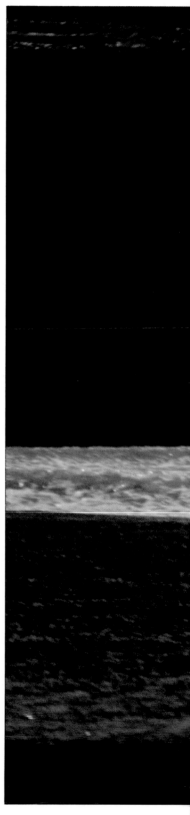

A waterskier skims the surface of a lake at dusk. A shutter speed of 1/1000 at f/5.6 with ISO 200 film froze the backlit subject and the curtain of spray behind.

A windsurfer (below) leans toward the water as he rides his board in. From a viewpoint on the beach, using a 200mm lens, the photographer was unable to close in on the subject. But the strong contrast, in line and color, between subject and setting powerfully conveys the mood and speed of the sport.

Indoor sports

With color slide photography, the available light of most halls, gymnasiums and other indoor sports arenas will often require the use of tungsten-balanced film. Because of the limited maximum speeds of such films, getting good color balance and saturation while stopping the action crisply is a special challenge. ISO 320 tungsten film can be pushed, with special processing, to give an effective speed of ISO 640. This may still not be adequate if you are using a telephoto lens with a small maximum aperture — an occasion when the extra stop or two of a fast lens will be most valuable.

If you are using color print film, you have a wide choice of fast daylight films — ISO 400 to 3200. And when photographing by available artificial light, you can always use a filter to correct any cast if color fidelity is crucial; but remember that this will limit the amount of light entering the lens. In dim light, it is better to rely on color correction during printing. Sometimes, however, a color cast can add mood to the picture — either subtly, as in the judo picture on the opposite page, or spectacularly, as shown in the photograph of skaters at right.

Flash enables you to take dramatically crisp pictures and, because flash is balanced to simulate daylight, you do not have to worry about color quality. Off-camera flash, as used below, produces a less flat lighting effect. Although flash may not be permitted at the event itself, this restriction is often lifted at practice sessions where you can create images as full of action as on the day of the event.

Ice skaters (above) execute a breathtaking turn. The photographer used fast ISO 400 daylight film at 1/500 to stop the action and to accentuate the colors of the red and blue spotlighting.

A gymnast (left) rotates on a vaulting horse. The photographer placed a portable flashgun on a stand to the right of the camera at about eight feet from the subject. This gave good modeling and showed up the gymnast's powerful muscles.

A judo blackbelt *(above)* *skillfully overcomes his adversary. To obtain a sharp image, the photographer used ISO 400 daylight film, which in tungsten spotlighting gave a warm, yellow cast.*

A boxer *(right)* *grimaces as he delivers a punch at a sparring session. The more relaxed atmosphere enabled the photographer to move in close and minimize the rapid fall-off of the flash.*

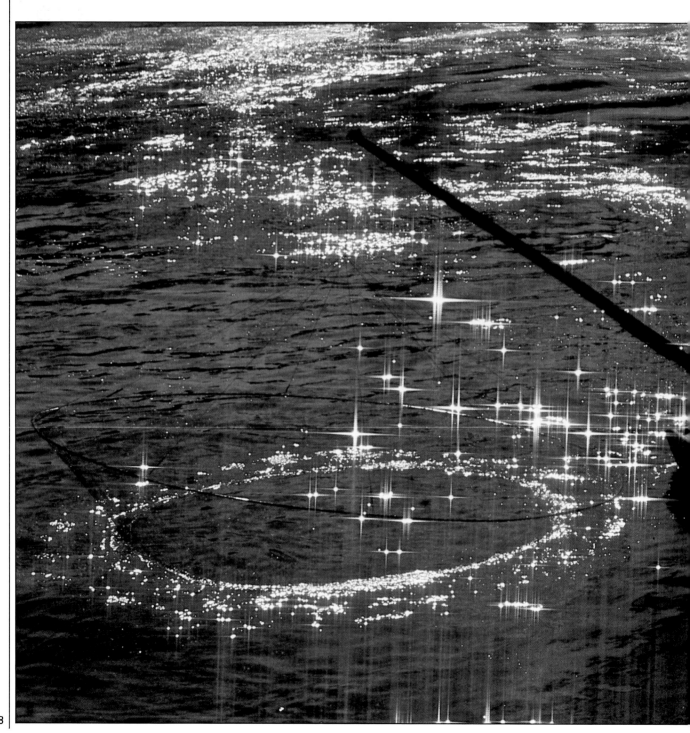

CREATING SPECIAL EFFECTS

Many photographers are content with the realistic pictures that reproduce the world as we perceive it. And because we are accustomed to such photographs, when the camera does create illusions the results are all the more striking. Taking reality as a starting point, these images surprise us with their weird juxtapositions or spin beautiful images with unearthly forms and colors.

This section introduces the fascinating world of special effects photography and explains some of the basic effects that you can exploit to make memorable surrealistic images. None of the techniques is beyond the reach of the amateur. For many, the only requirement is a willingness to experiment freely with ordinary equipment and film. Others require a little more in the way of camera attachments, like the relatively inexpensive filter that added glittering highlights to the view of a lake at left.

The basic techniques covered here should stimulate further exploration. Learn to break the rules uninhibitedly. And do not worry if the results are unpredictable – this is all part of the pleasure of special effects photography.

Two fishermen winch their net out of a lake to inspect their catch by the light of the early evening sun. A starburst filter over the lens turned the reflected highlights into a pattern of four-pointed stars.

Unexpected angles

Cups of Turkish coffee on a red cloth make a harmonious composition of shapes and colors. The photographer used a standard lens and took the picture from directly above. Soft shadows add tonal interest to the plain background.

Often, by finding an unusual camera position and viewpoint, you can turn ordinary subjects into intriguing images. When we look at something from an odd angle, we mentally correct distortions of perspective or scale. The camera cannot make such corrections, and by photographing from extreme angles you can exploit this limitation creatively.

As a simple example, pointing the camera directly down at a subject flattens the image: everything appears to lie on the same plane, so that forms are reduced to simple shapes. If you select a subject with strong shapes or lines against a plain, contrasting background, you can create almost abstract pictures such as the one at near right. The opposite technique, of pointing the camera straight up, can produce puzzling, ambiguous images in which the normal positions and relationships of objects are upset. The photograph of washing, below, is an example. With a very low viewpoint, you can also achieve distortions of scale and depth. If you use a wide-angle lens, the effect is exaggerated so that the nearer part of the scene appears unnaturally large, while the extended depth of field keeps the background sharp as in the two pictures opposite.

Household washing hung out to dry on clothes lines several floors up is buffeted by the wind into strange forms. Pointing the camera straight up took the subject out of its everyday context and gave the image strong background contrast.

The converging lines of a bridge suggest a giant kite balanced on the far horizon. From a camera position beneath the bridge, the photographer used a 24mm lens to exaggerate perspective and thus create a sense of extreme distance.

Giant pigeons point menacing beaks at the camera. The photographer lay down, resting the camera on the ground, and used a wide-angle lens in close-up. Seed scattered to attract the birds was cropped out to strengthen the effect.

Tricks with a slow shutter

The deliberate choice of a shutter speed that is too slow to stop a subject's movement can produce exciting and original pictures. Depending on the direction and speed of the subject, you can convey movement with slight blurring while still recording a recognizable image, as in the photograph of the flag below. Or you can create strange effects such as those in the picture on the opposite page, below, in which the central part of the image has dissolved into a formless blur.

To stop camera shake during slow shutter-speed exposures, you usually need to use a tripod. If you are photographing in daylight or bright light, you may also need to put a neutral density filter over your lens to compensate for the slower shutter speed: a 0.9 filter, for example, reduces the light reaching the film by three stops. Neutral density filters also enable you to set a wider aperture for shallow depth of field, so that you can throw a distracting background out of focus.

You can obtain beautiful abstract images by using a very slow shutter, of several seconds or more, for dusk scenes with colored lights. During lengthy exposures, even slight movement of the subject will cause highlights to spread into shadow areas and colors to flow. In the lower picture opposite, the effect was exaggerated by shining a colored light onto the subject. The reinforced glass of the balcony diffused the hues of the street lights below, adding texture to the composition.

A flag fluttering in the breeze appears as soft ripples of color at a slow shutter speed of 1/8 second. The photographer carefully framed the composition to include the tones and lines of the wall behind, which echo those of the flag.

Whirling chairs at a
fairground dissolve into
smoky shapes resembling the
dark clouds behind them. A
1/4 second exposure also
streaked the lights but
recorded the rest of the
scene sharply.

A wind-blown sheet
on a line glows with vivid,
fluorescent color against
a cool twilight setting. The
photographer shined a red
lamp on the sheet and set a
five-second exposure to get
the diaphanous effect against
the soft background hues.

Tricks with flash

With a little ingenuity and technical know-how, an electronic flash unit can be used to create exciting and unusual images – as these pictures show.

The easiest way to do this is to take pictures in dim light at a slow shutter speed – between 1/15 and one full second. When you press the shutter release, the flash fires but the shutter remains open, so that the ambient light continues to form an image. If the background is lit continuously from another source, a moving subject lit momentarily by flash will appear sharp but ghostlike, as on the opposite page below.

Some dedicated flash units, and the built-in flash units on many modern compact cameras, can balance the flash and ambient light levels automatically – this is often referred to as slow synch fill-in flash. However, this technique may not work when your SLR camera is set to program mode. On some SLRs, the slowest shutter speed the program will set on flash exposures is 1/60, which results in a brightly lit subject and a dark background. To solve the problem, switch to shutter priority mode or manual exposure mode.

A few, top-of-the-range flash units offer a second curtain synch option (sometimes known as rear curtain synch). Normally, the flash fires when the first shutter curtain opens fully, but when second curtain synch is set, the flash fires moments before the second shutter curtain starts to move. This has the advantage that the flash freezes a moving subject at the end of the exposure, rather than at the beginning, so trails of ambient light appear to follow the subject, giving a far more realistic effect.

If you have a tripod, you can produce interesting pictures by firing the flash several times on a moving subject, during a single exposure. This technique is known as multiple flash and is explained opposite. Similar, but more dynamic effects can be achieved using stroboscopic flash. In stroboscopic mode, a flash unit fires several, brief bursts of flash in quick succession. These record even fast moving subjects as a series of separate images on a single frame.

Another useful technique is to fit colored filters, or stretch brightly colored material, over the flash head. The photographer who took the picture on the opposite page, below, used the red cellophane wrapper from a candy bar to add brilliant color to the foreground.

A roller skater speeds backward past the camera, his motion frozen by a flash. By panning to follow the figure during the one-second exposure, the photographer spread the lights around him into brilliant streaks of color.

Multiple flash

In darkness, you can make several flash exposures on one frame. For multiple images of a single subject, attach the camera to a tripod, and lock the shutter open using the B setting and a lockable cable release. Then fire the flash to light the subject in several positions. For the example at left, the model moved away from the camera and the photographer followed her, firing a flash at each of three locations, as diagrammed below.

A splash of red from a filtered flash breaks the monotony of blank gray city slabs. A passer-by, frozen in motion by the flash, looks like an apparition, because the floodlit wall behind her formed an image on film during the 15-second exposure.

Zooming

Moving the focal-length control of a zoom lens during a long exposure is an excellent way to suggest dynamic movement in a static scene or to increase the sense of speed in a moving subject. For even more spectacular pictures, there are several ways of varying the characteristic zooming effect of lines radiating out from the center of the image.

If you move the zoom control through its full range for as long as the shutter is open, the result can be beautiful abstract patterns, as in the image at right. By operating the zoom for only part of the exposure time, you can create effects as dramatic or subtle as you wish, while keeping the main subject relatively sharp. Another approach is to pan or tilt the camera at the same time as zooming, so that you get horizontal or vertical streaking as well as radiating lines. These types of zooming work best on scenes with specular highlights – intense reflections or bright points of light – that form distinct streaks across the image, as in the picture opposite, below.

Christmas lights explode like a firework display. The photographer centered the subject and moved the zoom through its full range during exposure.

The front of a vintage car is dramatized by careful zooming, done during the latter half of a one-second exposure to retain sharp detail.

Horizontal and radial streaks convey a cyclist's speed. Panning the camera while zooming a 1/4-second exposure suggested hurtling movement.

Sunbeams pierce a gloomy wood. The photographer exposed the scene for a 1/2-second, then moved the zoom control for another 1/2-second exposure.

Filters for simple effects/1

By skillfully using filters to alter the color and quality of light, you can manipulate the mood of an image without making it obvious that a special effect is involved. The pictures on these pages owe their distinctive sense of atmosphere to the subtlety with which filters were used to support the compositions without intruding on them.

The ability of color to suggest mood often depends on creating an overall harmony of hues, and you can use pale color filters to achieve this – a brown filter to warm up overall tones or a blue one to give an impression of coolness. Diffusion and fog filters can evoke a dreamlike sense of the past, as in the picture opposite, below. And if you want to achieve a delicate pastel effect, you can try using a

fog filter and a pale color filter in combination.

Graduated filters, with a colored half that fades gradually into a clear half, are usually chosen to add drama to landscape pictures. But these filters, too, can be used unobtrusively – as in the photograph below, in which the darkening of the sky at the upper left of the image creates the naturalistic impression of a dust cloud or heat haze over the rest of the picture. A filter holder, illustrated on the opposite page, enables you to move a graduated filter to cover the desired part of the scene. Lens focal length and aperture will affect how the boundary zone between colored and clear areas blends in. The longer the lens and the wider the aperture, the less perceptible the boundary line will be.

An isolated stand of trees adds interest to a study of landscape colors. A blue graduated filter darkened the sky so that a dusty haze seems to hang over the cornfield. The photographer used a wide-angle lens at a narrow aperture to make the change in tone more apparent.

Filter systems
The filter holder above takes up to three square filters, or two square filters and one circular filter. It is attached to the lens by an adapter ring, and different adapter rings are available to fit any lens size.

An earth excavator (left) *makes an intriguing silhouette. The photographer used a No. 81EF brown filter to warm up the cool twilight tones and to unify the composition.*

Lines of bare trees reflected in a still pond convey a mood of pastoral tranquility. The photographer used a fog filter to achieve the delicate hues and soft outlines reminiscent of early photographs, and set a small aperture to suggest mist fading into the distance.

Filters for simple effects/2

Filters that radically transform nature require a very careful choice of subject matter if pictures are to avoid looking merely gimmicky. Filters are no substitute for imagination. However, used with sensitivity and understanding, they can help create effective images such as the one below, which cleverly exploits one of the optical properties of a polarizing filter.

One very simple technique is to put a strong color filter over the lens so that a scene appears bathed in an unnatural light, as in the beach view on the opposite page. Strong red, blue or green filters can deceive your TTL meter, so take the reading without the filter in place and increase the exposure by the manufacturer's recommended "filter factor". For good results with strong color filters, simple, bold compositions are best.

Instead of adding just one color to a picture, you can produce even more unearthly effects with two colors, provided you choose an apt subject such as the grassy landscape at right. Use a two-color filter (that is, a filter with each half in a different hue) or combine two single-color filters of equal strength, oriented in opposite positions in front of the lens. Alternatively, make your own two-color filter using pieces of gelatin taped together, as diagrammed opposite. Instead of setting a wide aperture to blur the division between the hues, you may prefer to keep the aperture small to provide a sharp line that you can incorporate into the composition for creative effect, as in the skyscraper picture at the bottom of the opposite page.

Brightly colored, wind ruffled grasses (above) stand out strongly against the ghostly shapes of gnarled trees in the background. The photographer used two graduated filters – a blue one and an inverted tobacco-colored one – to heighten the effect.

Streaks like heatwaves (left) fill a blue sky, giving the impression of an extreme weather phenomenon. For this effect, the picture was taken through a car windshield with a polarizing filter over the lens. The filter showed up light distortion caused by built-in stresses in the shatterproof glass.

The World Trade Center in New York (right) acquires new colors when viewed through a green and magenta two-color filter, which was oriented to align the sharp division between the hues with the diagonal line between the skyscrapers.

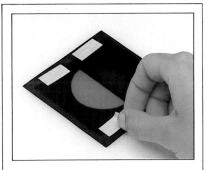

Making a two-color filter
Take a piece of cardboard and cut a circular hole in it slightly wider than the diameter of your lens. Then tape different-colored rectangles of gelatin over the hole as shown above, so that the pieces abut. You can then tape this home-made filter over your lens whenever you come across a suitable subject.

Riders on horseback (below) race along the gleaming wet sand of an empty shore, in a mystical light created by a deep blue filter. The photographer calculated an exposure increase of three stops to compensate for the blue filter's absorption of light, but set an increase of only one stop, underexposing to heighten the mood.

Starburst and diffraction filters

Dazzling flashes of sunlight on a pool of water enchant the eye, but on film they often look disappointing. A starburst or diffraction filter can restore the brilliance of the reflected light, as in the picture below, and create an image that more closely resembles what you remember seeing at the moment you released the shutter.

Tiny grooves on starburst filters and diffraction filters, as shown at the top of the opposite page, spread light from the bright highlights into the darker areas of a picture. Thus, both types of filters work best with scenes that show very bright subjects on a dim background. At night, for example, they enhance the twinkling brightness of street lights seen against the dark sky. A diffraction filter has an additional effect: it splits light into component colors, surrounding each bright highlight with rainbow-colored streaks or with halos, as at bottom right on the opposite page.

The effects of starburst and diffraction filters depend on the focal length of your lens and on the aperture you are using. However, the image in the camera's viewfinder does not always show precisely how the picture will appear, even if you stop the lens down to the working aperture. Take pictures at several different apertures, and choose the best effect after you have processed the film. Avoid using either a starburst or diffraction filter when a subject has a lot of fine detail; because both filters cause some diffusion, the picture may look blurred.

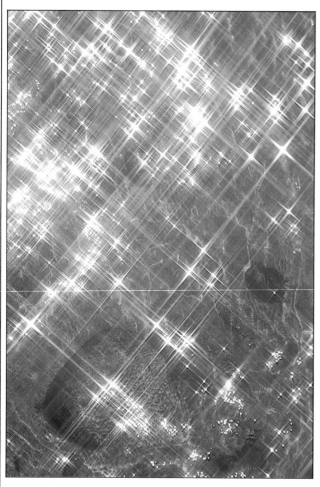

A rock pool glitters in the sun.
By attaching a starburst filter to
the lens, the photographer turned each
reflection into a four-point star. He
also oriented the spikes of each star
diagonally across the frame by rotating
the filter an eighth of a turn.

Choosing a filter

The pattern and spacing of lines etched on a starburst filter, illustrated below at right, control the appearance of the spokes that radiate from each light source. In the picture sequence, parallel lines create two-point starbursts (1), whereas lines at 90° and 22° produce four and 16 spikes on each highlight (2 and 3). On diffraction filters, the lines are too small and closely spaced to see; you can observe their effect only by holding the filter to the light.

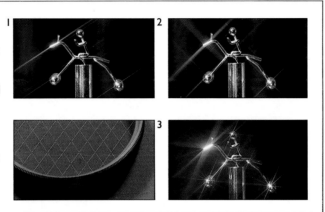

A misty window (below), when seen through a halo diffraction filter, spins rings of color around the reflected afternoon sun. By drawing a black curtain behind the window, the photographer ensured that the spectrum of colors appeared rich and saturated.

Spears of color (left), created by a diffraction filter, spill from the sun and its reflection in this upswept view of Fifth Avenue near St Patrick's Cathedral in New York City. Underexposure, and an additional magenta filter, helped make the rainbow streaks more prominent.

Photography through screens

A screen in front of the lens can turn pictures into colorful abstracts or overlay a recognizable image with an attractive texture, as in the picture below. You can make a screen of this sort from practically any clear or semitransparent material. Glass or acrylic sheets with textured surfaces are good choices. Alternatively, apply a diffusing medium to clear acrylic or glass, as was done for the picture below. To create this image the photographer smeared petroleum jelly across a plain sheet of glass: for a more permanent screen you can substitute varnish or clear nail polish for jelly. And by using inks, paints or dyes, you can add color to the image, as the picture below at right shows.

The focal length of the lens, its aperture, and the distance between the screen and lens will all affect the appearance of the picture, so that by varying these factors you can produce many different effects with the same screen. For example, if the screen is very close to the lens, the resultant image will be very diffuse. But if you shift the screen closer to the subject, outlines will become more easily recognizable – as in the image at right – though details will still be blurred.

The effects of aperture and focal length are less easy to predict. You should experiment by changing lenses and by stopping down the diaphragm, but always be sure to use the camera's depth of field preview button to check the viewfinder image before taking the picture.

A street carnival (*above*), seen through a prepared glass screen, takes on the appearance of an Impressionist painting. The photographer marked the screen with felt-tipped pens, then placed it on a tripod about a foot in front of the lens. A small aperture kept both the screen and the street beyond it sharp.

Silver birch trees (*left*) sparkle in the sun, and light from their white trunks catches the smeared surface of a glass sheet just in front of the lens. Smearing diagonal streaks of petroleum jelly created the corner-to-corner lines on the picture; horizontal smears would have made vertical lines, and vertical smears, horizontal lines.

Spring flowers in vases stand behind a pane of textured glass placed in front of the camera. The shaded background contrasts strongly with the sunlit blossoms, preventing the composition from looking cluttered.

Multi-image filters

Thread a multi-image filter onto the front of your lens, and with a single press of the shutter release you can create a picture that has all the appearance of a double or multiple exposure, as shown below. The polished facets of the filter bend rays of light before they enter the lens, so that several identical views of the subject reach the film. The arrangements of repeated images created by multi-image filters vary greatly. Usually there is one dominant image and a series of weaker, displaced ones.

When using a multi-image filter no exposure adjustments are necessary but you must choose your subject carefully. A filter that has five or more facets will scramble a complicated subject, making an almost unrecognizable picture. As in the picture of the car on the opposite page, it is best to choose a subject with very bold outlines and to use a filter that creates just three or four subsidiary images, especially if you want to generate a sense of motion.

Even when using filters of a simple design, you should try to ensure that at least one of the displaced images falls on a dark part of the frame. If the background is light, the images will be washed out and pale. Remember also to use the depth of field preview control, because the subject's appearance will change according to the aperture chosen.

An office building, *faced with mirrored glass, forms a forest of silver lines when seen through a parallel-image filter, which has a row of parallel sloping facets across half of the front surface.*

A stationary car reflected in water appears to leap forward, aided by a special multi-image filter which gives an effect of motion. The background showed up the repeated images clearly.

How multi-image filters work
Filters for multiple images are just glass or plastic blocks, cut and polished like the surface of a gem. The position and number of the facets determine the appearance of the picture. For example, the flat central face of the prism above allows light to reach the film directly, while the sloping faces form four images surrounding the central one.

A neon sign appears as a swirl of light when shot with a zoom lens and a multi-image filter. The zooming action of the lens turned the filter during the one second exposure, which made the outer images rotate around the central one.

377

Split-field close-up lenses

When objects in the viewfinder are very near the camera, you can usually show either the objects or the background sharply, but not both. However, with a split-field close-up lens screwed onto the front of your main lens, you will be able to keep foreground subjects just inches from the camera in focus, without sacrificing sharpness in the background, as these pictures show.

Such dramatic contrasts of scale will look convincing only if you take special care with composition. As explained in the box on the opposite page, the construction of the split-field lens results in a blurred zone across the middle of the picture. On one side of this zone, nearby subjects are sharp, and on the other side distant detail is recorded clearly.

So if possible you should compose the picture with only unimportant parts of the subject in the middle third of the frame.

Remember, too, that depth of field is very shallow when the subject is close to the camera; therefore, to keep all of the foreground sharp, you will have to stop down the main lens to a small aperture. Otherwise, confine your foreground subject to a shallow plane.

Never allow sunlight to fall directly on the split-field lens. The cut-glass edge causes light to scatter in a way that can veil your picture with flare, so use a lens hood or shade the lens with your hand. Also, you should focus an autofocus camera manually, as the split-field lens is likely to confuse the camera's autofocus system.

A shining trumpet and a brass band appear equally sharp, although a great distance separates them. The straight edge of the sheet of music was positioned just below the blurred central zone created by the split-field lens.

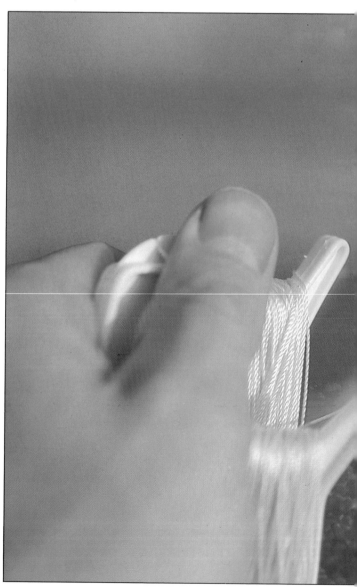

Cow parsley flowers close to the camera lift their heads against a background of distant trees and bushes. To record both the plant and a broad view of its habitat on one frame the photographer used a +1 diopter split-field close-up lens.

A red kite catches the breeze over a pebbly beach – and a split-field close-up lens brings the kite-flier's hand into focus. Here, the field is split vertically, but the blurred area of sky above the hand does not spoil the image.

Choosing a split-field lens

A split-field close-up lens is just half of a convex lens fitted into a rotating mount, as shown above. Like that of regular close-up lenses, the power of split-field lenses is measured in diopters. If you focus your camera lens on infinity, and attach a +1 diopter split-field lens over the bottom half of the camera lens, foreground subjects 40 inches (1 meter) from the camera will be sharp, and the distant background will be unaffected. This is true regardless of the focal length of the main camera lens. With a +2 split-field lens, the foreground will be sharp 20 inches (50cm) from the camera; and with a +3 lens, subjects one foot (30cm) away are sharp. The background will also be sharp, as long as the camera lens is focused correctly. Pick a split-field lens with the size of your foreground subject in mind: with a standard 50mm lens, a +1 split-field lens will fill the foreground with a subject just 27 inches (68cm) across. With a +2 and a +3, subjects 12 and 8 inches (32 and 20cm) across will fill the foreground. Wide-angle and telephoto lenses take in correspondingly broader and narrower foregrounds.

Transposing film

A simple way to obtain unusual color effects is to use a film that is incorrectly balanced for the light source. Daylight-balanced film, intended for use in natural light settings or with flash, is extra sensitive to yellow or red light, because daylight is predominantly blue. Tungsten-balanced film, on the other hand, is designed to make up the deficiency of blue in tungsten light or candlelight.

Color transparency film gives the best transposed effects. Daylight film in tungsten lighting gives a warm yellow tint to a scene; tungsten film in daylight records a cold blue cast. The depth of color depends not only on the type of light source but also on its intensity. For example, tungsten film used in weak, diffused daylight produces a subtle color cast,

as in the large picture below. For more dramatic effects, take your photographs outdoors at dusk, or just before dawn, when the natural light is very blue. To deepen the colors, simply underexpose by half to one stop.

When aiming for a strong color effect, choose the subject with care. A blue cast will make yellows and reds look muddy. But a scene of water and sky, such as the one below at left, can produce a beautiful atmospheric image with tungsten film.

Another approach with tungsten film is to juxtapose a naturally-colored foreground with a rich blue background by lighting the foreground with a tungsten photolamp or by covering the reflector of your camera flash with a No. 85B orange filter.

A seaside pavilion is picked out in lights against the deep blue of water and sky. The photographer used tungsten-balanced film at twilight to obtain the strong color cast, and made a double exposure to include the ornate street-light at an unusual angle to the subject.

Brilliant green light bathes the matted branches and gnarled trunk of an old tree. The photographer used daylight-balanced film to intensify the unnatural color of mercury floodlights.

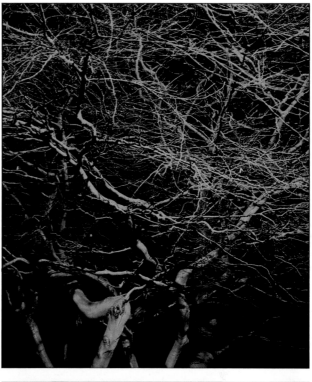

Soft sunlight through a window records a nude's natural skin tones on daylight film (above). By switching to tungsten film (left), the photographer gave an eerie bluish tinge to the scene, photographed in the same light but with a change of camera angle and pose.

Double exposure

Double or multiple views of the same person achieved by exposing a single frame more than once are intriguing. But they require careful planning and some practice. They work best against a dark background, preferably plain black. This way, a semi-transparent image of the background will not appear superimposed on the subject when you make the second exposure. Unless a ghostly effect is calculated, as at the bottom of the opposite page, a background overlap can simply look like a mistake.

Double exposures are easiest to control with large-format cameras that do not advance the film automatically and which have focusing screens on which you can trace with a wax crayon the exact position of images for each exposure. However, you can make double-exposed portraits with a 35mm camera by applying either of two techniques. One method is to put the camera on a tripod at night or in a dark room and set a time exposure. Take the lens cap off briefly and fire a flash unit twice with the subject in different positions, as at near right.

A more flexible approach is to disconnect the link between the film-advance mechanism and the shutter-release button. This link, designed to prevent inadvertent double exposures, can be freed on some cameras by means of a multiple exposure control, which cocks the shutter without advancing the film to the next frame. On other, generally older, cameras you can disconnect it yourself, as diagrammed and explained at top right on the opposite page, by using the camera's rewind knob and advance release button to free the film while operating the wind-on lever between one exposure and the next. With a dark background, you should be able to position your subject accurately enough to achieve clearly separated images, especially if the subject also wears dark clothes, as in the multiple exposure below.

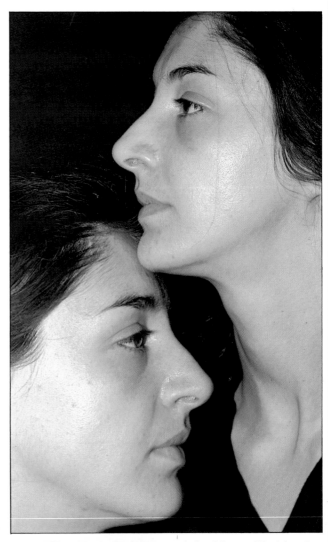

A double profile (above) *displays both sides of the same face. The woman turned around and posed slightly higher for the second of two flash-lit exposures against a black background.*

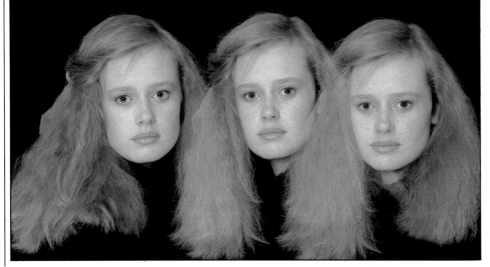

The triple image at left *was plotted on the focusing screen of a large-format camera to achieve a perfect arrangement of the subject's hair. Dark clothes are best for such well-defined images.*

A split personality is suggested by the overlapped images of this woman. To heighten this uncanny effect, she changed into white for the second exposure.

Exposing a frame twice

To free the shutter release on a 35mm camera for a second exposure, turn the rewind back to tighten the film (thumb at right). Then disconnect the film from the forward wind by using the advance release button (here on the camera front but often on the top or base). Maintain pressure and crank the lever forward with your other thumb.

The ghostly image of an artist appears out of the twining flowers and leaves of one of his own paintings. The photographer first made an exposure of the painting alone, as shown below. Then on the same film frame he photographed the artist against a black background.

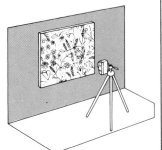

Projected images

Normally, you use a projection screen to display slides. But images projected onto a screen can also be incorporated in new compositions and then rephotographed. Or you can use the texture of a home-made screen to produce an image that is grainier and more atmospheric than the original transparency, as in the example below at left.

With two slide projectors you can combine different images on a screen to produce effects such as the one opposite. Make sure one image has light areas, so that details of the second image show through. If you wish, fix a piece of black cardboard in front of the projection lens to mask off unwanted parts of the image before rephotographing.

By projecting onto the back of a screen, you can combine a projected background with a foreground subject placed between the camera and the screen. The screen should be textureless, translucent material such as thick tracing paper. It can be difficult to match the lighting convincingly. One way around this is to use a foreground subject that does not require studio lighting, as in the image below.

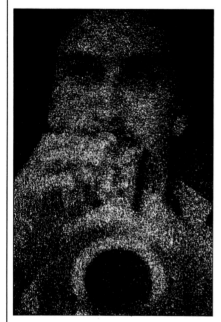

Speckly texture (above) adds atmosphere to a portrait of a trumpeter. The photographer obtained the effect by projecting a slide onto a metalized fabric screen and then rephotographing.

Two silhouetted shapes (right) combine in an intriguing composition. The photographer projected the background image onto the back of a screen and set up a cut-out figure in front, between the camera and the screen, as diagrammed above. No extra lighting was needed.

A wistful face appears between clouds
and foaming surf. The photographer
set up two slide projectors, one at each
side of the camera, and projected
the two transparencies onto the screen
simultaneously for a superimposed effect.

Sandwiching

Sandwiching is the term for combining two slides in one mount to produce a composite picture. The effect may be either naturalistic or surreal. As the two images on this page show, the technique is especially useful for dramatizing an uninteresting sky: for example, you can add a sun, moon, clouds, lightning, a flock of birds or an airplane's vapor trail to heighten the impact of a composition. (When photographing the sun, never look at it directly without protection; with an SLR, place a 5.0 neutral density filter over the lens and stop down manually to the smallest aperture.)

Generally, each slide in the combination should be overexposed by half a stop or a stop, or the final image will be too dense. However, no exposure adjustments are required when one of the subjects is a silhouette with a pale background.

For a realistic effect, you should usually match the two images in scale, perspective, and the quality and direction of the lighting, although you can sometimes use these discrepancies creatively. Avoid too much detail or the result will look cluttered.

The procedure for sandwiching, diagrammed on the opposite page, is extremely simple. Apart from

A town (above), *boldly silhouetted against distant hills, sits beneath threatening clouds and a half-obscured sun. The photographer combined a view taken on travels in Italy with one of the skyscapes that he photographs and files for such sandwiches. The bright cloud outline passing through the top of the tower adds a restrained touch of unreality to the composition.*

A windsurfer's sail (right) *forms a triangle that neatly bisects the sun. This is a sandwich of two images – the surfer was photographed with a 600mm lens combined with a x1.4 converter for extra magnification; the sun was taken with the sandwich in mind, using a 500mm lens fitted with an orange filter and a strong neutral density filter. The filter and small aperture protected the photographer's eye from the sun's rays; but as an added precaution he also wore sunglasses.*

slides and plastic mounts, all you need are a craft knife, adhesive tape, and a soft brush or can of compressed air for cleaning the slides. It also helps to have a light box and a magnifier, to facilitate sorting through slides and previewing the effect of various pairings. Having made your sandwich, you can show it with a slide viewer or projector, or you can send it to a photo lab for duplication or printing or you can make a duplicate yourself, using a slide copier.

The key to successful sandwiching is planning. For most photographers, the starting point is to identify a slide that will work well in a sandwich. If the slide you choose is too dense, you can have a paler overexposed duplicate made. Once you have selected the first image, you will often have to create the second especially for the sandwich. If so, take a sketch of the first image with you as a guide to composition. When you find the right subject, bracket by overexposing at half-stop intervals.

Another approach is to sandwich a slide with a piece of colored gel or paper rather than with another slide. In the photograph below at left, the lake owes its golden appearance to an experiment of this kind.

Making a sandwich

1 – Remove each slide from its mount. Very carefully use a craft knife to ease the cardboard pieces apart; if the mount is plastic, open it with your fingers. Handle the slides by the edges only. Clean each slide with a soft brush or jet of compressed air.

2 – Place the slides together. Using a narrow strip of transparent tape, join the slides along one edge, taking care not to cover any of the image. Remount the resulting sandwich. You can buy special mounts for this or reuse discarded mounts.

A fisherman (left) in a rowboat, silhouetted against a lake glittering with strange colors, examines his tackle. For this effect the photographer sandwiched a fishing scene, taken with a 500mm mirror lens, with some fogged film cut from the end of an exposed roll.

387

SPECIAL CONDITIONS

For the photographer inspired by challenge, unusual or extreme conditions provide one of the best means of getting remarkable and exciting images. Rain and snow, dawn and dusk, night lights and even harsh mid-day sunlight are among the conditions that can give you rewarding results as well as test your skill as a photographer. Equally challenging are the problems of using a camera underwater or in a theater.

Although the sheer difficulty or inconvenience involved may at times seem to be the chief obstacle, the challenge of most special conditions centers on problematic lighting. Today's sophisticated cameras can be relied upon to make proper exposures under normal conditions. But when light grows dim, creates sharp contrasts, or changes color, it is the photographer who must decide how to compensate.

Most of the techniques in this section require little more than paying close attention to choice of film, filter or exposure. But some activities, most notably underwater photography, require buying or renting special equipment. In the end, overcoming challenges to create memorable pictures is one of photography's most rewarding experiences.

Mountaineers and their tents stand out graphically against a mountain range. The photographer took advantage of a major picture-taking problem in snowy terrain – extreme contrast – to produce the dramatic silhouette.

Rain and storm

Many photographers see bad weather as a sign to pack away the camera and go home. By doing so, you may miss opportunities for really exciting pictures. Dull, overcast lighting can certainly drain most of the color from scenes and make everything seem drab. But often, light trapped beneath a lid of black rainclouds can give colors a dark, rich intensity never seen at other times. And although rain tends to soften and blur images, dampness often brings out subtle colors.

The spectacular brilliance of a thunderstorm, such as the one at far right, requires a long exposure to build up the overall effect. The best chance of exploiting the vivid contrasts produced by a break in the clouds is to choose a high viewpoint. With a clear view over a wide area you can sometimes follow the bright trace of a shaft of sunlight moving across the landscape.

You do not have to wait until a storm is at its height to find dramatic light effects. A gathering storm can be equally impressive, especially in tropical climates, as the picture at bottom right shows. To preserve the relatively rich colors in the sunlight, and some sense of the impending darkness, be careful to avoid overexposure. You can emphasize the color through contrast if you take a reading from the sunlit area, and then underexpose slightly to make the sky look still darker.

The picture below shows that the clouds which produce storm conditions may themselves form powerful aerial landscapes, especially if you photograph them from a distance with a wide-angle lens. The most exciting cloud formations of all are the tall, billowing thunderheads that form on hot afternoons in the tropics or in plains country such as the American Midwest.

The lowering blackness of the storm cloud gives this picture a power that seems all the more intense because the light is so richly colored. The photographer waited until the cloud just covered the sinking sun, leaving shafts of light piercing through to gleam on the sea.

Raindrops on a rose change its color to paler pink against a background muted both by the rain and by selective focusing. Delicate color effects can often be achieved just after a rainstorm, provided the light is good.

Searing backlight from an electrical storm produced this remarkable night shot of a train stopped on a bridge. The photographer put the shutter on a "B" setting for a time exposure that has captured several lightning flashes.

Glowing light bathes a landscape in South-East Asia moments before a gray sky releases a deluge of monsoon rain. In this rare and beautiful light, the contrast between light foreground and dark background heightens the color.

Ice and snow

The pictures on these two pages show that freezing cold has its own visual drama and that the silent, still enclosed feeling of a midwinter's day can come through strongly in photographs. Although colors often vanish and the scene is reduced to monochromatic patterns of just three or four tones, this often helps to simplify landscapes that would otherwise be too complex. The frozen pond and woodland below gain coherence and impact in this way.

However, the subtle whites of frost or snow demand a delicate touch, especially in judging exposure. A mere half-stop may make the difference between an effective picture and an underexposed image that comes out gray, or an overexposed one that comes out bleached. On a day when sky and land merge in a unifying whiteness, underexposure is the more likely risk, because your meter will be fooled by the preponderance of light tones. Start by allowing one stop more than the camera's meter indicates for a frost-covered scene, and one and a half stops extra for snow. Then bracket in half-stops on either side of this setting.

You can create impressions of brittle coldness with details just as convincingly as with broader views, as the pictures on the opposite page show. Look for details that provide a strong contrast of white against black or in which frost creates interesting patterns and textures.

Hoar-frost (below) covers the trees and grass around a frozen pond. To be sure of conveying the icy cold of the morning, the photographer bracketed the exposures. One and a half stops more than the meter indicated gave the best results.

Sparkling icicles (above) hang in sheets from a rock face usually dripping with water. Because of the amount of deep shadow in the frame, the photographer did not need to allow extra exposure to record the snow's whiteness.

Frosty leaves (left) create subtle textures and colors. The photographer closed in with a 50mm standard lens at its close-focusing limit and gave a half-stop more than the camera's meter suggested.

The glare of the sun

On a sunny day, every shiny surface can reflect a brilliant image of the sun's light. The surfaces of water, sand, stones, blades of grass or glossy leaves all can form bright reflections that dilute and desaturate color. And the glare of direct sunlight may make the sky itself look less blue. In these conditions, the best way to restore colors in your pictures is to use a polarizing filter.

Cutting glare can make the colors of foliage, fruit and flowers seem astonishingly vivid, as in the picture below. Against a sky darkened by a polarizing filter, even landscape features seem to be much brighter, as in the picture of crags on the opposite page at left. Keep the filter close at hand, so that you can check how it will affect the scene in front of you. You can use the filter alone to do this – just rotate it while looking through it.

However, removing glare is not always the best way to improve a picture. Occasionally, you can create a striking effect by pointing the camera almost directly at the sun, as the photographer did for the picture on the opposite page at right, taken from an airplane. Stop the lens down to a small aperture, and take pictures at several different shutter settings to be sure of getting at least one that is perfectly exposed.

Clusters of rich, red berries contrast brilliantly with the blue sky behind. To ensure full color saturation, the photographer used a polarizing filter. The camera's meter compensated for the light absorbed by the filter, setting an exposure of 1/60 at f/8.

Using a polarizing filter
Polarized light in the unfiltered picture (top) causes glare and weakens the color of the sky. In the second picture, a polarizing filter blocks the polarized light, reducing glare and darkening the sky. To record deep blue skies, simply fit the polarizer, as shown on the camera above, and twist it until you see the sky darken. Skies appear darkest when the sun is low and behind you.

The sun's rays strike the smeared surface of an airplane window, creating a brilliant splash of light at the top of this seascape. Pointing the camera at the clouds while taking the meter reading prevented the sun from totally dominating the exposure.

Twilight and night

The brief period of twilight that follows dusk is an enchanting time to take pictures. Twilight photographs have all the special, calm beauty of night, yet there is still enough light in the sky at this time to make photography quite easy.

Following an afternoon of clear sky, twilight is a rich blue, sometimes tinged with the pink of sunset. For the deepest, richest colors, take a meter reading from the sky itself. However, this will record the foreground as a silhouette, and you will need to open up the lens by a stop or two if you want to retain a little detail in the land, as in the image of the tree on the opposite page. If you can include a lake, the sea or a broad river in the scene, the water's surface will help to spread the colors of the sky across the whole picture. This is the technique used to create the beautiful image shown below.

At night, the brightest moonlight is very much weaker than sunlight. Even with Kodacolor Gold 400 film, a moonlit landscape will probably need an exposure of about four seconds at f/2 unless there is a large expanse of reflective water or snow in the picture. Bracket your exposures, and use a tripod to avoid camera shake.

One way to cope with the dim conditions of night is to include the bright surface of the moon itself in the picture, as in the images on the opposite page at left and at bottom. Such photographs are most effective when the sky is still quite light in relation to the moon – shortly after sunset – and when the moon is at least half full. Check a local newspaper for the times of moonrise and sunset.

A still pond in winter reflects the subtle shades of twilight. Just after the sun had set, the light was still bright enough to permit an exposure of 1/8 at f/8 on ISO 64 film.

Llamas in Peru *(above)*
stand motionless during a
1/4-second exposure. A slower
shutter speed would have
made the sky brighter, but
would have introduced the
risk of the moon blurring
due to its motion.

Moonlit clouds *(right)*
dapple the night sky with
silver and black. By pointing
the camera at the moon, the
photographer was able to set
a shutter speed of 1/60 and
thus handhold the camera.

A rosy sky *(above) forms*
a colorful backdrop for a
leafy beech tree. To ensure
that the distant hills did
not appear as featureless
silhouettes, the photographer
gave one stop more exposure
than his light meter indicated
(ISO 400, 1/4 at f/4).

Flames

The light of flames from burning candles or oil lamps, matches or fires provides the most natural form of illumination other than daylight. Although light is unpredictable, flames create such atmospheric images that pictures lit by this source can be enormously rewarding. Most flames burn at far lower temperatures than do indoor lights and so produce light of a distinctly orange, even red, color. Photographed on tungsten-balanced film, flame-lit scenes look a natural pale orange and on daylight film, which was used for all the pictures on these two pages, the warmer orange cast still looks acceptable, because even our eyes generally perceive flames as red or orange.

If you are taking pictures of only the flames themselves, accurate exposure is not particularly important – overexposed flames still appear yellowish while underexposure simply intensifies the red. Such moving flames as sparks or fireworks look attractive both when frozen by a fast shutter speed or when allowed to trace streaks of light during a time exposure. Choosing an exposure to record both the bright flames and the subjects they dimly illuminate is more of a problem. Place the subject as near as possible to the flame to minimize the brightness range. And read exposure from the subject, allowing the flames to be overexposed if necessary. You are likely to need fairly slow shutter speeds, even with high-speed ISO 400 film, and because exposure will be difficult to measure accurately, bracket your shots. Do not be tempted to supplement the light – using flash to photograph people around a campfire, for example, can destroy the entire mood of the scene.

A blacksmith, his face glowing red in the light from the fire, forges a horseshoe. Daylight supplements the flames, providing the general illumination for the smithy (ISO 400 film: 1/30 at f/4).

A row of houses, lit by a giant festival bonfire across the street, seems to be on fire as the flames reflect in the windows – an effect enhanced by the red light (ISO 200 film: 1/15 at f/2).

A glass of brandy, being warmed in a candle flame, makes an appealing still-life. The orange light creates mood, but is barely strong enough for an effective exposure (ISO 400 film: 1/30 at f/2).

A wood fire burns with orange flames in the snow. The scene is lit entirely by daylight, giving a very slight blue tint because of the overcast sky. The winter's day, stark trees and black dress make a monochromatic, even colorless, image, brought to life by the glow of the fire (ISO 100 film: 1/125 at f/8).

Fireworks burst orange and white over New York harbour, contrasting with the strong blue color cast on the floodlit Statue of Liberty at the bottom of the frame. (ISO 400 film: 1/30 at f/8).

Tungsten lighting

Mixed lighting is characteristic of many nighttime photographs, particularly at dusk, when ebbing daylight may provide as much or more light than tungsten or other lights that have been switched on. While sometimes presenting tricky problems in terms of exposure or film choice, this kind of lighting also produces some of the most attractive color effects. This is particularly true when one source of light predominates in the picture while another provides contrasting color accents.

The basic rule for mixing tungsten and daylight is to decide which light source dominates, and choose a film balanced to that. Outdoors, just before nightfall, the main illumination comes usually from the daylight. On daylight film, the tungsten lights will appear orange, as in the pictures below. When there is less daylight than tungsten light, you could decide to use a conversion filter – or a slide film balanced for tungsten light – in order to show tungsten-lit colors more accurately.

The choice between daylight and tungsten light film becomes more crucial for pictures of interiors in which you need to use a mixture of daylight and room lighting. If daylight from windows predominates, and particularly if the windows appear in the picture, there is no need to change from daylight film. The warm orange of tungsten room lights will add to the atmosphere, as in the interior scene on the opposite page.

In the early evening, or if the windows are small, the situation may be different, with the main light coming from the room lamps. To avoid everything turning orange, you should use a tungsten-light slide film – or a No. 80A blue conversion filter. Light from the windows will appear in the resulting picture as a shade of blue.

If you are undecided about whether daylight or tungsten dominates, always opt for daylight film. The warm glow of tungsten light exposed on this film is usually more acceptable than the cold blue of daylit subjects recorded on tungsten film, and looks closer to normal experience.

A streetlight glows in gathering dusk – daylight film records most of the scene in its true colors, but tints the lamp a warm orange (ISO 200 film: 1/30 at f/2).

The fish stall is lit by daylight, but the fish seller is lit by tungsten. On daylight film, his face looks orange (ISO 64 film: 1/60 at f/5.6).

A hotel lobby in Monte Carlo is lit by tungsten lamps, but daylight floods in through the glass doors. On daylight film, the tungsten-lit ceiling looks a rich orange, suiting the opulent decor. With tungsten light film or a color filter, the ceiling would have appeared in true colors, but the entrance would have looked a chilly blue. The photographer rightly chose to use daylight film unfiltered (ISO 200 film: 1/125 at f/4).

A Palm Springs street is lit bright by tungsten shop lights of varying strengths. Here, the use of tungsten film adds interest by deepening the dusk sky (ISO 25 film: 2 secs at f/5.6)

Other artificial lighting

A tungsten lamp produces light by heating a thin coil of wire inside a glass bulb, but some other common light sources do not rely on heat. Fluorescent lights and other vapor lights such as sodium and mercury work instead by passing an electrical current through a gas- or vapor-filled tube. Light produced by the resulting spark nearly always has a distinctive color – for example, sodium lighting, which is widely used on roads and industrial premises, is yellow. Sometimes the color of vapor lights gives visual interest to scenes that might otherwise look mundane. But when you are using vapor lighting to illuminate other subjects – especially people – the color cast may simply look wrong.

Sodium and mercury vapor lighting produces effects on daylight film similar to those produced by tungsten lights, but the color casts cannot be eliminated in the same way. Whereas the light wavelengths of tungsten lamps range across the whole spectrum – but with a bias toward red – vapor lamps other than fluorescent tubes produce light of just one or two colors. Putting a filter over a camera lens can only remove colors, not add them. Thus, although you can filter out the excess of red light from tungsten, you cannot put back the wavelengths missing from sodium or mercury light, whatever film or filter you use. The best thing to do is to accept the situation and make a virtue of the resulting color. For example, all the pictures here were taken on daylight film. In portraiture, where usually natural skin tones are important, you can introduce another light source, such as electronic flash, to light the foreground and counteract the color cast in the main area of the picture.

Fluorescent strip lamps differ from other vapor lamps, because their glass tubes carry a coating of phosphors, which make the tube glow with light in a broad range of wavelengths. Although this produces a light that looks white, all but the most expensive lamps are deficient in red or magenta, and pictures taken by their light have a greenish tint. The actual shade of green depends on the type of tube and its age. If you are taking a picture in fluorescent light, and color accuracy is important, you may need to make a series of exposures with different color compensation filters. But generally, a CC 30M (magenta) filter, or a special "fluorescent to daylight" filter will help.

City streetlights usually are either sodium or mercury vapor lamps. In the picture above, the photographer used a long exposure with the camera on a tripod and took advantage of the striking color of mercury lamps to turn roadside snow into a turquoise background for the lights of the passing cars *(ISO 200 film: 4secs at f/11).*

A pool enclosure, lit by fluorescent tubes, seems to be suffused with green light. The tinge is seen most clearly where the lights shine directly onto the blue-gray wall. The effect produced is one of subterranean chill and eeriness *(ISO 100 film: 1/60 at f/5.6).*

The Jefferson Memorial
*(above) appears the yellow
color of its floodlights. To the
eye, the building would have
appeared much whiter, but
complete color correction is
not necessary to achieve an
effective picture (ISO 400
film: 1/30 at f/2).*

A statue in Brasilia *glows
an unearthly green in the
light of mercury floodlights.
Such monuments often look
at their best by night, when
the strange and upredictable
colors of their lights show
up strongly in photographs
(ISO 200 film: 1/8 at f/5.6).*

403

Stage lighting

Stage lighting during just one performance may range from an overall glow to a kaleidoscope of colors to a single spotlight. Judging exposures in rapidly changing or high-contrast lighting conditions requires skill and experience. Exposure meters may prove unreliable, even when the lighting is stable, but they are useful for indicating a setting to bracket around. Spotmetering gives the most accurate readings, but be sure to meter from a mid tone, such as a performer's face. You can save vital moments by using your camera in the automatic mode, and

bracketing by adjusting the exposure-compensation dial. Cameras with an autobracketing function speed up the process and allow you to bracket exposures of fast moving action.

At a photocall, the lighting may be brighter than that for a public performance, and there is more time for careful metering. For the scene on the opposite page at left, the lighting was kept constant for photographers, making possible an accurate reading with a spot meter. However, photocalls often lack the atmosphere of a real performance.

A Buddhist monk
performs a religious ceremony
on stage at an outdoor concert
by Japanese percussionist
Stomu Yamashta. From a
central position in the
audience, the photographer
used tungsten-balanced ISO
160 film with a 50mm lens,
relying upon his experience to
judge the exposure at 1/30 at
f/2 to achieve this golden,
atmospheric picture.

Spotlights beam down on a
winged actor in a performance
of Salome. *To ensure maximum*
detail in both shadows and
highlights, the photographer
took an exposure reading for the
mid-tones. Because the overall
lighting was relatively bright,
he was able to freeze movement
with a shutter speed of 1/250.

The visual excitement of a rock concert or musical depends on rapid color changes and moving beams of light. These effects can look good even when frozen on film, but for less lavishly staged performances, the lighting may look dull. One solution is to use a starburst or diffraction filter, as in the picture below at right. Colored gels over stage lights affect color temperature, but it is unnecessary to attempt corrective filtration; even wildly unrealistic flesh tones seldom look disturbing on stage and can intensify the theatrical mood of an image.

A comedian entertains his audience at a nightclub (above). From his position on one side of the stage, the photographer used a 35mm lens, attaching a starburst filter to add interest to the upper area of the image. High-speed daylight-balanced film increased the feeling of warmth and intimacy common in such clubs.

Two Japanese dancers are frozen like marble statues under a spotlight at a photocall. The photographer took a spot meter reading and underexposed by one stop, preventing the bright highlights on the figures from burning out and emphasizing their sculptural quality by deepening the shadows.

405

Zooming challenges

Improved optical design has helped boost the reputation of zoom lenses, and professionals now regard them as capable of providing excellent image quality. Moreover, the range of zooms available has expanded in recent years: the familiar 80-200mm and 70-210mm models are now supplemented by wide-angle zooms (for example, 20-35mm), standard zooms (for example, 28-70mm as diagrammed opposite) and super-zooms (for example, 28-200mm or 50-350mm).

The complex construction of a zoom lens makes it heavier than any of the fixed-focal-length equivalents in the same range, even though it may be quite compact. However, if you treat a zoom lens as a convenient substitute for a multilens outfit, there is an overall saving in weight. With just two zoom lenses, you can cover an almost continuous range of settings from extreme wide-angle to medium telephoto, as shown by the photographs on these two pages. Furthermore, when the framing is critical and the viewpoint restricted, a zoom lens may enable you to obtain images that would be impossible with a fixed-focus lens. The wide range of framing options has special advantages for photographing moving subjects from a fixed camera position, for example in sports photography.

Using a zoom demands certain precautions and skills. With some "one-touch" manual focus zooms (that is, those with a single control ring to adjust the focal length and the focus), it is easy to shift the focus inadvertently while operating the zoom control. For critical focusing, you should focus with the lens at its longest focal length, pull back the control ring carefully and then make final adjustments to the focus. The number of glass elements in a zoom lens, often as many as 18, can cause flare when photographing into the sun. A lens hood will combat flare, but as an extra precaution you should preview the viewfinder image with the lens stopped down to its working aperture.

Another potential difficulty is reduced light-gathering power: the maximum aperture of a zoom is usually about one or two stops less than that of a fixed wide-angle or telephoto lens at the extreme end of its range. With the heavier, telephoto zooms, light loss may force you to set slower shutter speeds that result in a blurred image when the lens is hand-held. This problem of camera shake is particularly acute when you use such a lens at its longer focal-length settings. The best solution is to carry a tripod. Although adding to the weight of your outfit, this will give you wider scope for photography in dim light or for compositions that require a narrow aperture to provide sufficient depth of field.

80-200mm zoom, set at 80mm

35-70mm zoom, set at 55mm

80-200mm f/2.8 zoom lens

28-70mm f/3.5-4.5 zoom lens

80-200 zoom, set at 120mm

A two-zoom outfit
The 35-70mm wide-angle/
portrait zoom lens and the
80-200mm long-focus zoom
lens shown above make a
flexible outfit for travel, daily
life or architectural
photography. The precise
range of focal lengths available
will depend upon the make of
your camera body.

28-70mm zoom, set at 35mm

*Five nighttime views show
the versatility of a two-zoom
outfit. The photographer
carried the two zoom lenses
illustrated above, plus a
tripod. He took these pictures
within the space of three hours
in London's West End,
choosing a focal length
appropriate to each subject.
For example, the shortest
focal length available to him
was suitable for the dramatic
skyscraper view at right,
while the longest focal length
made possible an abstract
close-up from the same
viewpoint (below).*

80-200mm zoom, set at 200mm

Underwater photography

Taking photographs underwater is far more challenging than any photography you might undertake on land. Not only do you have to keep camera mechanisms and film dry and salt-free, but you must also contend with the fact that water is denser than air, creating problems of increased pressure, optical distortion and low light levels.

A variety of underwater camera equipment is available, some of which is shown at right. The least expensive amphibious cameras are single use cameras, which function to depths of about 18 feet (five meters). Never take equipment further than the maximum recommended depth, or water will penetrate the seals and the casing may even collapse, ruining your pictures and probably the camera.

To remove corrosive salt deposited by sea water, you should follow a stringent cleaning routine after every diving session. If you are using an amphibious camera, soak it in fresh water for at least half an hour, then hose it down with more fresh water. If you are using an ordinary camera in a waterproof housing, follow the same procedure, then, after letting the equipment air-dry, open up the housing and coat the O-rings, or rubber seals, with silicone grease. Never leave waterproof equipment standing in the sun after a dive or condensation will occur inside the case.

You must follow this procedure each time you reload, so use rolls with 36 exposures. ISO 200 slide film yields good results, although slower film is preferable for close-ups. Light meters underwater are unreliable. Always bracket your pictures widely.

As the two pictures at far right illustrate, light refraction underwater makes subjects appear closer and narrows the field of view. To compensate for this, use a wide-angle lens: a 35mm lens has an effective focal length of 47mm underwater. Always focus for the apparent distance, not the actual distance.

Light is absorbed rapidly as depth increases, as shown by the sequence at right. Red is absorbed most strongly, causing a blue cast that intensifies the deeper you dive. At depths between six and 15 feet, you can correct this blue cast successfully using red color correction filters. Calculate the required strength by adding 10CC for every three feet of subject-to-surface and subject-to-camera distance. Keep the subject within about 10 feet of the camera if possible. Note that water that is choppy on the surface absorbs more light than calm water.

When photographing underwater, remember that you are a diver first and a photographer second. Try out your equipment and technique in a swimming pool before venturing into the ocean. Avoid diving alone, and be particularly careful when investigating wrecks.

Light loss

As light diminishes underwater, color falls off from the red end of the spectrum first. At a depth of 10 feet (below top), color is still good. At 20 feet (center), yellow and red are weak. By 40 feet, most light has been absorbed and there is a strong blue color cast.

Underwater camera equipment

A wide variety of watertight equipment is available for the underwater photographer. The Kodak single use camera (at right) can be used to depths of 15 feet. The amphibious compact camera (at right, below) has a fixed 32mm lens, built-in flash and a depth capacity of about 100 feet. More sophisticated is the Nikonos RS (at right, above), an SLR camera that accepts interchangeable autofocus lenses and functions down to about 300 feet.

Another option is to use an underwater housing, available in different designs for specific land cameras. Housings are suitable for use down to about 150 feet, and are available with interchangeable "domed ports", to compensate for the water's very significant refracting effect.

Kodak waterproof single use camera

Nikonos RS autofocus SLR

Sea & Sea compact camera

Refraction
Both the pictures below were taken with the same lens at the same distance from the subject. Underwater, the diver appears closer, because the effective focal length of the lens is increased by 25 per cent. Correspondingly, the angle of view and depth of field are reduced.

The hull of a wrecked ship frames a tranquil seabed scene. The photographer used a Nikonos camera, bracketing to be sure of getting a correctly exposed image.

409

STUDIO TECHNIQUES

Some amateurs think of a studio as the exclusive domain of the professional and imagine that the skills and equipment required are beyond their reach. But the essence of studio photography is control, both of the subject and of the way it is lit. And mastery of studio techniques is a skill that anyone can perfect. As for space and equipment, a room with good daylight, some pieces of white cardboard and a tripod for your camera are all you need for a rudimentary studio. Portable flash or inexpensive photolamps extend the possibilities further. However, most amateurs will soon want to progress to small studio flash units for even greater control.

A studio can be temporary or permanent, depending on the space you have available. But lack of space need never hamper your creativity. However modest your home studio, the techniques described on the following pages will start you on your way to producing high-quality images in which every element is planned and nothing is left to chance.

A shiny kettle reflects broad, diffuse studio lighting from one side, creating a symphony of curves in black and white. The photographer constructed the still-life on a glass-topped table, covering one half with black cardboard, and the other with tracing paper. Then he lit the table from below. Most of the light, though, came from a six-foot-high diffusing screen placed to the right of the camera and lit strongly from behind.

One-lamp lighting

The simplest of all lighting arrangements is a single lamp. Since the great advantage of studio photography is full control over lighting, working with just one light source may seem limiting. In fact, many of the best professional studio photographs have been taken this way.

Because one-lamp lighting is simple, it is less likely to distract attention from the subject. It also resembles daylight most closely, but without the variables of intensity and color that can make daylight difficult to handle. Used unobtrusively, as in the picture on the opposite page below, a single photolamp gives sympathetic, natural illumination that is particularly suited to informal portraits.

By lighting the background rather than the subject, you can produce such brilliantly outlined silhouettes as the one at the top of the opposite page. Or, by lighting from below through diffusing material, you can obtain dramatic images combining simple shapes with intricate detail, as in the picture below. The degree of diffusion and reflection also affects the image. If you use a large diffuser for side or frontal lighting, with a reflector to fill in shadows, you can supply broad, soft illumination that is subtle rather than dramatic. But take care that the lighting is not too even, or the result may be flat and uninteresting. And to avoid flare make sure that the light does not shine directly into the lens.

Luminous color and *graphic shapes (right)* combine in an unusual still-life composition. The subjects were placed on a glass surface two feet off the floor, with a photolamp beneath it. Tracing paper was taped to the underside of the glass to diffuse the light, which reveals translucent items in fine structural detail.

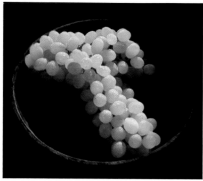

Droplets of water give a bunch of grapes *(above)* an appetizing luster. To create the pool of light on the subject, the photographer placed a photolamp behind the fruit bowl and used black cardboard *(diagram, top)* to prevent light from directly reaching the lens. The bowl's highlighted rim neatly encloses the subject.

A hatted figure (*right*) *makes an intriguing silhouette. The photographer posed the subject against a plain white backdrop, then angled a low photolamp up toward the background* (*above*). *The controlled lighting produced a perfectly clean-edged profile, which stands out sharply against the bright background.*

A man concentrates *on shaving* (*below*), *his face deeply shadowed by broad directional lighting. A large diffuser was placed in front of a photolamp set up directly to one side and about two feet away from the subject* (*diagram, above*). *The effect is close to that of natural light.*

Multiple light sources

Introducing extra lights to support a main source opens up many creative possibilities in studio work. But multiple lighting needs to be organized with some thought. Too many lights, indiscriminately placed, may cast conflicting shadows and produce effects that merely look showy, competing with one another for attention instead of focusing interest on the subject itself.

The best way to avoid overcomplicated and unnecessary lighting is to begin by positioning the dominant light. Only then can you evaluate the function of extra lights properly. Add these one by one, making sure that each serves a definite purpose. If the setup requires extra lights to fill in shadows and reduce the contrast range, these should be introduced only when the main scheme is established and should always be understated. The picture below illustrates the point: a powerful, undiffused frontal light here would have ruined the effect. Often, reflectors will lighten the shadows just as well.

Fill-in lighting frequently gives a softer, more flattering appearance to portraits and figure studies. However, for some subjects a contrasty treatment is much more suitable. In the portrait at the bottom of the opposite page, the areas of solid shadow make the image far more striking. This picture also shows the effectiveness of lighting a background separately to make the subject stand out and to avoid unwanted shadows on the background.

A light included for a particular effect, rather than for its contribution to overall illumination, is known as an effects light, and you should usually add this last of all. One example is a spotlight used to create a halo around the subject's hair, as in the picture below at left. Such special lighting can lend impact to a subject, as in the portrait opposite above.

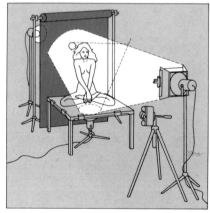

The symmetry of a nude pose (left) is enhanced by balanced lighting that emphasizes shape and color and casts a halo around the model's hair. The diagram above shows how the effect was achieved. The model was posed on a glass platform with tracing paper stretched across the underside to diffuse light from a photolamp beneath. Diffusing material placed over a fill-in light to one side of the camera gave soft modeling to the figure. A spotlight directed through a hole in the backdrop behind the woman's head provided the luminous halo effect.

A caped figure (left) appears to radiate intense beams of light. To create the strongly theatrical mood, the photographer combined two light sources (above). A photolamp behind the subject brilliantly outlined the dark shape and gave the fingers a spectral translucence. The narrow beam of a spotlight, aimed directly onto the face, defined the features sharply.

The rich tones and strong lines of a close-up portrait (left) are brought out by carefully controlled lighting (above). Diffused toplighting produced dense shadows without losing facial detail. A photolamp angled up toward the background gave clean, sharp definition to the subject. The photographer took an incident light reading from the face, and reduced the exposure setting by half a stop. Then he adjusted the lighting on the background so that it would be recorded overexposed by two stops. As a result, the background burned out to a creamy white.

Arranging the lighting/1

The lighting arrangement plays a crucial role in determining how a subject will appear on film. In still-life photography, the general rule is to position the lights to bring out the most important qualities of the objects. For example, the bottom-lit picture on the opposite page, below, displays to best advantage the rich yellow translucency of the bottle of oil, which appears to glow with color.

Frontlighting, from a position close to the camera, gives strong colors and minimizes shadows; a slightly more oblique angle is preferable if you want to reveal form, as in the picture below at left. Side-lighting can give dramatic effects, particularly with upright subjects such as bottles, as in the still-life below at right.

Unless you are photographing a uniform subject, such as a collection of glassware, you may have to compromise over lighting direction. For example, in the picture opposite at top, backlighting records the bottles of liquids successfully, but disguises the form and color of the opaque items, which appear as graphic silhouettes. Often, you can get around such problems by using mirrors or reflectors, or by adding extra lights to the setup.

Frontlighting
With the main light source just to one side of the camera, details and colors are clearly rendered without serious loss of modeling, as shown in the still-life above. White cardboard angled onto the subject from the back provides fill-in lighting (diagram, right). The reflection in the bottle is the diffuser used to soften the light; it creates a highlight that adds interest to this composition and helps define the bottle's shape.

Sidelighting
Placing the main light directly to one side of the subject creates dramatic lighting, as exemplified in the still-life above. However, unless you want shadows to hide parts of the subject farthest from the light source, always place a reflector on the far side, facing the main light – as the photographer did here (diagram, right). Placing light-toned subjects on the dimmer side of the frame also helps ''lift'' the shadow areas.

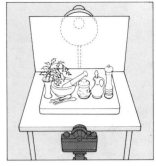

Backlighting
When the subject is opaque, lighting from behind, as diagrammed above, creates silhouettes. But with clear objects, such as the bottle and jar at left, backlighting emphasizes transparency and brings out the color of the contents. For a white, even tone at the back of the subject, diffuse the light thoroughly, using several layers of tracing paper or thick white plastic. Keep the light source well back from the diffuser.

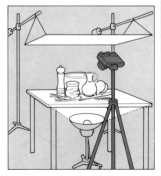

Bottomlighting
Because natural light very rarely comes from below, bottomlighting in a photograph has great impact. As demonstrated at left, bottomlighting can enhance the appearance of glassware, but, as with backlighting, opaque subjects will show as silhouettes. A white or silver reflector above the subject (diagram, above) will re-direct some of the light down onto the top of the still-life and help prevent this effect.

Arranging the lighting/2

In portraiture, the range of effective lighting schemes is much more restricted than with still-lifes. Many lighting configurations will yield an unflattering result. Devising an arrangement that does justice to the contours of the face and the tones and textures of the skin and hair requires practice. As a first step, try a time-honored setup such as the one illustrated in the picture sequence here. You can then go on to experiment with variations on this theme, such as an arrangement that gives a soft, shadowless effect.

The scheme shown uses three lights: one main light, one to illuminate the background and one more to add a highlight to the hair. Only rarely will you need more than three lights, and usually just one lamp will do. Avoid the temptation to overlight, or your portrait will look unnatural. For example, highlighting the hair is not vital for every portrait; it is essential only when the hair is very dark or is similar in color to the background.

Using foil reflectors is an excellent way to bounce light back into the shaded side of a face to lighten dark shadows. To avoid making the reflection too bright and losing the modeling altogether, crumple the foil. With color film, the darkest shadow should be no more than three stops darker than the brightest highlight. With black-and-white film, the latitude is four or four and a half stops.

A standard lighting scheme
The illustration sequence on these two pages shows how the photographer built up a standard scheme for a full-face portrait. As diagrammed at right, he used three lights, with reflectors to fill in unflattering shadows.

1 – Setting up a large photolamp with a diffuser over it provided the main light (left). This lamp, angled at 45° to the camera axis in both planes, lit the left side of the face but threw the other side into dark shadow. To prevent flare, the camera needed to be shaded.

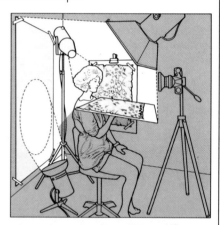

2 – Adding a foil reflector on the right of the face improved the effect by filling in some of the shadows. But there were still shadows under the chin and obvious folds of skin under the eyes.

3 – Adding a second foil reflector beneath the face resulted in a more sympathetic effect. It removed the shadows from the neck and chin and improved appearance around the eyes.

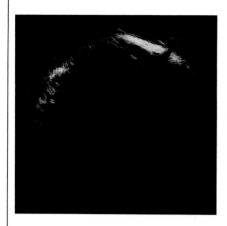

4 – *Highlighting the hair by means of a snooted light, aimed at 45° downward onto the head from a position just behind and to one side, subtly improved the portrait. The effect with the snooted light alone is shown above.*

5 – *Lighting the background, made of a sheet of warm yellow paper, completed the scheme. The light source was a lamp aimed upward from the floor behind the model's chair; this effect is isolated in the picture above.*

Composing the still-life

Still-life is the one area of photography where composition is wholly in your hands. The exact position of every element in the image is your choice. Yet this total freedom can be inhibiting; you may not know where to start. Following some basic compositional guidelines need not limit your creativity and will help you build pleasing, unified images.

A still-life should be self-contained, whether it is a detailed study such as the flower on the opposite page, above, or an elaborately constructed scene such as the one below. Each ingredient should make a real contribution to the overall effect, with subsidiary elements supporting the main subject. This can be done in many ways: for example, by using lines to frame and lead into the subject, by

juxtaposing complementary or contrasting tones and shapes, or by echoing a pattern on a smaller or larger scale. The precisely balanced picture opposite, below, makes use of all these techniques.

A good way to learn about composition is to start with just two or three simple objects and practice moving them around to find the strongest arrangement. With the camera on a tripod, you can keep the view constant while you adjust the set and lighting. For more complex still-life arrangements, it is especially important to keep a strong focus of interest. Once the background and main subject are in place, add secondary elements one at a time, checking through the viewfinder to gauge the effect of each addition.

A country life theme links an array of objects. The apparently haphazard arrangement was assembled in an elaborate studio set to produce a harmonious composition of natural tones and textures. Strong light from one side concentrates the eye on the main subject: the freshly cut foxgloves.

Lily blooms *(right)*
stand out in strong relief
against a black background.
Centering the subject brought
out its symmetrical pattern,
while lighting on each side
and slightly behind revealed
its subtle textures and hues.

Speckled eggs *(below)*
provide the main interest
in an intriguing still-life.
Each element contributes to
the unity of the composition,
in which the echoing colors,
lines and textures lead the
eye easily around the image.

The calculated illusion

One of the aims of a professional still-life photographer is to impart such three-dimensional immediacy to an image that the viewer almost feels that he can reach out and touch the objects within the picture frame. This demands grain-free transparencies with brilliant color rendition. Many studio photographers, including the ones represented here, use a large-format camera to achieve such critical results, although others obtain almost comparable quality with a 35mm SLR camera loaded with a slow slide film like Kodachrome 25 film.

Another goal is to idealize the subject, which means that every blemish must be removed. For example, the corkscrew still-life at right required no sophisticated lighting or camera techniques, but was a difficult subject because the shiny metal corkscrew and the surface it rested on would have shown up fingermarks glaringly. You can remove obstinate fingermarks from most metal surfaces with acetone or rubbing alcohol. Here, however, the photographer ensured that this emergency never arose by handling the corkscrew with a soft cloth and taking great pains not to touch the plastic base.

Outsiders sometimes regard the still-life studio as a problem-free environment. However, one mark of the professional is that he allows time to think about the problems inherent in the idea for a shot, and work out ways to solve them. If there is no instant solution, he must often resign himself to laborious approaches with which an amateur would soon lose patience. For example, in the study of guitars on the opposite page, above, the main difficulty was dust, which the raking lighting revealed with painful clarity. The only solution was to dust the surfaces frequently and thoroughly with a cloth. This task, added to those of adjusting lighting and composition and making a sequence of test photographs on instant film, stretched the total time required for the session to 10 hours.

A more unusual problem is exemplified by the still-life on the opposite page, below. The photographer wanted to include a drip on the verge of falling from the melting ice cube, which ruled out using an acrylic ice cube of the type often used in food studios. He knew that the studio lights would rapidly melt real ice, so that the cube would shrink and slip out of the tongs, which were held in place in a retort stand – a laboratory stand with a clamp mounted on it. The solution was simple but effective: a rubber band pulled the tongs together as the cube melted and so maintained a firm grip. The photographer also found that the cherry began to color the water if left in the glass for more than a few minutes; so he had to replace the water and cherry frequently before taking this final picture.

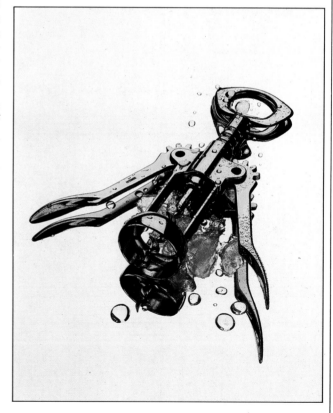

A corkscrew surrounded by crushed ice forms a double image. Before setting up the composition, the photographer polished the plastic base with an antistatic cloth; an ordinary cloth would have created a dust-attracting charge. An overhead window light provided diffused lighting, while two pieces of black cardboard, one on either side of the subject, edged the corkscrew with black reflections that defined its shape.

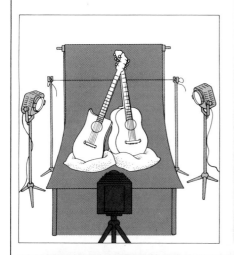

Guitars (above) nestle against each other in a still-life created for a record cover. The guitars rested on sandbags, their necks supported by an overhead wire. The angles of the guitars and of the two spotlights that illuminated them (diagrammed above at left) were critical: the spotlights had to define the edges of the instruments, highlight the strings and show enough overall detail without spoiling the subdued mood.

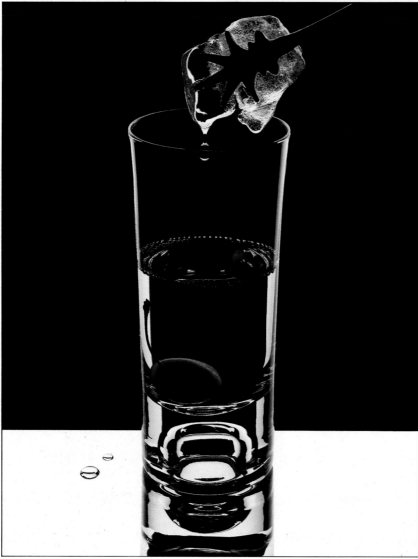

A droplet from a melting ice cube is poised to fall into a glass of water. To create the tiny bubbles, the photographer added a little wetting agent. The setup, diagrammed above, included a window light, black cardboard and a plastic base. The photographer took care to define the sides and rim of the glass against the black background and to silhouette the cherry stem against a highlight.

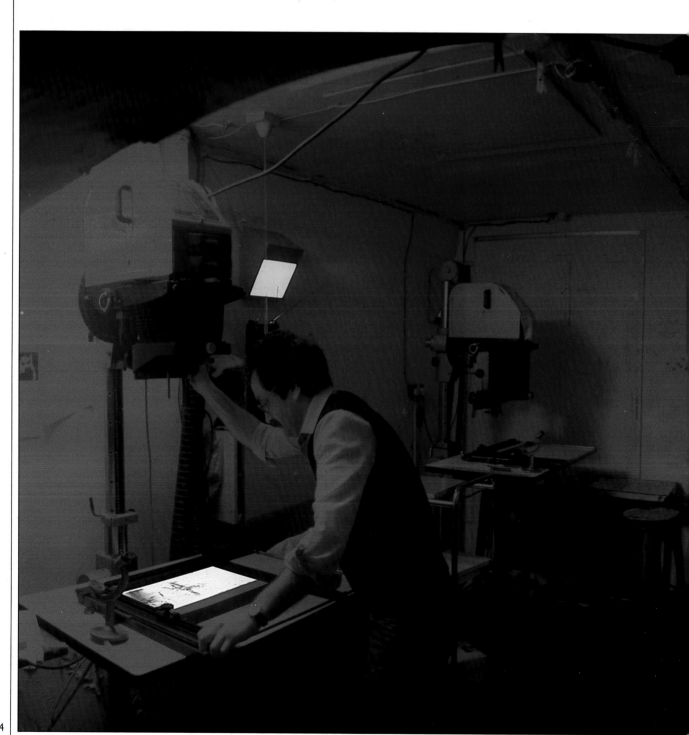

THE HOME DARKROOM

The marvelous advantage of home processing is that you have complete control over the results. You can make your images as small or large, light or dark as you wish. To begin with, you may decide to set up a darkroom just for black-and-white processing and printing. The basic procedures are relatively simple and will stand you in good stead if you later go on to making color pictures. However, with today's equipment and materials, there is no reason why you should not start with color processing if that is your main interest.

To start home processing you will not need a special room – just a work space that you can make completely dark. A bathroom, a kitchen or a dry basement laundry room makes a convenient temporary darkroom because there is running water to wash processed film and prints. But a large closet will do. Once film or color prints have been loaded into their lighttight processing containers, you can develop or wash them in another room. And black-and-white prints developed in the darkroom can be kept in a tray of water and later washed under running water.

To prevent damage from spills, keep trays and containers with chemicals away from the area where you make prints with the enlarger. And be sure the space is totally dark. Any chink of light will fog undeveloped film or paper. Consider making a removable window cover, using tightly fitted hardboard with black felt glued along the edges. Then cover that with a black curtain. A door may also need a curtain and a rolled-up mat to block the bottom crack.

A dry basement, with plenty of space for equipment, makes an ideal darkroom. Here, a black-and-white print is made on an enlarger. The red and yellow safelighting does not affect black-and-white printing paper yet provides a good level of light to work by.

425

Black-and-white darkroom equipment

A major piece of equipment used to print pictures is an enlarger, but you must also buy a number of smaller items. To develop film, you will need a developing tank and the reel that goes with it. Once you have wound your film onto the reel in darkness, and placed both inside the tank, you can turn on the lights and begin processing in normal room light.

To get consistent results, you must be able to measure three things accurately: time, temperature and volume. Any clock that has a sweep second hand will be precise enough to measure time, but to measure the other two variables you should buy a special photographic thermometer and at least two graduated cylinders.

To make prints, you can use the same thermometer and graduates as for processing film. You can also use the same clock, but more efficient is a timer that can be wired to the enlarger to automatically shut off the lamp after exposure. In addition you need three trays in which to develop and stabilize the paper prints and two pairs of tongs to transfer the chemical-soaked paper from one tray to the next. A safelight is also essential.

The enlarger magnifies your negative to the size of the print you choose to make, much as a movie projector throws an enlarged image onto a screen. Although an enlarger is not cheap, it is a one-time investment, and often you can use the same enlarger to print both black-and-white and color prints.

Finally, you will need an enlarging easel, often called a masking frame. This holds the photographic paper flat and positions it on the enlarger baseboard. Adjustable blades enable you to print pictures with borders of variable width.

Film developing equipment

Choose a developing tank and reel that match the size of the film you use. Some reels are adjustable, so that you can use them to develop both 35mm film and rollfilm. Buy two graduates, a large one for mixing chemicals and a small one for measuring concentrated solutions. A good choice of size is 32 and 8fl oz (1000 and 250ml). Many pieces of equipment you can find around the house. For example, although special film clips are available to hang up film while it dries, clothespins will do the job almost as well. A bottle opener is useful for opening 35mm film cassettes. However, household thermometers are not precise enough, so buy a darkroom thermometer. Rubber gloves should be worn whenever you handle undiluted chemicals.

Storage bottles for chemicals

Graduates

Rubber gloves

Protective envelope for negatives

Developing tank

Darkroom thermometer

Clock

Reel

Clothespins

Scissors

Bottle opener

Printing equipment

When buying printing equipment, always make sure that the easel and trays will accommodate the largest size of print you are likely to make. The enlarger itself should be capable of making a print 50 percent bigger than this, because you may want to enlarge just the central portion of a negative. A wide range of safelights is available from photo dealers. Be sure to use the appropriate filter recommended by the printing paper manufacturers.

Washing and drying prints

After processing, you must wash each print in running water for four or five minutes. An automatic tray siphon converts any print tray into an efficient print washer. If your darkroom does not have any running water, wash prints in a deep sink elsewhere. A length of hose attached to the faucet and a plastic pipe in the outlet will ensure a continuous flow of water, as shown in the diagram below.

You can dry most types of printing paper by laying the prints out flat on an absorbent surface, such as a clean towel or a blotter; by hanging the pictures on a line; or, more quickly, by using a hair dryer.

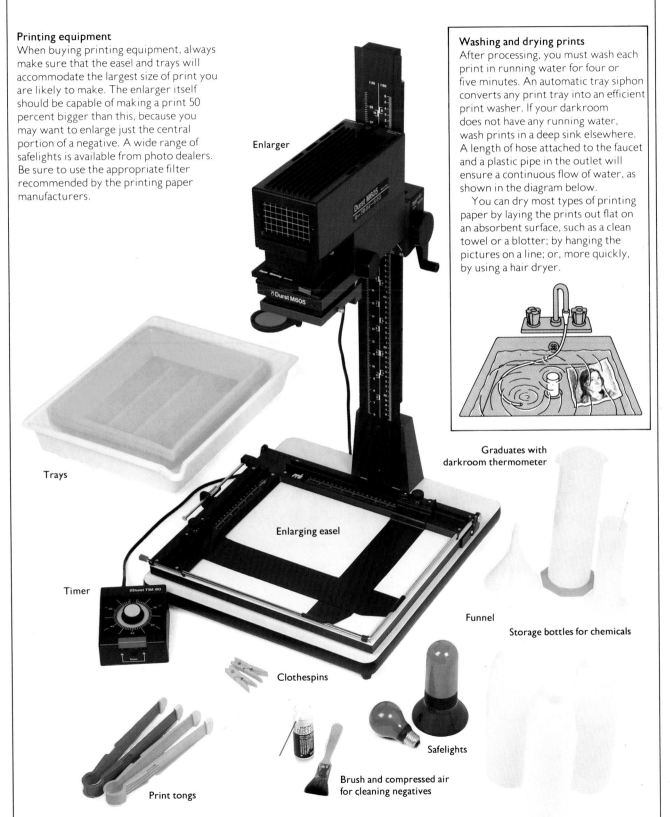

Enlarger

Trays

Graduates with darkroom thermometer

Enlarging easel

Timer

Funnel

Storage bottles for chemicals

Clothespins

Print tongs

Brush and compressed air for cleaning negatives

Safelights

Developing black-and-white film / 1

Because black-and-white film is highly sensitive to all the colors of light, you have to open the film and load it into the developing tank in complete darkness. If you are not sure that your darkroom is absolutely lighttight, you can use a changing bag, illustrated among the equipment at right. This is a special double-lined cloth bag that you can close and manipulate with the equipment inside, thus creating a totally dark environment for loading.

Developing tanks are designed to be lighttight so once the film is loaded and the lid of the tank is in place, you can continue processing in normal light. Two different types of tank are shown on the opposite page. Both are available in various sizes; the larger sizes are able to hold more than one reel of film for multiple developing. Each type of reel has advantages and disadvantages. The plastic edge-loading reel adjusts to fit any size film and is slightly easier for beginners to load. However, the reel must be absolutely dry before you load, or the film may stick or buckle instead of lying flat in the spiral grooves. The center-loading reel cannot be adjusted for different films, and the loading method may require a little practice. But once you have mastered the technique, the film will slide on smoothly even if the reel is not completely dry.

The techniques involved in loading film into a tank are quite straightforward. However, it is easy to make mistakes when you are working in the dark. A good idea is to practice the procedures a few times with the lights on, using an old roll of film. When you can handle each stage successfully with your eyes shut, have a final run-through in the dark. Following a few general rules will minimize the chance of error. Always begin with a tidy, well-organized working area. Put away anything you will not be using, and keep all necessary equipment where you can locate it easily. Work with blunt-end scissors to avoid scratching the film, and close the blades after use. If you are loading in a changing bag, check that everything is inside the bag before you remove the film from its light-tight casing. With 120 roll film, make sure you can feel the difference between the film and its paper backing, so that you do not load the paper into the tank by mistake. With 35mm film, cut off the film leader and then make two short, diagonal cuts across the corners of the film strip. This makes loading the film easier.

When you load the film onto the reel, take your time and never try to force the film if there is resistance. If the film jams, do not panic. Carefully unwind and reload it, checking that the reel is dry and the edges of the film are square with the spiral grooves. Drop the reel in the tank and replace the lid before turning on the lights.

Equipment checklist
1 Developing tank
2 Reel
3 Changing bag
4 Bottle opener
5 Blunt-end scissors

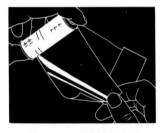

Opening 120 film
Carefully tear the paper seal on the roll and separate the film from the paper backing. Peel away the tape that attaches the end of the film to the paper.

Opening 35mm film
With a bottle opener, pry off the cover at the end opposite to that from which the spool protrudes. Slide the film spool out of the cassette. Use scissors to square off the tapered film leader.

Preparing 35mm film
Using a pair of scissors, cut off the film leader and snip the corners off the film strip. This makes it easier to load the film onto the developing reel.

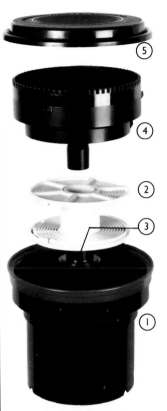

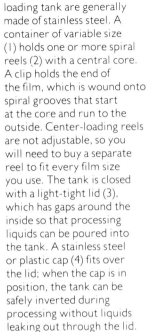

Tank with edge-loading reel

The components of an edge-loading tank are generally made of plastic. A light-tight container (1) holds one or more reels (2) with spiral grooves. The film is wound on from the outside toward the center, with two clips on the outer groove holding the leading edge of the film in position. Plastic edge-loading reels have adjustable halves to take different film sizes. A hollow black tube (3) fits inside the reel to funnel solutions into the tank. The tank lid (4) has a funnel that forms a light-tight channel to admit the liquid. When the lid is closed, the tank is completely lighttight. A cap (5) fits tightly onto the lid so that the tank can be turned upside down during processing.

Tank with center-loading reel

The components of a center-loading tank are generally made of stainless steel. A container of variable size (1) holds one or more spiral reels (2) with a central core. A clip holds the end of the film, which is wound onto spiral grooves that start at the core and run to the outside. Center-loading reels are not adjustable, so you will need to buy a separate reel to fit every film size you use. The tank is closed with a light-tight lid (3), which has gaps around the inside so that processing liquids can be poured into the tank. A stainless steel or plastic cap (4) fits over the lid; when the cap is in position, the tank can be safely inverted during processing without liquids leaking out through the lid.

1 – Set an adjustable reel to the right width by sharply twisting the halves until they click into position.

2 – Line up the slots on the outer rim and, holding the film by the edges, feed the end into the outer groove.

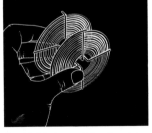

1 – Hold the reel firmly with the sides vertical. Rotate the reel until the blunt ends of the spiral are at the top.

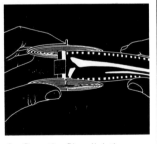

2 – Bow the film slightly between thumb and forefinger and insert the end into the clip in the core of the reel.

3 – Rotate the two halves of the reel alternately and in opposite directions, keeping the film smooth and straight.

4 – Cut the end off the roll or magazine to leave a neat edge when the whole film has been wound into the grooves.

3 – Continue to bow the film as you rotate the reel away from it. Gently slide the film on; do not scrape the edges.

4 – When the film is wound on, cut it free. Check that each coil of film lies flat and that each groove is used.

Developing black-and-white film/2

Developing film is the most crucial of all darkroom tasks. Although errors at later stages in the darkroom process can be remedied, careless development techniques can waste all the effort put into taking the pictures by ruining the film. You can get good-quality negatives only if you follow methodical procedures, as shown on the opposite page.

The key to good processing is consistency. Try to use just one type of film and developer at first, and keep strictly to the recommended time and temperature – usually 68°F (20°C) – whenever you develop a film. Take special care when pouring solutions into and out of the tank. Some tanks take as long as 20 seconds to empty or fill, and if you vary your filling and emptying routine you can increase development time by up to 15 percent. Thus, follow a regular procedure, such as starting to time development as soon as the tank is full and stopping when it is

completely empty. Overly-vigorous agitation of the developing tank can cause as much variation in development as inaccurate timing or poor temperature control can, and may result in streaks forming on your film. So standardize the way you invert the tank, too.

After developing and fixing, you must wash and dry the film. Care at this stage can save much time and effort later. Particles of dust or grit that land on the wet film will show up on your prints as white spots, which you must laboriously spot out with a brush. To prevent such marks, give your film a final rinse in filtered or distilled water, then add the correct amount of wetting agent so that water drains evenly off the film without leaving drying marks. You can speed up this process by gently removing excess water with your fingers or with a soft sponge. Finally, hang the film to dry in a dust-free place.

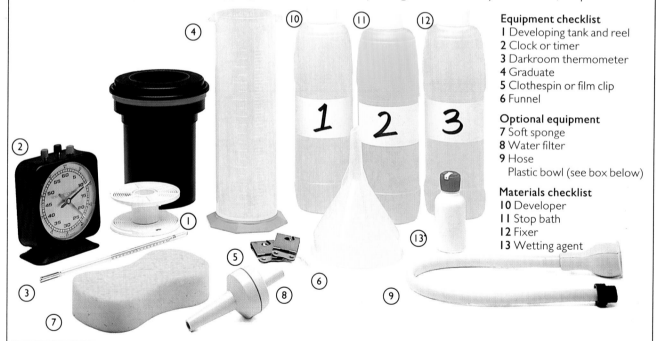

Equipment checklist
1 Developing tank and reel
2 Clock or timer
3 Darkroom thermometer
4 Graduate
5 Clothespin or film clip
6 Funnel

Optional equipment
7 Soft sponge
8 Water filter
9 Hose
   Plastic bowl (see box below)

Materials checklist
10 Developer
11 Stop bath
12 Fixer
13 Wetting agent

Temperature control
The usual temperature for developing black-and-white film is 68°F (20°C), and developer should be within 2°F (1°C) of this for consistent results. If you dilute your chemical stock with water at the right temperature, you should have little difficulty maintaining this temperature during development; but in very cold or hot rooms you may have to stabilize the temperature of the developer by using a bath of water warmed or chilled to 68°F. Keep the chemicals and tank in this water bath just prior to processing, and store the tank in the bath when not agitating it.

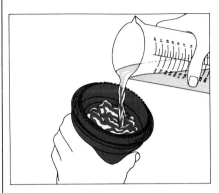

1 – Fill the developing tank with developer, tilting the tank to help speed the flow of solution. Remember to check that the developer is at the correct temperature and that there is enough of it to cover the film reel.

2 – Start timing as soon as the tank is full, then replace the cap and tap the tank a couple of times on the work surface to dislodge air bubbles from the surface of the film. Air bubbles leave small round marks on the negatives.

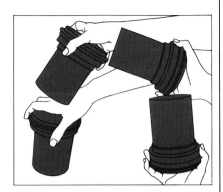

3 – Agitate the tank for five seconds every minute by gently inverting it several times. Hold the lid tightly on the tank. A minute or so before the full development time has elapsed, measure out the correct quantity of stop bath.

4 – Remove the cap and pour out the developer the instant the specified time has elapsed (see the instructions packed with the chemicals). Funnel reusable developer into a storage bottle. Pour single-use developer down the drain.

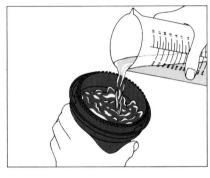

5 – Pour in stop bath immediately after draining the developer, and agitate continuously for about 30 seconds. Without opening the tank, pour the solution into a bottle. You can reuse stop until it turns from yellow to blue.

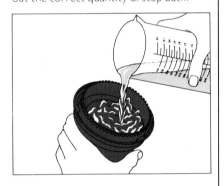

6 – Fill the tank with fixer. Agitate continuously for half a minute, then intermittently until the full fixing time is up. Drain the fixer back into its bottle, and remove the lid from the tank to wash the film.

7 – Wash the film for at least half an hour in running tap water at between 65 and 75 F (18 –24 C). A hose pushed to the base of the tank makes the washing process more efficient. Give the film a final rinse in filtered or distilled water.

8 – Add the correct amount of wetting agent to the water in the tank. This helps water drain evenly off the drying film. With too little wetting agent, water drops will leave drying marks; too much leaves greasy smears on the film.

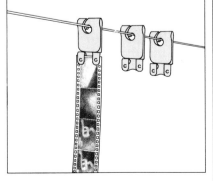

9 – Hang up the film to dry in an area that is as dust-free as possible – the bathroom is usually a good place. Then thoroughly wash and dry the tank, reel, and all other equipment to remove chemical residues.

Making a contact sheet

A contact sheet shows a positive image of every frame on a roll of film, so that you can easily assess which of your pictures you want to enlarge. And because a ring binder can hold, side by side, both the negatives and the contact sheets made from them, you can use a contact sheet to locate a negative quickly without examining each strip of negatives against the light.

Making a contact sheet is simple, as the pictures at right show. Using a sheet of glass to press your negatives tightly against a piece of photographic paper, you shine light through this sandwich of glass and negatives onto the paper. Then you make the image visible just as you do when processing film – by immersing the paper in developer, stop and fixer. The developer must be specially formulated to process paper prints. However, the other two solutions can come from the same concentrates or powders that you used when processing the film, though you may have to follow different diluting instructions.

The process of exposing and developing a contact sheet can take place in yellow safelighting, giving you a clear view of what you are doing. Unlike film, conventional black-and-white photographic paper is sensitive to only one color of light – blue. Thus, the yellow safelighting has no effect on the printed image.

The fixer bath removes even this sensitivity to blue light, so once your contact print has been in the fixer for half a minute or so, you can switch on the normal room lighting and examine the results. Now is the time to judge whether you gave your print the correct exposure. If the sheet is too dark, have another try, cutting the exposure time by half, or else closing down the enlarger lens by one stop. Conversely, if the sheet is too light, double the time, or open up the lens aperture by one stop.

Making and storing contacts
A finished contact sheet (1) shows every negative actual-size, but with the tones reversed. To press negative and paper together for a contact print, use a sheet of glass with taped or polished edges (2). A contact printing frame (3) makes the job easier by holding all the materials. If you use transparent negative file pages (4), you need not remove individual negative strips; you can lay the whole page on the printing paper. This saves time and keeps negatives cleaner, though it does require a larger size of paper than printing with individual strips. Store the contact sheets in a file (5) alongside the negatives.

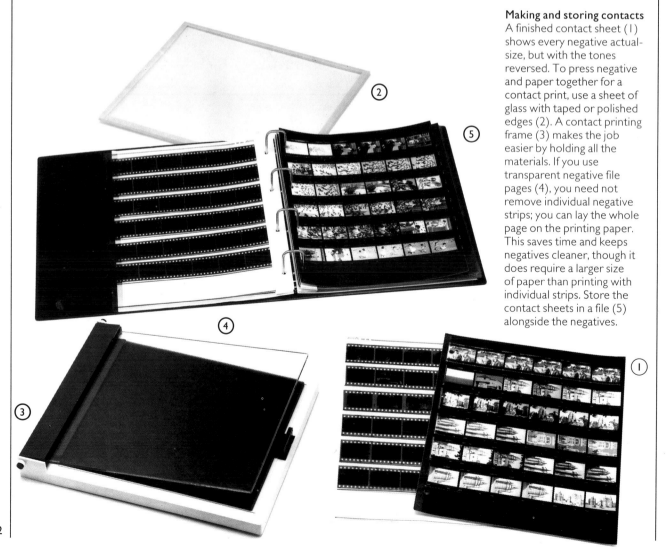

Equipment checklist
Enlarger
Safelight
Clock or timer
Darkroom thermometer
Graduates
Three processing trays
Two pairs of print tongs
Sheet of glass, or special contact
    printing frame
(Rubber gloves are advisable if you
    have sensitive skin)

Materials checklist
Box of resin-coated printing paper
    (see pages 52-3)
Developer, stop and fixer

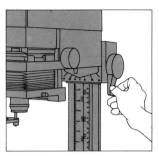

1 – Fill trays with developer, stop and fixer to a depth of about $\frac{3}{4}$in ($1\frac{1}{2}$cm). The solutions should ideally be at 68 F (20 C), though temperature is not critical; processing simply gets faster as the temperature rises.

2 – Move the enlarger head up the column until the light from the lens easily covers the glass or contact frame. Close the lens aperture to f/11, and turn out the room lights and the enlarger lamp. Switch on the safelight.

3 – Take a sheet of paper out of its box and inner envelope and reseal the package against light. Place the paper, emulsion (shinier) side up, on the enlarger baseboard or on the foam base of the contact frame.

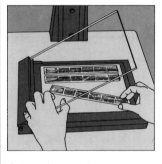

4 – Lay the negatives, emulsion (duller) side down, on the paper, handling them by the edges. Cover with the glass sheet. If you are using a contact frame, lower the glass surface and lock it into position.

5 – Switch on the enlarger lamp for about 15 seconds to expose the paper, then lift the glass carefully and put the negative strips back into their filing sheet before removing the printing paper for processing.

6 – Slide the paper, emulsion side down, into the tray of developer, then gently rock the tray by lifting and lowering one corner. After half a minute, you can turn the paper over. Development takes about 90 seconds.

7 – Lift the paper from the developer, using a pair of print tongs. Allow the print to drain for a moment, then lower it into the stop bath. Make sure that you do not contaminate the tongs with the acidic stop solution.

8 – Rock the tray of stop for about half a minute, then – using the second pair of tongs – transfer the paper to the fixer tray. Both stop and fixer are acidic, so you can safely use one pair of tongs.

9 – Agitate the fixer continuously for the first 15 to 30 seconds, then occasionally until a total of about two minutes has elapsed. Lift the paper out of the fixer, and lower it into a tray of water.

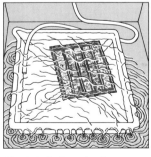

10 – Wash the print in tap water for four minutes. The water temperature should be between 70 and 75 F (21 – 24 C). If your tap water is too cold, use five changes of warmed water instead.

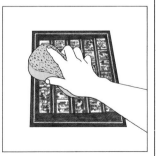

11 – Wipe drops of water from the surface of the print, then dry the paper, either by hanging it up or by laying it out on a flat, absorbent surface. You can speed drying with a hair dryer.

Black-and-white printing/1

By examining your contact sheet with a magnifier, you can get an approximate idea of which negatives are worth printing. However, do not discard images simply because they are darker or lighter than the rest. This is a result of over- or underexposure in the camera, and within limits you can correct the faults at the enlarging stage.

Once you have identified the most promising images on the contact sheet, refer back to your negatives and locate the selected frames. Use a loupe or a powerful magnifying glass, and look very carefully at the negatives. Fine detail that was indistinct on the contact sheet will be clearly visible. Make sure each picture is perfectly sharp, with no evidence of camera shake, and that no processing faults are visible. Care in picking out only the best frames

to print will save you from a discouraging struggle with indifferent negatives, which invariably produce mediocre results.

Having chosen the negative you want to print, follow the step-by-step procedure illustrated on the opposite page in preparation for printing. Resist the temptation to rush through or skip any of the nine steps, because every one of them is an essential part of the enlarging process. For example, cleaning the negative – step 2 – is tedious, yet every speck of dust that lands on your negative will show up as a white speck on the print. As you gain experience in darkroom work, you may want to introduce refinements. For example, to focus the image on the easel with extra precision, you can use a focusing magnifier, as described below.

Equipment checklist
1 Enlarger
2 Enlarging easel
3 Soft brush or compressed air can

Optional equipment
4 Focusing magnifier

Using a focusing magnifier
For really sharp prints, you must focus the enlarger precisely. If you are making a big enlargement, or printing from a very dense negative, you may find that the image on the easel is so dim that you have difficulty in finding the precise point of sharp focus. A focusing magnifier makes this much easier. Place the magnifier in the center of the easel, so that the mirror of the magnifier reflects a greatly enlarged view of the center of the negative up into the eyepiece. If the picture is sharp, you will clearly see a sharp image of the grain of the film, as at left below. Out-of-focus images show as a gray blur, as illustrated at right below.

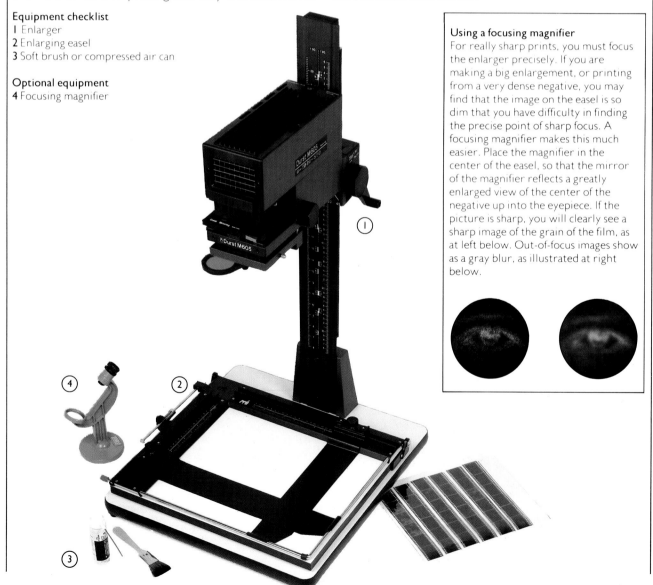

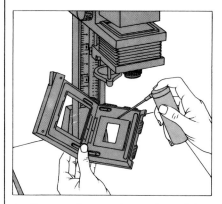

1 – Remove the negative carrier and dust it with a brush or a jet of compressed air. If the holders are glass, check that each surface is free of fingerprints.

2 – Clean the negative in a similar way. To reveal dust, hold the negative in the enlarger's beam, so that the light falls obliquely across the film surface.

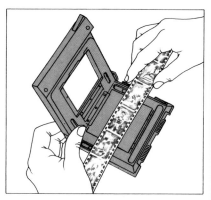

3 – Slip the negative into the carrier, emulsion side downwards, and check that all of the frame you plan to print is visible within the window of the carrier.

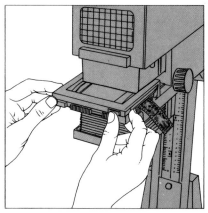

4 – Replace the carrier. With some enlargers, you have to lower the lamp housing onto the carrier to press the negative flat. Turn out the room lights.

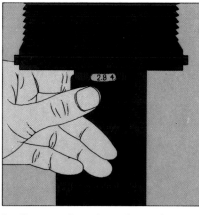

5 – Open up the enlarger lens to its largest aperture. This ensures that the image on the baseboard is as bright as possible – and thus easy to focus.

6 – Set the easel to the paper size. Then slide in a sheet of blank processed paper to cover the easel and provide a white surface on which you can get exact focus.

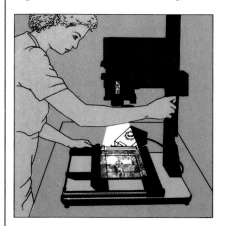

7 – Switch on the enlarger lamp, and raise or lower the head until the negative image on the easel is composed roughly as you want it on the print.

8 – Turn the focusing control until the picture appears sharp. This changes the image size, so you may have to readjust the head, then fine-tune the focusing.

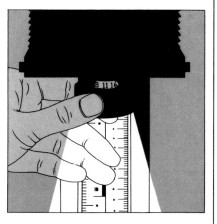

9 – Close down the lens to the working aperture – f/11 is a good starting point – then remove the focusing sheet from the easel and switch off the enlarger.

435

Black-and-white printing/2

Just as film requires carefully judged exposure to produce a good negative, a sheet of printing paper requires just the right amount of light to produce a print that is neither too dark nor too pale.

To find out how much light the paper needs for the image you are projecting, you must make a test print. This is a strip of paper cut from a full sheet, on which you print a section of the negative. But instead of giving the whole strip the same exposure, you follow the procedure shown on the opposite page (steps 1 to 8) to make a series of exposures of increasing duration. After processing the test strip, you can judge which time produced the best results, and expose the full print accordingly (steps 9 to 12). The box below will help you to work out how much exposure each section of the test should receive.

For the test to provide a reliable guide to exposure, you must process the strip – and the print that follows – with a little more care than you take when processing a contact print. When you mix the developer, use water at 68°F (20°C), or warmer if the developer concentrate is cold. This way the temperature of the developer should be right for developing both the test and the print. Do not worry if the developer temperature falls one degree during your printing session – such a small change is unimportant. In a cold room, you can prevent excessive cooling by standing the tray of developer in a larger tray of warm water. The temperatures of the stop and fixer baths are less crucial than that of the developer.

Processing time is significant, too. With resin-coated paper (the most common type of photographic paper), your test and print will need about one and a half minutes in the developer. Make sure that you use exactly the same developing time for the print as you did for the test, or your result may be unsatisfactory. If the test strip appears to be darkening much too rapidly in the developer, resist the temptation to lift the paper from the tray prematurely. A half-developed test strip has about as much value for exposure estimates as no test at all.

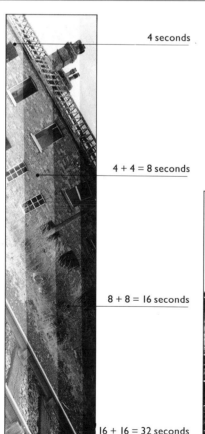

4 seconds

4 + 4 = 8 seconds

8 + 8 = 16 seconds

16 + 16 = 32 seconds

Judging a test print
The test procedure illustrated opposite (steps 1 to 8) results in a strip of paper divided into four zones, each darker than the one before. If your enlarger lens was set to f/11, one of these zones should show approximately the correct tones. However, if the whole strip is too pale, make another test with the lens set to f/5.6. If all the zones are too dark, close down the lens to f/16 or f/22 and repeat the test. In the example at left, the best zone had an 8-second exposure, so the photographer printed the whole negative for this length of time, and produced the correctly exposed result shown below.

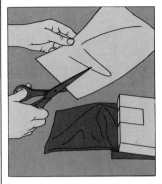

1 – Cut a strip of printing paper about two inches (5cm) wide. Put the remainder back in the black envelope, and close the box.

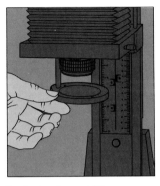

2 – Swing the red filter over the lens to prevent the blue-light-sensitive paper from being exposed. Turn on the enlarger lamp.

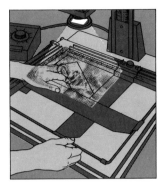

3 – Position the paper in an area of the image that shows both dark and light tones. Turn off the lamp and swing the red filter aside.

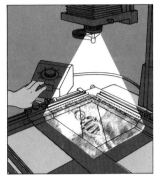

4 – Turn on the enlarger lamp to expose the whole test strip. After four seconds have elapsed, switch the lamp off again.

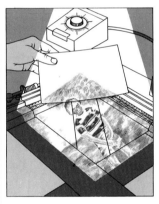

5 – Cover a quarter of the paper with a piece of cardboard and expose the rest of the test print – again, for a four-second period.

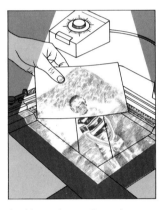

6 – Move the cardboard so that it covers half the strip of paper, and make another exposure, this time for eight seconds.

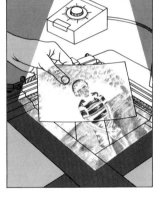

7 – Move the cardboard again, so that it now covers three-quarters of the paper. Expose the remaining quarter for 16 seconds.

8 – Process the test print and then pick the zone in the strip that shows the best tones. Note the exposure time given for that zone.

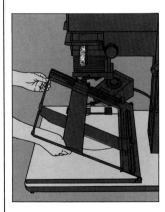

9 – Place a full sheet of paper on the easel, swing the red filter across, and turn on the enlarger to make a final check on composition.

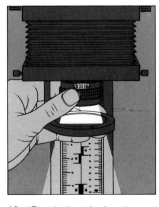

10 – Check that the lens is set to the correct aperture, then switch off the enlarger lamp and swing the red filter out of the light path.

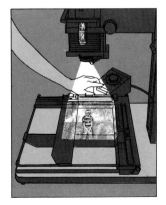

11 – Switch on the enlarger to expose the paper. After the time indicated by the test print has elapsed, switch off the enlarger lamp.

12 – Process the print as before. Make sure that the print stays in the developer for the same time as the exposure test.

Basic control techniques

By using special control methods during enlarging, you can improve the overall appearance of prints and make good pictures into excellent ones. The two main techniques of control involve reducing or increasing exposure for selected areas of the print so as to achieve a correct overall density and avoid having some areas too dark and others too light.

In dodging (left-hand diagrams below), you shade areas of the printing paper during exposure so that they receive less light than the rest of the image and print lighter than they would during a uniform exposure. As a result, dodging can reveal detail in shadow areas that would be too dark in an otherwise correctly exposed print.

Burning-in, also known as printing-in (right-hand diagrams below), is the exact opposite of dodging. Areas that are too light in relation to the rest of the picture get extra exposure so that they print darker. Whereas dodging is done during the main exposure, burning-in requires a second exposure with all but the selected areas shaded from the light.

To use either technique effectively, you need to know how much lighter or darker a particular area should be. The surest way to calculate this is to make a test strip that includes the full range of tones in the subject, as illustrated on the opposite page. The test strip will show the best exposure time for the main part of the image, and also indicate how many seconds more or less you need to expose areas that are too light or too dark.

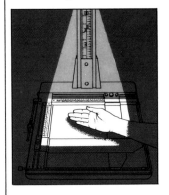

Dodging with a hand
Use your hand to dodge, or hold back light, in large areas of a print. Position your hand to the size and shape of the area to be shaded, and move it to and fro continuously to avoid an abrupt change of tone in the print.

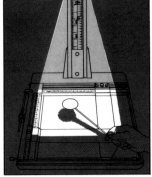

Dodging with a tool
Use a dodging implement (see below) of a suitable size and shape to shade small or isolated areas. Keep the tool moving from side to side all the time during exposure, so that you do not get obvious edges where the shadow falls.

Burning-in with cupped hands
Cup your hands over the paper around the area of the print that you wish to burn-in (give extra exposure to). By moving your hands closer together or farther apart, you can reduce or increase the part of the picture you burn-in.

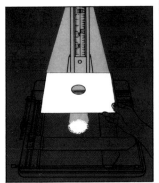

Burning-in with a card
Use a sheet of cardboard with a hole cut out to burn-in a small area of a print that needs darkening. Again, keep the card moving across the area during the additional exposure to avoid leaving discernible edges.

Equipment for dodging and burning-in
Dodging tools and burning-in cards (right) can be made very simply at home by using squares of cardboard and fairly stiff wire. For burning-in, cut out holes of different shapes and sizes in the cardboard. The cut-out pieces can then be glued or taped to lengths of wire to make dodging tools. Do not try to make the edges of the shapes too symmetrical: generally rounded or serrated edges will be best, because any shadow lines around the burnt-in or dodged area will be less noticeable. To avoid light from the enlarger reflecting back onto the printing paper, use black cardboard; alternatively, paint the cardboard black or cover it with black tape. Supplement a selection of different cards and tools by using your hands for larger areas.

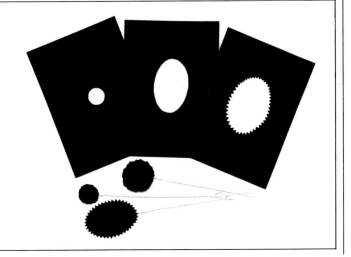

Burning-in a print

A test strip of the scene below revealed extremes of
light and dark. A print made at two seconds' exposure
clearly showed the backstage figures and details of
the audience. But the figures on the stage were much
too light. At 16 seconds, the stage figures printed
correctly, but detail was lost in the darker areas. The
final print was made by exposing for two seconds, then
burning-in the highlights for 14 seconds.

| 64 seconds | 32 seconds | 16 seconds | 8 seconds | 4 seconds | 2 seconds | 1 second |

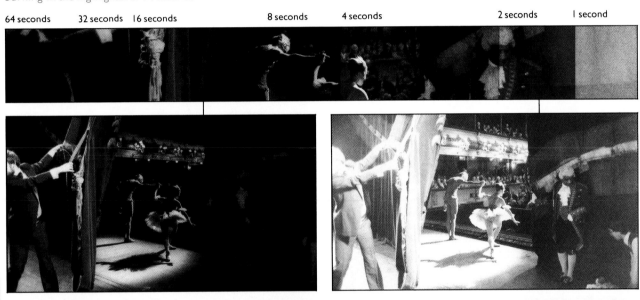

Color darkroom equipment

The equipment used to develop color materials in a home darkroom differs only slightly from that used for black-and-white work. Because most color processes involve more stages, you need extra bottles and graduates to store chemicals and to measure and hold made-up solutions. You also need to have a temperature-control bath that will hold enough warm water to keep the solutions in graduates at the specified temperature; a large bowl will do. Temperatures are higher and more critical than in black-and-white processing, so the third requirement is an accurate high-temperature thermometer.

The key item in color printmaking is the enlarger, which you should use with a voltage regulator because even small fluctuations in voltage can cause color changes in the print. Some enlargers have a filter drawer, as shown in the example on the opposite page, for holding special filters that modify the color of the enlarger light source to produce the correct color balance. Other enlargers have a color head, which contains permanently fitted filters. The filtration is adjusted by turning color coded dials on the enlarger head.

The only other important item of additional equipment needed for a color darkroom is a processing drum, which is relatively inexpensive to buy. Although you can process color prints in trays, a processing drum is more convenient because it allows you to carry out most of the process in normal light.

Film developing equipment (below)
You can process color films in the same daylight developing tanks that are used for black-and-white developing. Color chemicals can be harmful to sensitive skin, so be sure to wear rubber gloves when handling them.

To time the developing process, an ordinary clock with a second hand is adequate. The thermometer should be capable of accurately measuring temperatures in the range of 74°F to 105°F (23° to 41°C).

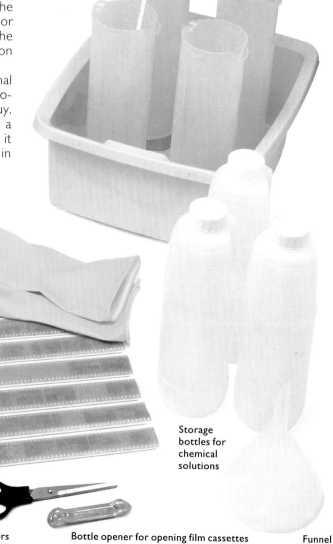

Bowl, graduates and high-temperature thermometer

Developing tank

Rubber gloves

Protective envelopes for negatives

Clock

Reel

Clothespins

Scissors

Bottle opener for opening film cassettes

Storage bottles for chemical solutions

Funnel

Printing equipment (below)
Color printing filters come in three hues – yellow, cyan and magenta. You need a full set (usually several filters per hue, each of a different density), plus an ultraviolet and an infrared heat filter. If you plan to make color prints in any quantity, you may prefer to buy an enlarger fitted with a color head. This device, which contains up to three adjustable color filters, greatly simplifies filtration.

Other essential items for color printing include a processing drum, a bowl (used as a temperature-control bath), a bucket (for soaking the loaded drum in warm water before processing) and a timer wired to the enlarger to time exposures.

Color analyzers
If you make a lot of prints from color negatives, you may eventually wish to add a color analyzer to your darkroom inventory. Color analyzers measure light just as exposure meters do. However, they measure not only the brightness of light from the enlarger, but also its color. After suitable calibration with a standard negative, a color analyzer can thus determine the correct filtration and exposure for virtually any negative, greatly reducing the need for test prints.

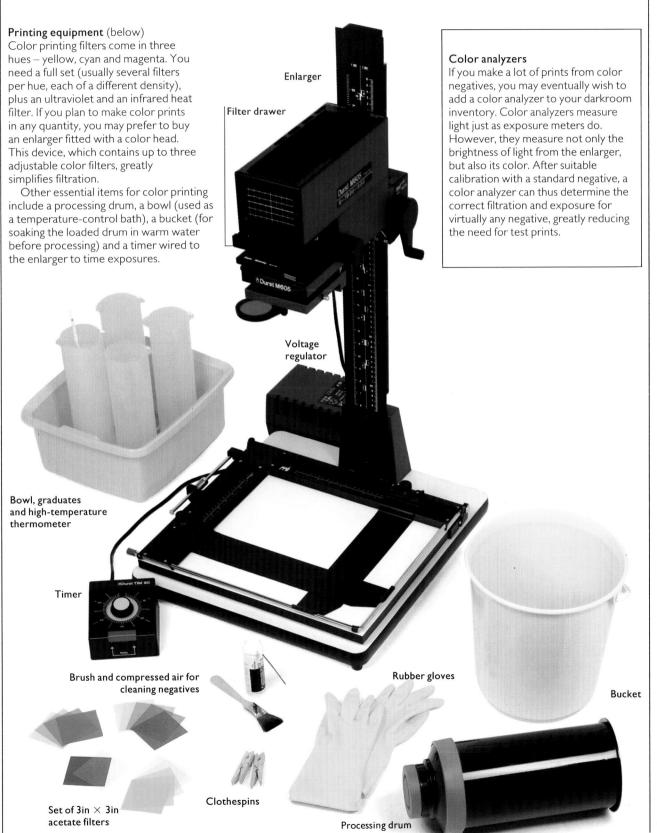

Enlarger

Filter drawer

Voltage regulator

Bowl, graduates and high-temperature thermometer

Timer

Brush and compressed air for cleaning negatives

Rubber gloves

Bucket

Set of 3in × 3in acetate filters

Clothespins

Processing drum

Processing color negatives/1

You can process most kinds of color negative film in a home darkroom without much expense or difficulty, although there are some types that must be sent to a laboratory for processing.

If you already have all the equipment for processing black-and-white film, you are well set up for color and will require only a few additional items such as a high-temperature darkroom thermometer marked in 0.5°F (0.3°C) divisions, and a couple of extra graduates and storage bottles for mixing and storing solutions.

Chemicals for processing color film come in kit form. Be sure to buy a kit containing chemicals compatible with the film you use – a Kodak C-41 kit will process Kodacolor and most other color negative films. Some kits can be used for processing color prints as well as color negatives.

When preparing chemicals for processing, always follow the manufacturer's instructions with the utmost accuracy. Store any leftover or reusable solutions in tightly stopped bottles. The bleach used in color processing lasts indefinitely, but the useful life of other solutions is limited: developer usually keeps for about six weeks, fixer and stabilizer for about eight weeks. Always label all storage bottles clearly, indicating solution type and expiration date.

To prevent skin irritation, wear rubber gloves whenever you are preparing or using color process-ing solutions; wash the gloves before you take them off at the end of session. Try to avoid splashes, and if you do spill chemicals, rinse them away as soon as you can. To stop staining on enamelled and porcelain sinks, wash them down frequently with fresh water. The chemicals involved in color processing are all more corrosive than those used for black-and-white.

Temperatures for processing color negative film are higher, and more critical, than for black-and-white film. For example, Kodak Flexicolor chemicals work at 100 F (37.8 C), and you must maintain the developer within an average of $\frac{1}{4}$ F (0.15 C) of this level throughout development. Usually, you can allow the other solutions and the wash water to vary within a wider range – 75 F to 105 F (24–40 C). The box below describes alternative ways to maintain the correct temperature during processing. Some kits are designed for lower temperatures, which makes them easier to use, although processing times are correspondingly longer.

Timing is also a critical factor. Control the time allowed for each processing stage by one of the methods described at the top of the opposite page. Note that the time of each step (given overleaf) includes the time it takes you to drain the developing tank. This is usually about 10 seconds. Have a few practice runs first, and always start draining the tank so that it empties precisely on schedule.

Controlling the temperature

To maintain all the processing solutions at the recommended temperatures for the kit in use, put them in graduates or beakers in a deep bowl filled with warm water, as shown at right. Before using a solution, check its temperature and if necessary add hot or cold water to the water bath to bring it to the correct warmth. Wash the thermometer after checking each solution.

If you want infallible temperature regulation, invest in a thermostatically controlled unit of the kind illustrated at right.

Warm water bath

Thermostatic unit

Electronic timer

Tape recorder

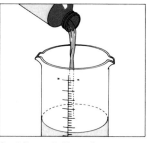

Clockwork timers

Controlling the time

A clock with a sweep hand is sufficient to time the various stages of color processing. However, you may prefer to buy a special darkroom timer, which you can set to make an audible signal when the required period has elapsed. Clockwise timers are the cheapest. One popular model, shown directly at left, has three projecting buttons. Pressing the green button starts the hands moving to indicate elapsed time. The red button stops the clock at the end of each processing step, and the black button sets the hands back to zero.

Another type of clockwork timer (shown at far left) has a dial into which you insert small stop pegs at preselected intervals. When the first peg turns against a special feeler, a bell rings and the clock stops. Electronic timers, as shown at left above, are also available. Some types can be operated by a foot switch.

An alternative timing method is to make a tape-recording of yourself speaking the processing instructions at precisely timed intervals.

Equipment checklist

Developing tank and reel
Warm water bath or
    thermostatic unit
Clock or timer
High-temperature darkroom
    thermometer
Graduates
Storage bottles
Funnel for filling bottles
Clothespin or film clip
Rubber gloves

Optional equipment

Light-tight changing bag
Soft sponge
Water filter
Hose

Materials checklist

Kodak Flexicolor processing kit
    (Process C-41) or similar

Preparing to process

Give yourself plenty of time to process color negative film. Loading the film into the developing tank, mixing the chemicals and bringing them to the right temperature, as described below, should take about half an hour. With most kits, you need to allow about half an hour for the processing itself, excluding drying time.

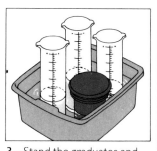

1 – Load the exposed film into the developing tank in total darkness. The procedure for this is exactly the same as for black-and-white processing. If you think your darkroom may have a light leak, use a light-tight changing bag. Make sure that your hands are clean and dry. Handle the film only by its edges.

2 – Mix and dilute the chemicals to the working strengths recommended in the manufacturer's instructions. Take care to avoid the slightest contamination of one chemical by another. One way to ensure this is to use a separate graduate for measuring out each of the chemical solutions.

3 – Stand the graduates and developing tank in a warm water bath. Start with the bath at a higher temperature than you need, and let the developer cool slowly. When the solution is still about $\frac{1}{2}$ °F too high, begin processing so that the temperature reaches the correct level mid-way through.

Processing color negatives/2

The processing stages for color negatives vary in number according to the kit you are using. For example, the Kodak Flexicolor processing kit has seven steps including drying, as shown in the table on the opposite page at top left.

Once you have loaded the exposed film into the developing tank, mixed all the solutions, and brought both the tank and the solutions to the correct temperature, you can start processing. The boxed text on the opposite page at far right, below, describes, in simplified form, the chemical principles underlying each stage. But you need not understand the precise chemistry to produce excellent negatives.

A meticulous approach to timing, temperature control and agitation is a prime requirement in color processing, particularly during the critical developer stage. As when mixing, follow the manufacturer's instructions with care and avoid contaminating any chemical solution with any other solution. Carry out the washing stages thoroughly, with warm water as explained in the box on the opposite page at top right.

You can agitate your film by inverting the developing tank, rotating the tank or rotating the reel within the tank. The method you use will depend on the design of your tank. To ensure consistently good results, remember to use the same method each time you process; the sooner it becomes a habit, the better.

The step-by-step instructions given below apply to the seven-stage Process C-41. Other processes differ from this in detail, but the general procedure is essentially similar.

Processing the negative

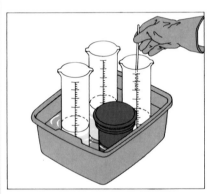

1 – Check the temperature of the developer. If necessary, adjust it to the correct level by adding hot or cold water to the warm water bath. Remove the developer from the bath.

2 – Pour the developer into the developing tank. Tap the tank sharply on the work surface to remove any air bubbles from the film. Then start the timer (or note the time on the clock).

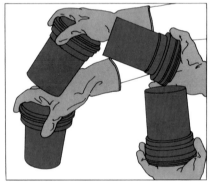

3 – Agitate the tank. After an initial agitation that begins the process, you generally need to agitate at regular intervals, following manufacturer's instructions about timing.

6 – Empty the tank at the end of the bleach step. Timing is not as critical as for development, but the duration of this step should not fall short of the specified period.

7 – Wash the film in running water, or else use several changes of water, agitating constantly. You can take the lid off the tank at this stage if this makes washing easier.

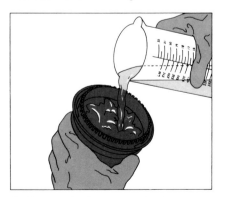

8 – Pour in the fixer, reset the timer, and agitate as directed until the film has been fixed for at least the time specified. Then drain the tank, and wash the film as in step 7.

The Kodak Flexicolor processing kit

The table below breaks down the stages in the processing of color negative film, using Process C-41. The time for each step includes a drain time of 10 seconds. If you reuse solutions, extend the times as recommended in the manufacturer's instructions included with the kit.

Processing step	Minutes
1 Developer	$3\frac{1}{4}$
2 Bleach	$6\frac{1}{2}$
Remaining steps in normal room light	
3 Wash	$3\frac{1}{4}$
4 Fixer	$6\frac{1}{2}$
5 Wash	$3\frac{1}{4}$
6 Stabilizer	$1\frac{1}{2}$
7 Drying	10–20

Washing the film

One way to wash the film after the bleach and fixer stages is to fill the tank with warm water, agitate vigorously, then repeat the operation six times. However, a better method is to use a hose attached to a faucet. Push the nozzle of the hose down the center of the reel (cross-section, right) and turn on the faucet. Use a water filter on your faucet to remove any impurities.

Washing times depend on the temperature of the water. A wash at 95 F (35 C) needs only five minutes, while 69 F (20 C) – the lowest you should allow the water temperature to fall – requires at least 15 minutes.

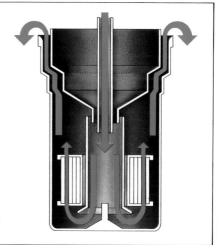

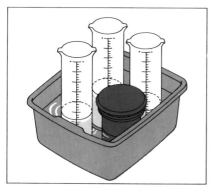

4 – Leave the tank in the water bath when you are not agitating it to maintain the solutions at the correct temperature. Do this after each agitation step throughout the process.

5 – Drain the tank after the alloted time, pouring reusable developer into a bottle. Quickly refill the tank with bleach and reset the timer, then agitate according to the instructions.

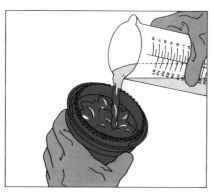

9 – Pour in the stabilizer. With kits that omit this stage, rinse the film in water treated with a wetting agent; but do not rinse film that you have stabilized. Remove the film from the reel.

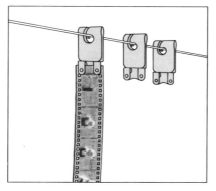

10 – Hang the film up to dry in a warm, dust-free room, using a film clip or clothespin. To stop the film from curling, you can attach another clip or pin to the bottom end.

What happens during processing

When you take a picture, light reaches silver halide crystals in the emulsion and creates minute specks of silver that form latent images in each of the three emulsion layers. As in black-and-white processing, developer turns these light-struck crystals black. At the same time, the by-products of development combine with chemicals in the film to form color dyes varying in placement and strength according to the pattern and density of silver grains in the three layers.

After development, the next step is to remove the silver grains by means of a bleach bath that reconverts them to silver halide crystals but leaves the dyes in place. Then you add a fixing solution. This removes all silver crystals and thus stabilizes the image so that light cannot fog it. Some processing kits have a combined bleach and fixer, known as a blix. The final stage of processing is to make the image stable, either by washing the negative to remove residue chemicals or by adding a stabilizing solution.

Making a test print

In color printmaking, you control not only the density of the image but also the color balance. As with black-and-white printing, the first step is to make a test print. But because two variables are involved – the exposure time and the color of the exposing light – the procedure differs slightly. To control the color of the light reaching the paper emulsion, you can either adapt a black-and-white enlarger for color with acetate filters, or use a special color head with filtration adjusted by dials, as shown at right. For your test print, select a starting filtration of 50 magenta, 90 yellow and 0 cyan. Then adjust this according to the manufacturer's directions on the box of printing paper you are using. Next, expose your test strip, as demonstrated on the opposite page.

Color printing paper is much more sensitive to all the colors of light than is black-and-white paper. For this reason, you must work in total darkness, or use a color safelight, until the paper is sealed in a light-tight processing drum. The safelight must be at least four feet from the paper; do not expose the paper to it for longer than three minutes.

The number of chemical stages in print processing varies from one processing kit to another, but all kits follow approximately the procedure diagrammed in the sequence below. Read the manufacturer's instructions carefully. Both when exposing and processing, make sure you follow exactly the same procedures every time. Take particular care over the temperatures of solutions and the timing of each stage. Remember to note down the details of each step – exposure time, filtration used, processing times and temperatures – so that you can repeat or modify your results after assessing the test print.

Equipment checklist
Enlarger with wired-in voltage regulator
Color printing filters or color head
Enlarging easel
Soft brush and compressed air can
Cardboard mask
Print-processing drum
Timer
High-accuracy darkroom thermometer

Bucket for presoak water
Water bath
Graduates
Bottles for made-up solutions
Rubber gloves
Soft sponge

Materials checklist
Kodak Ektaprint RA4 processing kit or similar
Color printing paper

Color filtration systems
A color head has built-in filtration that you can control by dials (shown at right). Acetate color printing filters (see below) are placed in the filter drawer of a basic enlarger. Filter kits contain cyan, yellow and magenta filters of varying densities, from five to 80. The filters are stacked together to make up the color and density values of the required filtration. Usually, a CP2B filter is included to filter ultraviolet radiation.

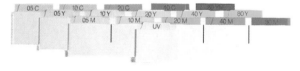

Processing a color print

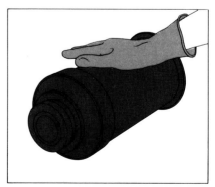

I – Fill the processing drum with presoak water at the correct temperature, as instructed on the processing kit. Set the timer and agitate for the required length of time, then drain the drum.

2 – Place the developer solution in a water bath to bring it to the right temperature. Test with a high-accuracy thermometer. Pour the solution into the processing drum and set the timer.

3 – Agitate the drum by rolling it back and forth on the work surface, or use a motorized roller. Agitate 30 to 60 times a minute, or as instructed on the kit, and rest the drum between agitations.

Exposing the print

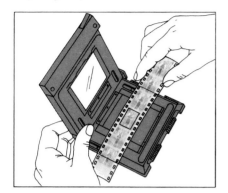

1 – Select a negative that will show up color balance variations: one with flesh tones is ideal. Clean the carrier of dust. Insert the negative.

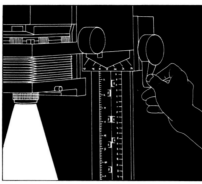

2 – Adjust the height of the enlarger and position the enlarging easel frame over the test area. Switch off the lights and focus the lens on the test area.

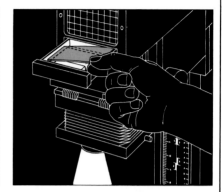

3 – Insert filters, or set the dials on a color head, to obtain the correct value for starting filtration; follow the directions on the printing paper pack.

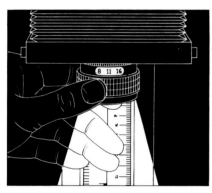

4 – Stop down the enlarger lens to f/11 and switch off the lamp. In the dark or under a color safelight, place a sheet of printing paper in the easel.

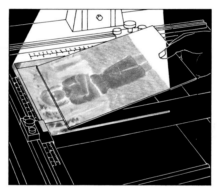

5 – Make a test strip using a cardboard mask. Move the mask along every five seconds during a total exposure of 20 seconds, to get four exposure bands.

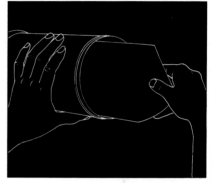

6 – Place the exposed paper carefully in the print-processing drum, with the emulsion facing inward. Seal the lid of the drum tightly. Turn on the room lights.

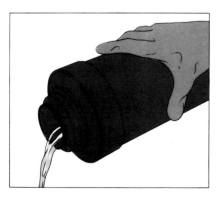

4 – Begin to drain the drum within 10 seconds of the end of developing time. Repeat steps 2, 3, and 4 for each of the remaining processing stages, following the manufacturer's directions precisely.

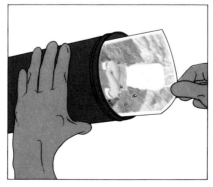

5 – After the final processing stage, remove the lid of the drum and take out the print, handling it carefully by the edges. Place the print in a tray and wash it thoroughly under running water.

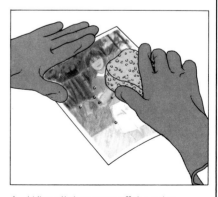

6 – Wipe all the water off the print to prevent spots appearing as it dries. Hang the print up to dry. For more rapid drying, use a hair dryer, but do not let the print get hotter than 200°F (93°C).

Testing filtration

After your test print is dry, you can begin to assess it. The picture may have one or more of the faults shown below, particularly if this is your first attempt at color printing. Use the illustrations to diagnose and correct basic errors of processing technique, then turn your attention to the density and colors achieved in the test print.

One of the strips on your test should be just about the right density. If all the strips are too dark or too light, repeat the exposure test using more or less exposure before making any decisions about changing the filtration.

A half-visible image indicates that you rolled the processing drum on a slanted surface, wetting only one end of the print.

Pink streaks are caused by water inside the drum. Remember to dry it thoroughly each time you make a print.

A very dark print with a pronounced color cast shows that you omitted the filters from the enlarger when making the exposure.

A strong magenta cast indicates that you have contaminated the developer with bleach-fix. Wash all graduates thoroughly.

Undeveloped patches on your print indicate that you loaded the paper into the drum with the emulsion side outward, not inward.

Unless you are very lucky, your test print will have a color cast. This may be either a pale tint or a strong, saturated hue that suffuses the whole frame. Do not be put off by this; the cast arises because all enlargers have an inherent color bias and a first print seldom has perfect color.

To eliminate the color cast, make a second test, this time to check color. Do so by exposing each quarter of a sheet of printing paper with the enlarger set to a different filtration for each exposure, as explained below at right and diagrammed on the opposite page.

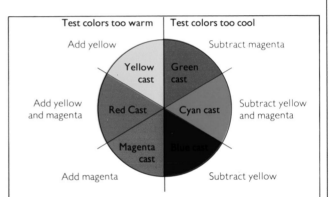

Adjusting filtration

Before you make your color filtration test, examine the earlier exposure test and decide whether the colors look too warm or too cool. If too warm, make three exposures with added filtration as indicated at the left of the diagram above. If too cool, make subtractions as indicated at the right of the diagram. (A 10-unit change in filtration corrects most pale color casts.)

For example, if filtration for the exposure test is 50Y (yellow), 90M (magenta) and 0C (cyan) and the colors are too warm, try the following changes in filtration for separate quarters of the test sheet:

	first quarter	second quarter	third quarter
Starting filtration	50Y 90M 0C	50Y 90M 0C	50Y 90M 0C
Change	+10Y	+10Y +10M	+10M
New filtration	60Y 90M 0C	60Y 100M 0C	50Y 100M 0C

You can use the fourth quarter of the test sheet either for a more extreme filtration change or for a more moderate change in one filtration density.

None of the filter packs suggested above includes cyan filtration because in printing from color negatives you need use only yellow and magenta filters. To remove a cyan cast from a print, simply reduce the amounts of both magenta and yellow in the filter pack.

Making a color test

Select the part of the exposure test that looks properly exposed – here an area exposed for 10 seconds – and use it as a guide to the color correction needed.

5 seconds   10 seconds   15 seconds   20 seconds

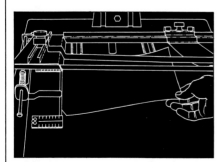

1 – From a piece of cardboard the size of your paper, cut away a quarter so that the cardboard forms an L-shaped mask that covers three-quarters of the paper.

2 – Decide on an initial change of filtration from the one used in the test, and insert the filters or set the dials of the color head. Turn off the room lights.

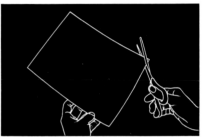

3 – Take out a sheet of paper and snip off one corner. This will enable you to position the paper in the easel in the same way for each test.

4 – Place the paper in the easel with the cardboard mask in position on top so that one quadrant is uncovered for the first color test.

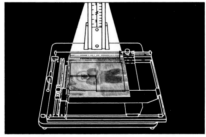

5 – Expose the first quadrant for the time determined from the exposure test. Replace the paper in its pack and turn on the room lights.

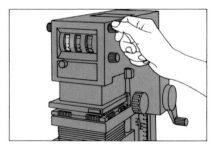

6 – Reset the filtration, then move the easel so that the image area that appeared on the first quadrant falls on a new quadrant. Turn off the lights.

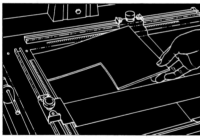

7 – Place the paper back on the easel, and check that the cut corner of the sheet is in the same position as it was for the previous test.

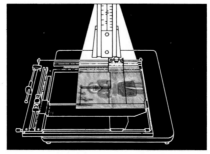

8 – Reposition the mask to uncover the new quadrant, and repeat steps 6, 7 and 8 twice more until you have exposed each quadrant with a different filtration.

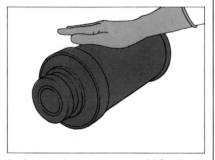

9 – Process the paper as you did for the exposure test. Make sure the print is dry before evaluating colors, as hues will look different when the paper is wet.

Making a final print

Your color test will show four different zones, one of which should have more or less correct color balance. On the back of the sheet, jot down the filtration that you used for each quadrant. One or two of the four zones may be lighter than the others. This is quite normal. The cause is the absorption of light by the enlarger's color filters, and when you make the finished print you must make an exposure adjustment, as explained at right, to compensate for the absorbed light.

If none of your tests has perfect color, you will have to make a further filter change. Usually, the required change in the filter pack will be quite small, but this process of fine-tuning the color can actually be more difficult than the earlier correction of heavy color casts. This is because subtle color casts are hard to identify; it is easy to see that there is something wrong, but the remedy is not quite so clear. The ring-around chart on the opposite page will help you to identify an elusive color cast. You may also find it useful to look at the color test through gelatin color-printing filters. Remember that the color of filter that makes the test look right is the one you should remove from the filter pack before making the final print.

Filter factors

Filter value	05	10	20	30	40	50
Yellow	1.0	1.1	1.1	1.1	1.1	1.1
Magenta	1.2	1.3	1.5	1.7	1.9	2.3

When you change filtration, you increase or decrease the amount of light that reaches the negative and the paper; to maintain the print density, you must adjust the exposure time to compensate. If you *add* an extra filter, you should *multiply* the exposure time by the corresponding factor shown in the chart above. And remember to *divide* by the same factor when you *remove* filters from the enlarger.

A color test (below left) shows how changes in filtration affect the print color. The photographer made the final print (below) at the filtration used for the bottom left quadrant but gave extra exposure to compensate for the added filters, as explained above.

Filter ring-around

If you cannot identify the color cast in your print, try to match it with the color bias of one of the twelve patches on this chart, then note the corrective filtration that you must apply to make a good color print. You may even wish to make your own ring-around instead of using a printed one. Do this by systematically changing filtration between prints, but remember to adjust exposure, as explained in the box on the opposite page.

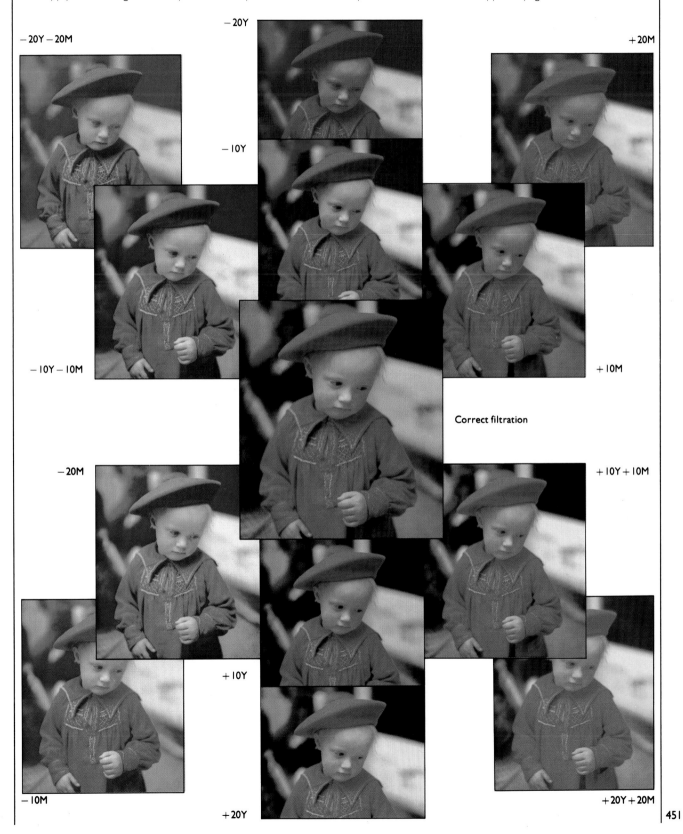

−20Y −20M

−20Y

+20M

−10Y

−10Y −10M

+10M

Correct filtration

−20M

+10Y +10M

−10M

+10Y

+20Y +20M

+20Y

Printing from transparencies/1

One way to make a color print from a color transparency is to produce an intermediate negative, or "internegative," and then print this exactly as you would any other color negative. Although you can make your own internegative by photographing the slide using color negative film with a duplicating attachment on your camera, you will usually get more accurate results if you send your slides to a photolab for copying.

Another approach, which is both cheaper and more satisfying, is to make a color print directly from the transparency onto color reversal paper, such as Kodak Ektachrome paper. This gives a positive image from the positive image on the slide. You can use the same equipment as for printing color negatives, but you will need additional filters – printing on color reversal paper often requires cyan filtration, whereas printing on color negative paper requires only magenta and yellow filtration. Filtration assessment is much easier than with negative/positive printing, because you can directly compare the colors of your test strip with the original.

You can easily judge by eye whether a transparency is good enough for printing; thus there is no need to make a contact sheet. Choose an example that is correctly exposed and not too contrasty.

Transparencies have a greater range of brightness than printing paper can reproduce, so a print from a contrasty image would lose details in the highlights and shadows.

Reversal paper reacts differently than negative/positive papers. The image becomes lighter as the paper receives more exposure and darker as the exposure is reduced. The border areas of the print that are masked during exposure will come out black. Since reversal paper is sensitive to all visible colors of the spectrum, you must handle it in total darkness before and during processing.

The procedure for exposing and processing a test strip from a transparency is essentially the same as it is for a color negative. To expose a test strip, follow the diagrams in the upper sequence on the opposite page. For processing, you must be sure to buy chemicals that are compatible with the paper you are using. The processing stages given below are typical, but will vary in details from kit to kit. Follow meticulously the manufacturer's instructions for mixing the chemicals, controlling temperature and time, and agitating the processing drum. Processing is likely to take between 15 and 25 minutes. Usually the temperature is critical for the first developer and color developer, but not for the other stages.

Equipment checklist

Enlarger with wired-in voltage regulator
Color printing filters or color head
Enlarging easel
Soft brush or can of compressed air
Cardboard mask

Print-processing drum
High-accuracy darkroom thermometer
Timer
Bucket of presoak water
Water bath
Graduates
Rubber gloves
Print-washing tray

Soft sponge
Bottles for made-up solutions

Optional equipment
Focus magnifier
Motor-driven agitator

Materials checklist
Color reversal processing kit
Color reversal printing paper
Sheet of exposed, processed printing paper for use when focusing

Processing a color reversal test print

1 – Fill the processing drum with presoak water at the correct temperature, as instructed on the processing kit. Set the timer and agitate for the required length of time, then drain the drum.

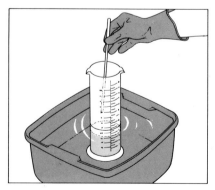

2 – Place the first developer solution in a water bath to bring it to the right temperature. Test with a high-accuracy thermometer. Pour the developer into the processing drum and set the timer.

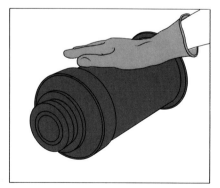

3 – Agitate the drum by rolling it back and forth on the work surface, or use a motorized roller. Agitate 30 or 60 times a minute, or as instructed on the kit, and rest the drum between agitations.

Exposing a color reversal test print

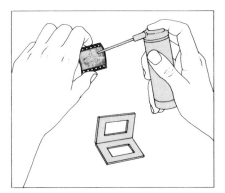

1 – Remove the slide from its mount and clean it using a soft brush or a compressed air jet. Insert the slide in the carrier and place the carrier in the enlarger.

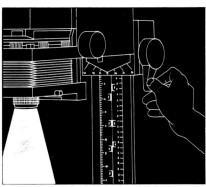

2 – Adjust the enlarger height and place a focusing sheet under the masking frame. Switch off the room light and focus the image. Set the lens at f/8.

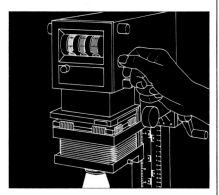

3 – Insert filters, or adjust dials on a color head, to give the correct value for starting filtration (follow the instructions given on the printing paper pack).

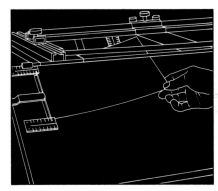

4 – With the enlarger lamp switched off, replace the focusing sheet under the masking frame with a sheet of unexposed printing paper, emulsion side up.

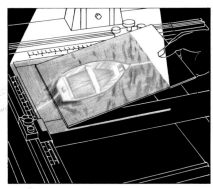

5 – Make a test strip using a piece of cardboard as a mask. Move the cardboard along to give four bands, exposed for exactly 2, 4, 8 and 16 seconds.

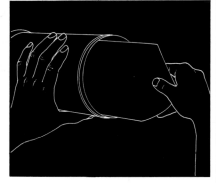

6 – Place the exposed paper in the print-processing drum, with the emulsion facing inward. Seal the lid of the drum tightly to exclude light. Turn on the room light.

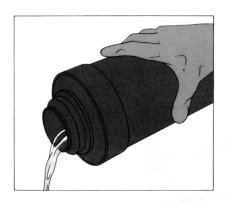

4 – Begin to drain the drum within 10 seconds of the end of developing time. Repeat steps 2, 3 and 4 for each of the remaining processing stages, following the manufacturer's directions precisely.

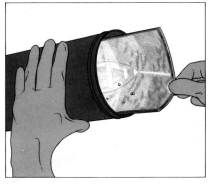

5 – After the final processing stage, remove the lid of the drum and take out the print, handling it carefully by the edges. Place the print in a tray and wash it thoroughly under running water.

6 – Wipe all the water off the print to prevent spots appearing as it drains. Hang the print up to dry. For more rapid drying, use a hairdryer, but do not allow the print to get hotter than 200 F (93 C).

Printing from transparencies/2

After your test print is dry, the first thing to do is examine it for faults. The examples at right (shown for convenience on a properly exposed print) illustrate some of the most frequent errors. To make excellent prints from your transparencies consistently, you must diagnose your mistakes accurately and be sure that they do not recur.

The next step is to examine closely the four exposure bands on your print. Decide which band shows correct tones and make careful note of the exposure time. If all bands are too dark or too light, repeat the exposure test using more or less exposure. As the test strip below shows, reduced exposure results in a darker print, not a lighter one as with color negatives; increased exposure results in a lighter print, not a darker one.

When you are satisfied that one of the bands of your exposure test print is correctly exposed, compare the colors in that band with the colors in the same area on the original slide. Generally, the print will have a color cast caused by the inherent color bias of your enlarger. To eliminate this cast, you must make a second test, this time of filtration. You can make this test by following the procedures described for printing from a color negative, using an L-shaped piece of cardboard to uncover each quarter of the color reversal paper with the enlarger set to a different filtration for each exposure. Alternatively, you can use a quartered masking frame as shown on the opposite page at top right. The filtration adjustments required to correct color balance in prints from transparencies are different from those adopted when printing from color negatives. To compensate for a color bias, subtract filters of the same color or add filters of the other two colors. The principle is illustrated in the box on the opposite page. As a rough instant-filtration guide, you can use a print viewing filter card, as illustrated on the opposite page, below right.

Common printing faults

A deep orange cast indicates that the paper was fogged before processing by exposure to a safelight. Always handle color reversal paper in total darkness.

A pale print with a color cast may occur if you print without filtration – for example, if you forget to set the filtration after focusing the image.

A weak print with loss of highlights and no shadows occurs when you exceed the first development time, or use first developer at too high a temperature.

Random blotches correspond with undeveloped patches. You probably loaded the paper into the drum with the emulsion on the outside instead of the inside.

Excessive contrast with a blue-black or magenta stain may be caused by contamination of one of the solutions by bleach-fix. Mix a new batch of chemicals, using a separate graduate for each.

A muddy appearance overall indicates that the bleach-fix solution was probably too diluted or exhausted, or that the drain time for the wash preceding the bleach-fix was insufficient.

A band of white is caused by the color developer failing to reach across the print during processing. Check that the drum is on a level work surface.

Judging the right exposure

16 seconds   8 seconds   4 seconds   2 seconds

The test strip above was exposed for 2, 4, 8 and 16 seconds at f/8. The 16-second exposure produced the best density but was still slightly too light. Thus for the filtration test, the photographer chose an exposure of 12 seconds.

Choosing filtration

When you are ready to make your filtration tests, first look at your initial exposure test strip and determine whether the correctly exposed band looks too warm or too cool in hue. If it is too warm, make three exposures using the filtration changes indicated on the left-hand side of the color wheel below. If it is too cool, follow the adjustments given on the right-hand side.

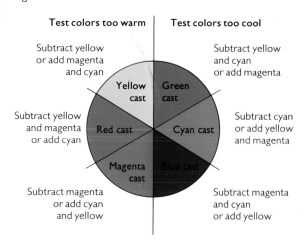

Test colors too warm

Subtract yellow or add magenta and cyan

Subtract yellow and magenta or add cyan

Subtract magenta or add cyan and yellow

Test colors too cool

Subtract yellow and cyan or add magenta

Subtract cyan or add yellow and magenta

Subtract magenta and cyan or add yellow

Color wheel labels: Yellow cast, Green cast, Red cast, Cyan cast, Magenta cast, Blue cast

You will need to make greater adjustments than are necessary to correct color casts on prints from color negatives: for a pronounced color cast, a change of 15 units is a good starting point. With practice, you will be able to judge the degree of correction needed by comparing the print with the original slide. Always subtract filters if you can, rather than add them. This will ensure that there are not more than two filter colors in the enlarger. A combination of three colors would reduce exposure without accomplishing any color correction.

For example, suppose that the filtration for the exposure test was 0Y (yellow), 45M (magenta) and 45C (cyan), and the test came out too cool. The changes needed for the filtration test, as determined from the color wheel above, would be as follows:

	first test	second test	third test
Starting filtration	0Y 45M 45C	0Y 45M 45C	0Y 45M 45C
Change	+15M +15C	−15C	15M −15C
New filtration	0Y 60M 60C	0Y 45M 30C	0Y 30M 30C

You can use the fourth quarter of your test sheet for a more extreme filtration, or for one that is somewhere between these values.

Quartered masking frames

Some masking frames come with four separate hinged, light-tight covers, each of which can mask off a different quarter of the total area of the printing paper, as shown above. This simplifies making an exposure or filtration test. In total darkness you can easily lift one cover before you expose a quarter of the print, then close that cover and lift another one to expose a second quarter, and so on.

Print-viewing filters

Some manufacturers produce color print-viewing filters of the type shown below. These are actual filters mounted in cardboard. Look through the windows to see what your print will look like if you add or subtract a specific filter or pair of filters. By comparing the effect with the original slide you can determine the correct filtration and set the enlarger head accordingly.

Printing from transparencies/3

A filtration test from a color transparency requires evaluation and interpretation in much the same way as does a test print made from a color negative. But in looking at the four different quadrants from the transparency test, it is much easier to understand the relationship between the color changes and the changes that you made to the filter pack, because there is an exact correlation. For example, putting in extra yellow filtration makes the print yellower – just as putting on yellow-tinted sunglasses makes everything look yellowish.

On the back of the test sheet, make a note of the filtration you used when exposing each individual quadrant. You will probably find that one of the four quadrants has good color, so you can go straight to a final print without making any further tests or changes in filtration. One reason why you can often proceed directly to a successful print is that you probably started with a slide that you knew would print well. (It is easier to recognize and discard a poor transparency than it is to pick out and reject a poor negative.)

Even so, you may find that the best quadrant from your filter test still has a slight color cast. To check this, examine the print in daylight. When deciding what final filtration corrections to make, look especially at light areas and flesh tones, where color casts will be most evident. You may also find it helpful to compare your test print with the ring-around on the opposite page.

Once you have decided on the correct filtration for a particular film type, make a careful note of it together with exposure details. Provided that it does not have a color cast, any other transparency of this film type will print equally well with the same filter pack and exposure setting.

Filter factors

Filter value	05	10	20	30	40	50
Yellow	1.0	1.1	1.1	1.1	1.1	1.1
Magenta	1.2	1.3	1.5	1.7	1.9	2.1
Cyan	1.1	1.2	1.3	1.4	1.5	1.6

If you change the filter pack in the enlarger, you must adjust exposure time to compensate. As with negatives, multiply the exposure time by the factors shown above when adding filtration, and divide when you take filters out. In all but the most critical applications, you can effectively ignore the corrections for yellow.

A color test (above) from a transparency clearly shows the effect of changing the filtration. The photographer picked out the quadrant at lower left as best and used the same yellow filtration to make the final print (right). The exposure time was not altered, because the small correction factor – 1.1 – was not enough to make a significant difference to the print density, as explained at right above.

Filter ring-around for reversal printing

Compare your test with this chart to identify elusive color casts, then apply one of the two recommended filtration changes to correct the color of your final print. Once you have a perfect print from one of your transparencies, you can make your own ring-around. Such a homemade chart gives you useful practical experience in filtration changes and a better grasp of the specific combination of materials that you use.

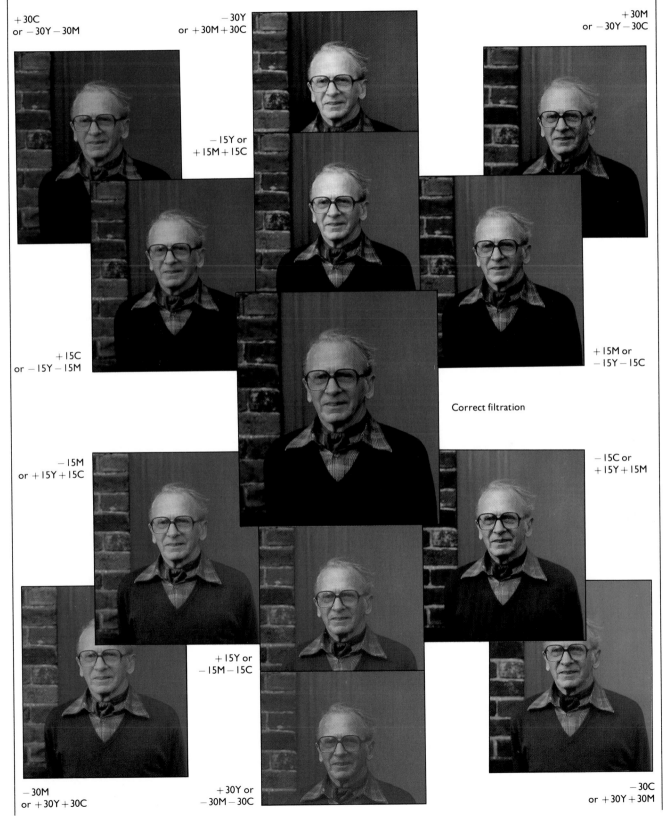

+30C
or −30Y −30M

−30Y
or +30M +30C

+30M
or −30Y −30C

−15Y or
+15M +15C

+15C
or −15Y −15M

+15M or
−15Y −15C

Correct filtration

−15M
or +15Y +15C

−15C or
+15Y +15M

+15Y or
−15M −15C

−30M
or +30Y +30C

+30Y or
−30M −30C

−30C
or +30Y +30M

PRESENTING YOUR PICTURES

Photographs are meant to be seen, and the lasting pleasure of photography comes after the pictures are taken and processed and you can browse through your prints and slides. Selecting, arranging and presenting your pictures are as much parts of the creative process of photography as composing and lighting, and deserve as much care.

The following pages explain how to put your pictures in order, and then how to show them to best effect – either in the form of an album or as a slide show, perhaps using a soundtrack with commentary. Whatever the mode of presentation, you should try to arrange your pictures in some logical order suggested by the pictures themselves. You might arrange them consecutively in a chronological or story-telling sequence. Or you might link together images that share themes or motifs. Keeping this in mind when you are taking pictures can pay off nicely when you show them.

When you begin to sort through your pictures, make sure you can study the images together. Allow plenty of space to spread out your prints or, as shown here, use a light box for viewing slides. And no matter how well you have planned your shots, keep an open mind – you may find that an unexpected theme suddenly occurs to you.

A photographer examines her slides on a light box and lists their details in a notebook. Being organized is as much a key to producing an interesting slide show as creativity.

Editing photographs

After processing, the first step in selecting prints for enlargement or slides for projection is to sort through them. Throw away those that are spoiled by camera shake, inaccurate focus or exposure errors, and carefully examine the others to pick the best. Images that look good at first glance may fail to live up to your expectations when you examine them with a magnifier. However, keep any second-choice pictures; later they may fill a small gap in a slide show or album. To make sense of the pictures, sort them into categories, grouping images together by subject matter or in chronological sequence. It is essential to be systematic – especially if you have many rolls from a special event or a trip.

If you used slide film, a light box, shown in the picture below, makes editing easier. You can impro-

Sorting slides (below)
With the aid of a light box, you can see immediately which slides are usable and which to discard. A 4x or 8x magnifier is an essential aid in making a selection. Note any special details on the back of the slide mounts and put the slides in vinyl sheets. Many laboratories will, at your request, return slides unmounted, in clear plastic sheets such as the example at left below. You can mark these sleeves with a wax pencil to indicate your chosen pictures.

Mounting slides (right)
If you order color slide film from a lab unmounted, you can put frames you want to save in simple, inexpensive cardboard mounts (1). These hold the slide in place with adhesive. Optional plastic sleeves (2) protect the film from scratches. Processors mount slides in cardboard or simple plastic mounts (3). For maximum protection against marks and fingerprints, use mounts with glass covers (4).

Plastic slide boxes (below)
These are fine for storing rarely needed slides, but finding a particular image means emptying the whole box – and this takes time.

vise one by lighting a sheet of translucent white plastic from below. Mounted slides form precarious piles when stacked up. Put them in vinyl sheets with pockets. Or ask the processing lab to leave off the mounts and return the film in easy-to-handle strips. Mount the images you want later.

You can have color negative film printed either as individual postcard-sized prints or as a contact sheet.

A contact sheet can be filed alongside the originals and often makes it easier to compare pictures with one another. But you do need a magnifier to see the images clearly. Postcard-sized prints are simpler to look at. But to avoid problems when ordering reprints, you should be sure to write the roll and frame number of the corresponding negative on the back of each print.

Card index (left)
This will effectively store large numbers of postcard-sized prints. Roll and frame numbers on the back of each picture enable each one to be quickly matched to its own original. Store the negatives separately.

Cardboard L-frame (below)
This is a useful aid to visualize how a small print will look if you want to have it cropped and enlarged.

Postcard-sized prints
These are what customers ordinarily receive from lab-processed negatives and are good for looking at with friends. But stored in the processer's envelopes, specific pictures are hard to find. Instead, you can order a contact sheet (right) that shows every frame on a single sheet and thus makes it easier to locate those images that you want to have enlarged. Here the photographer has examined the contact sheet with a magnifier, crossing through faulty images.

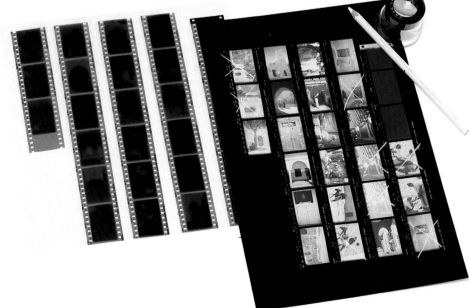

Showing slides

No doubt the most impressive way to present pictures is in a slide show. Even at the simplest level, using only a manual projector (below, top) and an accompanying script, images enlarged on a screen come to life and take on a narrative flow.

The essentials for a slide presentation are a projector, a screen and a viewing area that can be thoroughly darkened. In a fully darkened room, a white wall can serve as a screen, but a wall-hung or tripod-mounted screen, as at right, will normally work better. The conditions you create for viewing are just as important as the show itself. Any light spilling onto the screen will weaken the images, so if you cannot successfully black out a room, present the slides at night. Check that the projector and screen are at the correct heights and distance apart (see the diagram on the opposite page). Make sure, too, that your viewers will be comfortable and have a clear view of the screen.

For a more ambitious show, you might use one of the semi- or fully automatic projectors shown below at right and at bottom. Automatic focusing is a useful feature – in some cases you adjust focus by remote control; in others the projector focuses entirely automatically. A rotary slide tray helps to ensure a smooth sequence of images; and for a truly sophisticated show, you might link two projectors to a dissolve unit. With this unit you can fade out one projector lamp as the other brightens so that one image dissolves into the next and the screen is never blank. Most dissolve units can also be programmed to synchronize the slide show with a tape recorder.

Slide projectors

The illustrations below show the three main types of slide projectors that are available, which range from completely manual machines to those that are fully automatic. Some models have timers to change slides automatically.

A simple manual projector (right) has a push-and-pull slide carrier. The fixed lens offers only limited focusing control.

The automatic projector below takes a tray of 30 to 40 slides, and has an interchangeable lens. Autofocusing corrects the image if slides vary in thickness.

A Carousel projector (above) holds a rotary tray of 80 slides. It has remote control and focusing, and a timer for projecting slides automatically at preset intervals. Gravity feed lessens the risk of slides getting jammed.

150mm lens
12ft 6ins distance

100mm lens
8ft 4ins distance

60mm lens
5ft distance

Projection distances
The size of the screen image depends on the focal length of the projecting lens and the distance from the projector to the screen. The diagram above suggests the lenses and corresponding distances to project a good-sized image onto an average 3 × 3ft screen, as at left.

Compact projection
The illustrations at right show two projectors suitable for small slide presentations. A daylight projector, near right, has a built-in screen to view and show slides without the need for a darkened room. A back-projection console, far right, incorporates a tray for 80 slides, a display screen and an audio input unit, so that a soundtrack can be synchronized with the slides.

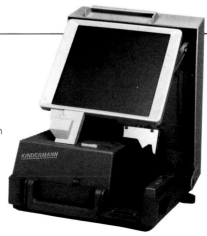

Sequencing a slide show

There are two basic rules for organizing a slide show: first, prepare everything in advance, and second, keep your presentation short. Try to work out a logical order, one that tells the story in a straightforward way. Some techniques are shown in the panel below. You should also look for visual continuity; several ways of linking sequences of pictures are shown at right.

Above all, avoid straining your audience's span of attention. If in doubt, err on the side of brevity. Your subject will have to be extremely interesting to warrant a showing time longer than 20 minutes, and 15 minutes is a sensible maximum. Plan to have the majority of your slides on the screen for less than 10 seconds, and never leave them up for more than 30 seconds unless you are answering questions. Try to vary the pace of the show: several views of the same scene should be given a few seconds each; one overall view with lots of detail, a longer time. As a starting point, you should aim to select about 80 slides for a typical show — the capacity of an average slide tray.

Creating a script
To see how your planned order will work out, sketch the slides in numbered sequence on large sheets of paper. Use these storyboards for final adjustments and to decide how long to hold each picture. Then write your commentary in a notebook and use a watch to keep on schedule during the show itself.

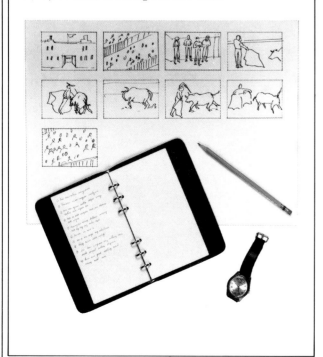

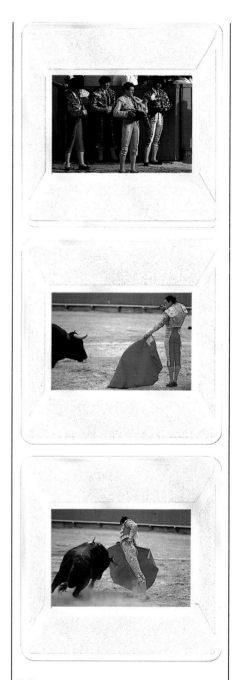

Tell a story
The simplest way to link a series of slides within an overall presentation is to follow the time sequence in which the pictures were taken. This is very effective with action events such as the Colombian bullfight shown here, where we see the matadors waiting and then move on to the actual playing of the bull. Sports events, processions and ceremonies all work well in this way.

Repeat a motif
You may find that several of your pictures include similar subjects such as the hand-shaped door knockers from Athens above. These can be effectively run together as a sequence within your show, but be careful not to hold them on the screen for too long.

Make transitions gradual
This sequence illustrates how to move smoothly from one place to another by including a linking slide. The top picture is from a sequence showing a Greek island's fishing port. To link this with inland pictures, the photographer included a slide of a fisherman mending his nets. The following slide picks up the theme of local characters, with an old man sitting outside a bar.

Repeat shapes or colors
You can use the abstract qualities of certain pictures to connect seemingly random groups. The sequence above, in London's commercial center, repeats the use of a distinctive oval shape – in a brass bell push for bank messengers; the center of a famous gold plate; and an oval window framing one of the Bank of England's towers. You can also repeat areas of color for a similar effect.

Showing prints

Florida

Photo albums

Probably the best photo album is one you make yourself after buying the raw materials from an art supplier. The example above, showing a selection of pictures taken in Florida, uses a ring binder with clear plastic sleeves. The photographer first designed the layout of each page, then had the prints made to a suitable size and mounted them on stiff black paper. For captions, you can use transfer lettering, here in white, or ink. If you want to caption every picture, a designer's stencil is a good tool. For a less ambitious approach, use a ready-made album such as the two shown at right. One has a clear-plastic film that you peel back and then place over the picture, and the other has plastic sleeves into which you can neatly slide postcard-size prints.

Prints can form the basis of a coherent story just as effectively as slides can. With a little flair and imagination, you can preserve and present them as a kind of personal publishing venture in the form of a photo album specially devoted to a favorite subject.

Decide first on the organization of the album; perhaps a time sequence following the itinerary of a trip or presenting a year in the life of your family. Or consider having a series of chapterlike sections, each centering on a specific subject. For example, in a travel sequence, you could establish the setting with landscapes, then move on to people, then to interesting buildings and so on. Always think of two facing pages in an album as a unit to be arranged at the same time. If you have an isolated sequence, a story within a story, you can devote two to four pages to that alone, and feature it by mounting the pictures on stiff paper backing of a different color or by drawing box rules around the prints.

Planning is equally important when you present prints in other ways. If you want to frame and display some favorite prints, try grouping images with related themes. Sometimes it is possible to create a miniature exhibition by clustering pictures on a wall or lining them up along a hallway. Other ways to present prints are shown below. However you show prints, always remember that judicious cropping can often greatly heighten a print's impact.

Other display systems
The standing folder (above at left) displays several pictures on the same theme – California's Death Valley. Mount prints on paper or cardboard and then glue a framing mat to the front. Use heavy adhesive tape at the back to secure the accordion joints. For a boxed set (above), find a suitably sized box or make one out of cardboard. Have the prints made to a regular size and mount and frame them with cardboard. For a wall display, frame pictures individually in the normal way or mount them up together, as with the studies of the Greek island of Corfu at left. This ready-made frame consists of a simple clear-plastic box which is so easy to fill with pictures that you can change the display periodically.

Glossary

Accessory shoe
A fitting on top of the camera that incorporates one or more electrical contacts for linking the camera to the flash. The most basic accessory shoe has one contact, which synchronizes the firing of the flash with the firing of the shutter. On more advanced cameras there may be as many as five contacts, which pass information, such as exposure readings, between the camera and dedicated flash units. The term "hot shoe" is sometimes used as an alternative to accessory shoe.

Angle of view
The angle over which a lens accepts light or "sees" a subject. The longer the focal length of a lens, the narrower its angle of view will be.

Aperture
The opening in a lens that admits light. Except in very simple cameras, the aperture can be varied in size by a diaphragm, which regulates the amount of light passing through the lens.

ASA see FILM SPEED

Artificial light
Any light source used in photography other than that from natural sources (usually the sun). Generally the term refers to light specially set up by the photographer, such as flash or photo-lamps. Photographic emulsions have different sensitivity to daylight and artificial light, and films may be rated for either type.

Autobracketing
A system that automatically makes a series of exposures at different exposure settings when the shutter is released, to increase the chances of obtaining a correctly exposed image.

Automatic exposure
A system that automatically sets correct exposure by linking a camera's exposure meter with the shutter or aperture or both. There are three main types: aperture priority, when the photo-grapher sets the aperture and the camera selects the appropriate speed; shutter priority, when the photographer chooses the speed and the camera sets the correct aperture; and programmed, when the camera sets both aperture and shutter speed. Aperture priority is advantageous when you want to control depth of field; shutter priority comes into its own particularly in action photography; and programmed exposure can be useful when the photographer has to react quickly.

Automatic focusing
A camera system that automatically brings the lens into sharp focus on the subject. Autofocus systems operate very quickly and reliably, and can usually focus more rapidly than the photographer can unaided. However, there are instances when manual focusing is preferable to automatic: for example, few autofocus systems can cope adequately when the subject is behind bars, such as animals in a zoo.

Available light
The existing light (natural or artificial) in any situation, without the introduction of supplementary light (for example, flash) by the photographer. The term usually refers to low light levels, for example indoors or at dusk.

Backlighting
A form of lighting in which the principal light source shines toward the camera and lights the subject from behind.

Bleach
A chemical bath to convert the black metallic silver that forms a photographic image into a compound such as a silver halide, which can then be dissolved or dyed. Bleach is used in toning and in many color processes.

Blix (bleach-fix)
A combined bleach and fixer bath used to shorten color processing.

Bounce flash
A technique of softening the light from a flash source by directing it onto a ceiling, wall, board or similar reflective surface before it reaches the subject.

Bracketing
A way to ensure accurate exposure by taking several pictures of the same subject at slightly different exposure settings above and below (that is, bracketing) the presumed correct setting.

Burning-in (printing-in)
A technique used in printing photographs whereby selected areas of an image are given more exposure than the rest. Other areas are shaded from the light during this time.

Cable release
A thin cable encased in a flexible rubber or metal tube, used to release the shutter when the camera is not being handheld. Newer cameras may not have a mechanical cable release socket; instead they have a pair of electrical contacts which trigger the shutter when connected. For these cameras, the cable release comprises a length of electrical flex with a push button at one end and a connector that fits into a socket on the camera at the other.

Cast
An overall tinge of a particular color in a print or slide.

Close-up lens (supplementary lens)
A simple one-element lens placed over a normal lens, in the same way as a screw-on filter, allowing the camera to be focused closer to a subject.

Color compensating filters
Filters designated by the letters CC and used to alter the color balance of a slide, particularly to compensate for a color bias in the light source.

Color conversion filters
Filters used to adjust the color balance of a light source when it differs substantially from the color temperature for which a film type is designed. Such filters can effectively convert tungsten slide film into daylight film or vice versa.

Color correction filter
Comparatively weak color filter used to correct small differences between the color temperature of the illumination used for a particular exposure and that for which the film was manufactured. An 85B filter is used with tungsten film in daylight, an 80A filter with daylight film in tungsten light. The term is also sometimes rather loosely used to describe the cyan, magenta and yellow filters that are placed in an enlarger to balance the color of prints made from color negatives.

Color head
A device on an enlarger that contains adjustable built-in filters (yellow, cyan and magenta) for color printing.

Color negative (print) film
Film processed as a negative image from which positive prints can be made.

Color paper
A light-sensitive material on a paper base for making color prints from color negatives or transparencies. The paper is coated with three emulsion layers, which respond to red, green and blue light, forming cyan, magenta and yellow dye, respectively.

Color temperature
Term describing the color quality (particularly the redness or blueness) of the light source.

Color transparency (slide) film
Film giving direct color positives in the form of transparencies. It is also known as reversal film.

Compact camera
A simple-to-use 35mm camera that has a non-interchangeable lens and is intended primarily for taking snapshots.

Condenser
A lens or lens system used in an enlarger or slide projector to concentrate light from the lamp source and focus it evenly on the negative or slide.

Contact sheet
A sheet of negative-sized photographs made simply by placing the printing paper in direct contact with the negatives during exposure.

Contrast
The difference in brightness between the lightest and darkest parts of a photographic subject, negative, print or slide. Contrast is affected by the subject brightness, lighting, film type, degree of development, the grade and surface of the printing paper, and the type of enlarger used.

Cropping
Trimming an image along one or more of its edges to eliminate unnecessary parts, or framing a scene to leave out parts of the subject.

Daylight film
Film balanced to give accurate colors when exposed to a subject lit by daylight or light of similar color-temperature – for example, electronic flash.

Dedicated flash
A flash unit, made for a specific make of camera or range of makes, that uses the camera's TTL metering system to control light output automatically.

Depth of field
The zone of acceptable sharpness in a picture, extending in front of and behind the plane of the subject, that is most precisely focused by the lens. You can control or exploit depth of field by varying three facors: the size of the aperture; the distance of the camera from the subject; and the focal length of the lens. If you decrease the size of the aperture, the depth of field increases; if you focus on a distant subject, depth of field will be greater than if you focus on a near subject; and if you fit a wide-angle lens to your camera, it will give you greater depth of field than a normal lens viewing the same scene. Many SLRs have a depth of field preview control – a button that closes the lens diaphragm to the aperature selected for an exposure so that the depth of field in the image can be checked on the viewing screen first.

Developer
A solution containing a number of chemicals that will convert a latent image on an exposed photographic material to a visible image.

Developing tank
A light-tight container, made of plastic or

steel, in which film is developed. The exposed film is loaded into the tank in complete darkness, and temperature-controlled chemicals are added at precisely timed intervals to make the image visible and stable.

Diaphragm
The part of the camera that governs the size of the aperture. The most common type is the iris diaphragm – a system of curved, overlapping metal blades that form a roughly circular opening similar to the iris of the eye. It varies in size to control the amount of light.

Diffraction filter
A colorless filter inscribed with a network of parallel grooves. These break white light up into its component colors, giving a prism-like effect to highlights.

Diffused light
Light that has lost some if its intensity by being reflected or by passing through a translucent material. Diffusion softens light, eliminating both glare and harsh shadows, and thus can be of great value in photography, notably in portraiture.

DIN see FILM SPEED

Dodging (shading)
Means of reducing exposure in selected areas during printing by holding a solid object between the lens and the light-sensitive paper. By moving the object, abrupt changes in tone can be avoided.

Double exposure
The recording of two images on the same frame of film. When more than two images are recorded, the term "multiple exposure" is used.

Emulsion
The light-sensitive layer of a film. In black-and-white films the emulsion usually consists of very fine grains of silver halide suspended in gelatin, which blacken when exposed to light. The emulsion of color films contains molecules of dye in addition to the silver halide.

Enlarger
An apparatus that makes enlarged prints by projecting and focusing an image from a negative or transparency onto light-sensitive paper, which must then be processed to reveal the final print.

Enlarger head
The part of an enlarger that contains the light source, the negative carrier and the lens. An enlarger head also houses a filter drawer or a built-in filtration system.

Enlarging easel (masking frame)
A board used with an enlarger for positioning printing paper and keeping it flat and still during exposure.

Exposure
The amount of light that passes through a lens (in either a camera or an enlarger) onto a light-sensitive material (film or photographic paper) to form an image. In the camera, too much light causes over-

exposure – this makes negative film look too dark and reversal film look too light. Underexposure (too little light) has the reverse effect. In enlarging, overexposure makes a print from a negative too dark and a print from a slide too light. Underexposure has the reverse effect.

Exposure meter
An instrument for measuring the intensity of light so as to determine the shutter and aperture setting necessary to obtain correct exposure. Exposure meters may be built into the camera or be completely separate units. Separate meters can sometimes measure the light falling on the subject (incident reading) as well as the light reflected by it (reflected reading); built-in meters measure only reflected light. Both types of meter may be capable of measuring light from a particular part of the subject (spot metering) as well as taking an overall reading.

Extension attachment
A camera accessory used in close-up photography to increase the distance between the lens and the film, thus allowing you to focus on very near objects. Extension tubes are metal tubes that can be added in different combinations between the lens and the camera to give various increases in lens-to-film distance. Extension bellows are continuously variable between the longest and shortest extension. Bellows are considerably more cumbersome than tubes and must be used with a tripod.

Fast lens
A lens of wide maximum aperature, relative to its focal length, allowing maximum light into the camera in minimum time. The speed of a lens – its relative ability to take in light – is an important measure of its optical efficiency: fast lenses are more difficult to design and manufacture than slow lenses, and consequently cost more.

Fill-in light
Additional lighting used to supplement the principal light source and brighten shadows. Fill-in light may be supplied by redirecting light with a card reflector or by using a flash unit, for example.

Film speed
A film's sensitivity to light, rated numerically so that it can be matched to the camera's exposure controls. The two most commonly used scales, ASA (American Standards Association) and DIN (Deutsche Industrie Norm), are now superseded by the system known as ISO (International Standards Organization). ASA 100 (21° DIN) is expressed as ISO 100/21° or simply ISO 100.

Filter
A thin sheet of glass, plastic or gelatin placed in front of the camera's lens to control or change the appearance of the picture. Some filters affect color or tone;

others can, for example, cut out unwanted reflections, help to reduce haze or be used to create a variety of special effects.

Filtration
In color printing, the use of filters to control the colors of the enlarged image and thus of the final print.

Fixer
A chemical bath used to make a photographic image stable after it has been developed. The fixer stabilizes the emulsion by converting the undeveloped silver halides into water-soluble compounds, which can then be dissolved away.

Flash
A very brief but intense burst of artificial light, used in photography as a supplement or alternative to any existing light in a scene. Flash sources take various forms. Some small cameras have built-in flash, but for SLRs the most popular flash units slot into the top of the camera.

F-number
The number resulting when the focal length of a lens is divided by the diameter of the aperture. A sequence of f-numbers calibrates the aperture in regular steps (known as stops) between the minimum and maximum openings of the lens. The f-numbers generally follow a standard sequence, in such a way that the interval between one full stop and the next represents a halving or doubling in the image brightness. The f-numbers become progressively higher as the aperture is reduced to allow in less light.

Focal length
The distance, usually given in millimeters, between the optical center of a lens and the point at which rays of light from objects at infinity are brought to focus. In general, the greater the focal length of a lens, the smaller and more magnified the part of the scene it includes in the picture frame. A standard lens for a 35mm camera typically has a focal length of 50mm, a wide-angle lens one of 28mm and a telephoto lens one of 135mm.

Focal plane
The plane on which the image of a subject is brought to focus behind a lens. To produce a sharp picture, the lens must be focused so that this place coincides with the plane on which the film sits.

Focusing
Adjusting the distance between the lens and the film to form a sharp image of the subject on the film. The nearer the object you wish to focus on, the farther you have to move the lens from the film. On manual cameras you focus by moving the lens forward or backward by rotating a focusing control ring.

Format
The size or shape of a negative or print. The term usually refers to a particular film size, for example 35mm format, but in its most general sense can mean simply whether a picture is upright (vertical format) or longitudinal (horizontal format). Cameras are usually categorized by the format of the film they use.

Frontlighting
A form of lighting in which the principal light source shines from the direction of the camera toward the subject.

Graduated filter
A filter in which a clear and tinted half gradually blend into each other. A graduated filter can be used, for example, to enliven a dull sky in a landscape without affecting the rest of the image.

Grain
The granular texture appearing to some degree in all processed photographic materials. In black-and-white photographs the grains are minute particles of black metallic silver that constitute the dark areas of a photograph. In color photographs the silver is removed chemically, but tiny blotches of dye retain the appearance of grain. The more sensitive – or faster – the film, the coarser the grain.

Hot shoe see ACCESSORY SHOE

Incident light reading
A method of measuring the light that falls on a subject as distinct from the light that is reflected from it. To take this kind of reading, the exposure meter is pointed from the subject toward the camera.

Intelligent metering
Many modern autofocus SLRs have computer controlled metering systems. These systems can measure the light falling on different areas of the frame and then compare the pattern of brightness levels to thousands of stored brightness patterns in the computer's memory. In this way, the camera's meter is able to recognize the level of brightness and give accurate exposure readings, even under difficult exposure situations such as strong backlighting.

ISO see FILM SPEED

Latitude
The ability of a film to record an image satisfactorily if exposure is not exactly correct. Black-and-white and color print films have more latitude than color transparency films, and fast films have greater latitude than slow ones.

Lens
An optical device made of glass or other transparent material that forms images by bending and focusing rays of light. A lens made of a single piece of glass cannot produce very sharp or exact images, so camera lenses are made up of a number of glass "elements" that cancel out each other's weaknesses and work together to give a sharp true image. The size, curvature and positioning of the elements determine the focal length and angle of view of a lens.

Lens hood
A simple lens accessory made of thin metal or rubber, used to shield the lens from stray light that does not come from the subject and can impair the image.

Macro lens
A lens specifically constructed for close-up photography, having its elements designed to give their best results when the subject is close to the camera. The special focusing mechanism of a macro lens permits sharp pictures from as close as three inches, which makes it possible to record subjects life-size on film. Macro lenses are also used for normal photography at ordinary subject distances.

Masking
The act of blocking out light from selected areas of an image for various purposes; for example, to cover the edges of a piece of printing paper during exposure to produce white borders.

Mirror lens
A lens that uses curved mirrors to reflect light back and forth and so create a long focal length within a physically compact body. The main disadvantage of the mirror lens is that the aperture is fixed and usually quite small, preventing any control of depth of field. Light intensity can be regulated to a degree by use of a neutral density (ND) filter. Otherwise, exposures must be controlled by shutter speeds. The telltale product of the mirror lens is the ringed appearance of out-of-focus highlights, known as "doughnuts", which can be used to striking effect. Such distortion is due to a blind spot in the lens, caused by placing the front mirror in the center of the first lens element.

Multiple exposure
The recording of two or more images on the same frame of film. This can be achieved in a number of ways. Some cameras have a multiple exposure control that lets you recock the shutter without advancing the film. On cameras without this facility you can recock the shutter after pressing in the rewind release, keeping the film taut by constant pressure on the rewind lever. Another technique is to expose the same film twice, taking care to align it so the frame positions match up for the second exposure.

Negative
A developed photographic image in which light tones are recorded as dark and dark ones as light. In color negatives, each color of the original subject is represented by its complementary. Usually, a negative is made up on a transparent base so that light can be beamed through it onto light-sensitive printing paper to form a positive image.

Panning
A technique of moving the camera to

follow the motion of a subject, used to convey speed or to freeze a moving subject at slower shutter speeds. Often, a relatively slow shutter speed is used to blur the background while panning keeps the moving object sharp.

Photographic paper (printing paper)
Paper coated with a light-sensitive emulsion, used for making photographic prints. When a negative or slide is projected onto printing paper, a latent image forms, and this is revealed by processing. Printing paper may be fiber-based or resin-coated (RC); the resin-coated papers offer speedier processing because they are water-repellent. Papers come in grades according to their contrast range.

Photolamp
A tungsten light bulb specially designed for photographic use. Photolamps are similar to household bulbs, but bigger and brighter. They give off light that is matched to tungsten-balanced film.

Polarizing filter
A filter that changes the vibration pattern of the light passing through it. Chief uses are to remove unwanted reflections from a photographic image or to darken the blue of the sky.

Prefocusing
The technique of setting the camera's focus in anticipation of the subject's movements as an aid to quick picture-taking. Usually the focus is set on a motionless feature toward which the subject is moving.

Processing
The sequence of activities (usually developing, stopping, fixing, washing and drying) that will convert a latent image on film or photographic paper into a visible, stable image.

Processing drum (processing tube)
A light-tight container in which photographic paper is processed in daylight. The drum is used particularly for color print processing, in which temperature, solution consistency, timing and agitation need careful control.

Pushing film
Setting the camera's ISO dial to a number higher than the nominal speed of the film, so that the photographer can use a faster shutter speed or smaller aperture. To compensate for the deliberate underexposure that pushing produces, the film must be push-processed.

Push-processing
Extending development time, usually to compensate for underexposure caused by a film being uprated to permit a faster shutter speed than the light allows.

Red eye
The bright red color of the pupil of the eye that sometimes disfigures pictures taken by flash. It is caused by reflection of the flash unit's light from layers of the retina rich in blood vessels. Red eye can

be avoided by making sure that the subject is not looking directly at the camera or by using off-camera or bounce flash. Some cameras with built-in flash units have a red eye reduction control. When this is activated, the flash emits a beam of light just before the flash fires, causing the subject's pupils to contract, which lessens the risk of red eye.

Reflector
Any surface capable of reflecting light; in photography, generally understood to mean sheets of white, gray or silvered cardboard used to reflect light into shadow areas. Lamp reflectors are generally dish-shaped mirrors, with the lamp recessed into the concave interior, which points toward the subject. Studio electronic flash equipment is often combined with an umbrella reflector, usually silvered, mounted on a stand.

Reflex camera
A camera employing a mirror in the viewing system to reflect the image onto a viewing screen. The most popular type is the single lens reflex (SLR), which reflects the light from the same lens that is used to take the picture. The twin lens reflex (TLR) has an additional lens for viewing. A single lens reflex camera shows the image in the viewfinder as it will appear on the film, whatever the focal length of the lens used.

Rimlighting
Lighting in which the subject appears outlined against a dark background. Usually the light source is above and behind the subject, but rimlit photographs can look quite different from conventional backlit images, in which the background is usually bright.

Safelight
A special darkroom lamp whose light is of a color and intensity that will not affect light-sensitive photographic materials. Not all such materials can be handled under a safelight, and some require a type designed specifically for them.

Sandwiching
Combining two or more negatives or slides to produce a composite image either on one sheet of printing paper or on a slide-projecting screen.

Second curtain synch
A flash mode in which the flash unit fires just before the camera's second shutter curtain begins to move during the exposure. This causes any ambient light trails in the picture to appear as though they follow the flashlit subject.

Self-timer
A device found on many cameras that delays the operation of the shutter, usually until about eight to ten seconds after the release is pressed. This allows the photographer to set up the camera and then pose in front of the lens.

Shutter
The camera mechanism that controls the duration of the exposure. There are two main types – between-the-lens shutters are built into the lens barrel close to the diaphragm; focal plane shutters are in the camera body, in front of the film.

Sidelighting
A form of lighting in which light falls on the subject from one side. Sidelighting produces some dramatic effects, casting long shadows and emphasizing texture and form.

Silver halide
A chemical compound of silver (usually silver bromide) used as the light-sensitive constituent in films. The invisible image produced when the halides are exposed to light is converted to metallic silver when the film is subsequently developed.

Single use camera
A 24 exposure roll of color print film housed in a cardboard or a plastic box, with a low quality, plastic lens on the front and some form of rudimentary film advance control and shutter release. At the end of the roll of film, the camera is sent to the processing lab, which returns a set of prints, but not the camera. The cameras cost about two or three times the price of a roll of film and are designed for taking snapshots.

Skylight filter
A filter, usually pale pink, used to eliminate a blue color cast caused by haze. As a skylight filter does not affect exposure, it may be kept in place permanently to protect the lens from dust and scratching.

SLR see REFLEX CAMERA

Soft focus
Deliberately diffused or blurred definition of an image, often used to create a dreamy, romantic look in portraiture. Soft-focus effects are usually created with special lenses or filters embossed so that the glass surface breaks up the light by means of refraction.

Split-field close-up lens
A lens attachment that consists of half a close-up lens fitted into a rotating mount. The attachment is used to keep foreground subjects that are close to the camera in sharp focus, without sacrificing sharpness in the background.

Spotlight
A photographic lamp designed to emit a concentrated beam of light.

Spot meter
An exposure meter with a 1° angle of coverage, used to take readings of small areas within the subject.

Sprocket
A small projection on the camera spool that winds the film forward or back in the film chamber. The sprockets connect with the perforations ("sprocket holes")

along the edges of the film, and move the film through the camera.

Stabilizer
A processing solution used in color processing to make the dyes produced by development more stable.

Standard lens (normal lens)
A lens producing an image that is close to the way the eye sees the world in terms of scale, angle of view and perspective. For most SLRs the standard lens has a focal length of about 50mm.

Starburst filter
A filter with crossed horizontal and vertical lines etched into its surface. Any sharp point of light viewed through the filter forms radiating lines of light, resembling a star.

Stop
A comparative measure of exposure. Each one-stage change of the shutter speed or aperture (for example, from 1/60 to 1/125 or from f/2.8 to f/4) represents a stop and doubles or halves the amount of light reaching the film.

Stop bath
A weak acidic solution used in processing as an intermediate bath between the developer and the fixer. The stop bath halts development and at the same time neutralizes the alkaline developer, thus preventing it from lowering the acidity of the fixer.

Stop down
A colloquial term for reducing the aperture of the lens.

Supplementary close-up lens
A simple lens used as an accessory for close-ups. The supplementary lens fits over a normal lens to produce a slightly magnified image.

Teleconverter
A device that fits between a lens and camera body to increase (usually to double or treble) the effective focal length of a lens and produce a magnified image.

Telephoto lens
A lens that includes a narrow view of the subject in the picture frame, making distant objects appear closer and magnified. In the 35mm format, lenses with a focal length of 85mm or longer are generally considered telephoto lenses. Telephoto focal lengths stretch to 1200mm, and lenses that are longer than 400mm are sometimes referred to as "long toms".

Thirds, rule of
A simple compositional principle whereby the main point of interest of a scene is placed approximately one-third from one of the edges of the picture frame. The term "intersection of thirds" is used when the subject is centered on a point approximately one-third in from two adjacent edges.

Time exposure
An exposure in which the shutter stays open for as long as the photographer keeps the shutter release depressed. Time exposures may be necessary in dim light and are usually made using a cable release and with the camera mounted on a tripod.

Transparency
A positive image viewed by transmitted rather than reflected light. When mounted in a metal, plastic or cardboard mount, a transparency is called a slide.

Tripod
A three-legged camera support. The legs (usually collapsible) are hinged to a head to which the camera is attached.

TTL
An abbreviation for "through-the-lens", generally used to refer to exposure metering systems that read the intensity of light that passes through the lens.

Tungsten light
A common type of electric light for both household and photographic purposes, named after the filament of the metal tungsten through which the current passes. Tungsten light is much warmer in color (more orange) than daylight or electronic flash, and with daylight-balanced slide film you must use a blue filter to reproduce colors accurately. Alternatively, you can use a special tungsten-balanced slide film.

UV filter
Lens filter used to absorb ultraviolet radiation, which is prevalent on hazy days. Like skylight filters, UV filters have no effect on the exposure.

Vapor lamp
A lamp containing a gas or vapor that glows with light when an electric current passes through it. Mercury, neon and sodium vapor lamps produce strongly colored light. The light from fluorescent tubes is closer to daylight.

Viewfinder
The window, screen or frame on a camera through which the photographer can see the area of a scene that will appear in the picture.

Wide-angle lens
A lens with a short focal length that takes in a wide view of the subject. In the 35mm format, lenses with a focal length of 35mm or shorter are generally considered wide-angle lenses.

Zoom lens
A lens of variable focal length. For example, in an 80-200mm zoom lens, the focal length can be changed anywhere between the lower limit of 80mm and the upper of 200mm. This affects the scale of the image on which the lens is focused without throwing the image out of focus.

Index

Picture credits

Abbreviations used are: t top; c center; b bottom; l left; r right. All Magnum pictures are from the John Hillelson Agency.

WHAT MAKES A GOOD PICTURE?
17 Graeme Harris. 18 Alfonse Iseli. 19 Robin Bath. 20 Luis Huesco. 21 Russell D. Arthur. 22-23 John Garrett. 24-25 Robert Farber/Image Bank. 26 Peter Knapps/Image Bank. 27 Geg Germany. 28 John Garrett. 29 James B. Rinaldi. 30 Nadia MacKenzie. 31 Ronald Kaufman.

You, the Photographer
32-33 F. Damm/Zefa. 34 bl Audrey Stirling/Daily Telegraph Colour Library, tl c Michael Freeman. 34-35 Michael Freeman. 35 c Michael Freeman. 36 t David W. Hamilton/Image Bank, l R. Phillips/Image Bank, br Jean & C. Fichter/Image Bank. 37 Larry Dale Gordon/Image Bank. 38 Cecil Jospé. 39 tl Sally & Richard Greenhill, tr Geg Germany/Daily Telegraph Colour Library, b John Sims. 40 tl Sergio Dorantes, bl R. Nuettgens/Zefa, r Herb Gustafson. 41 Pablo Ortiz. 42 Michael Freeman. 43 John Sims. 44 t Jerry Young, c Robin Laurance, b Neill Menneer. 45 Jerry Young. 46 l Kodak-Pathé, r Uli Butz. 47 l Steve Powell/All-Sport, r Ian McKinnell. 48 l Neill Menneer, 48-49 Hans Woolf/Image Bank. 49 Michelle Garrett. 50 l Patricia Birdman, r Graeme Harris. 51 t Michael Freeman, b Sergio Dorantes. 52 t Robert J. Walcyak, b Vautier/de Nanxe. 52-53 Brain Seed/Click/Chicago. 54 t Timothy Beddow, b John Garrett. 55 Richard Brook. 56 t John Roberts, b John Veasey. 57 tl Linda Burgess, tr Ed Buziak, b Graeme Harris.

You and Your Camera
58-59 P. Pfander/Image Bank. 65 tr Michelle Garrett. 67 tl c John Garrett, bl D. Brownwell/Image Bank, br Robert Saxton. 68 br Ian McKinnell. 68-69 l c r Michael Freeman. 69 bl Stuart Windsor, br Leo Mason. 70-71 All Michael Freeman. 72-73 All Vautier/de Nanxe. 74 t Michael Freeman, b Laura Clark. 75 J.-C. Lozouet/Image Bank. 76 t Pete Turner/Image Bank, b Andrew Lawson. 76-77 Brian Seed/Click/Chicago. 78 Walter Looss/Image Bank. 79 l Julian Calder, r Michael Freeman. 80 r Brian Seed/Click/Chicago. 81 John Hedgecoe. 82 l Simon Yeo, r Thomas W. Wienand. 83 Julian Calder. 84 t John Sims, b Jerry Young. 85 John Sims. 86 tr John Topham Picture Library, b Barry Lewis/Network. 87 Carol Sharp. 88 Linda Burgess. 89 tr Graeme Harris, l John Starr. 90 bl br Colin Molyneux/Image Bank. 91 tl tr Linda Burgess, bl br Colin Molyneux/Image Bank. 92 F. C. Gundlach/Image Bank. 93 Peter Gittoes.

Make Light Work for You
94-95 Michael Abrahams/Network. 97 t Christian Kempf, b John Garrett. 99 tl tc tr Michael Busselle, b Alastair Black. 100 b Michael Busselle. 101 t Dick Scott-Stewart, b John Garrett. 102-103 All Michael Freeman. 104-105 Linda Burgess. 106 tl S. & O. Matthews, tr Graeme Harris, b Jürg Blatter. 107 Martin Elliott. 108 Michael Freeman. 108-109 Heather Angel. 109 Jerry Young. 110 Andreas Heumann. 111 Linda Burgess. 112 t Vince Streano/Aspect Picture Library. 113 t Michael Freeman, b Frank Wing/Image Bank. 115 Neill Menneer. 116 t Michael Freeman, b Paul Damien/Click/Chicago. 117 t Geg Germany, b C. Thomson/Image Bank.

Using Color Creatively
118-119 Noble Beheler. 120 Mike Burgess. 121 t Cyril Isy-Schwart/Image Bank, b Simon Yeo. 122 Ashvin Gatha. 122-123 Robin Laurance. 124 tr Brian Seed/Click/Chicago, bl Vautier/de Nanxe. 125 t Brian Seed/Click/Chicago, b Ashvin Gatha. 126 Linda Burgess. 127 t Pete Turner/Image Bank, b Marcel Nauer. 128 tr Linda Burgess, b Ashvin Gatha. 129 Kate Salway. 130 Ian McKinnell. 131 J. P. Lescouret/fotogram. 132 Michelle Garrett. 133 t John Garrett, b Linda Burgess. 134 Michael Freeman. 135 Michael Borum/Image Bank. 136 Michael Freeman. 137 tl tr bc Michael Freeman, ct Ashvin Gatha. 138 Roger Payling. 139 Michael Freeman.

PICTURES OF OURSELVES
141 Brian Seed/Click/Chicago. 142-143 Both John Garrett. 144 Douglas Kirkland/Image Bank. 145 Steve Wall/Click/Chicago. 146 Al Satterwhite/Image Bank. 147 Dick Scott-Stewart. 148 Lise St. Denis. 148-149 Mike Harker/Image Bank. 150 Joseph Brignolo/Image Bank. 151 Adam Woolfit/Susan Griggs Agency. 152-153 David Hamilton/Image Bank. 154 Paulo Curto/Image Bank. 155 Pete Turner/Image Bank.

People at Their Best
156-157 Peter Thompson. 158 l Herbie Yamaguchi/Xenon, tr Didier Derambur/fotogram, br John Sims. 159 Walter R. Gyr. 160-161 Francoise Bouillot/Kodak. 162 Jay Freis/Image Bank. 163 l Tim Ashley, r Digiacomo/Image Bank. 164 t Kodak-Pathé, b Robert Littlepage. 165 Timothy Woodcock. 166 Francoise Bouillot/Kodak. 167 t Trevor Wood, b Sebastian Keep/Robert Harding Associates. 168 t John Garrett, b Robert Harding Picture Library. 169 David Hamilton/Daily Telegraph Colour Library. 170 t Janice Keene, b Anne Conway. 170-171 Alain Bourdes/Explorer. 172-173 Michael Freeman. 174 l Barry Lewis/Network, r John Garrett. 175 A. J. Bedding/Tony Stone Associates. 176 Nikita Kolmikow. 177 t Nikita Kolmikow, b J. Tisne/Explorer. 178 C. Sommer/Explorer. 179 t D. Sparks/Image Bank, bl R. Gunther/Explorer, br Michael Busselle. 180 Wayne Miller/Magnum. 181 b Bard Martin/Image Bank. 182 John Hedgecoe. 183 l Dan Budnik/John Hillelson Agency, r John Hedgecoe. 184-185 Nancy Durrell McKenna. 186 t George Skirrin, b Paula Marie Elston. 187 tl Frank T. Wood, tr Jim Dennis, b Michael Freeman. 188 l Robin Laurance, r John Lewis Stage/Image Bank. 189 Pete Turner. 190 l Leo Mason, r Steve Benbow/Network. 190-191 Michael Freeman. 191 Ian Berry/Magnum.

The Art of Portraits
192-193 Chris Barker. 194 l John Marmaras/Woodfin Camp Associates, r Michael Freeman. 195 tl John Hedgecoe, bl Ph. Ledru/Sygma, r Graham Harrison/Daily Telegraph Colour Library. 196 l Ian Miles/Image Bank, r l. Thoma/Image Bank. 197 Th. Rouchon/Explorer. 198 t Julian Calder, b David Whyte. 199 t Clive Barda, b David Whyte. 200 John Sims. 201 tl bl Frank Herrmann, r John Miller. 202 John Bulmer/Susan Griggs Agency. 202-203 Elliot Erwitt/Magnum. 203 Paul Fusco/Magnum. 204-205 All John Garrett. 206 bl Patrick Ward, r Julian Calder and John Garrett. 207 tl Th. Rouchon/Explorer, tr John Garrett, b Nancy Brown/Image Bank. 208 bl br John Garrett. 208-209 Graham Harrison/Daily Telegraph Colour Library. 209 t Ted Streshinsky/Image Bank, bl br John Garrett. 210-213 Mayotte Magnus. 214 t Julian Calder, b Robin Laurance. 215 Robert Gelberg/Image Bank. 216 Michael Busselle. 217 l Michael Busselle, tr John Sims, br Linda Burgess.

Photographing the Nude
218-219 John Garrett. 220-221 All John Garrett. 222 Michael Boys/Susan Griggs Agency. 222-223 Michael Busselle. 223 John Garrett. 224 bl David Hamilton/Image Bank, tc bl Trevor Wood. 225 Ph. Rouchon/Explorer. 226 t Larry Dale Gordon/Image Bank, b Michael Busselle. 227 Larry Dale Gordon/Image Bank. 228 t Ph. Roy/Explorer, b Chris Thomson/Image Bank. 229 Josef Neumann. 230 l Chris Thomson/Image Bank. r John Hedgecoe. 230-231 Gerard Petreman. 232 l Hideki Fujii/Image Bank, r Tony Stone Associates. 233 Pete Turner/Image Bank.

THE WORLD AROUND US
235 Joseph F. Viesti/Susan Griggs Agency. 236-237 John Garrett. 237 Ted Spiegel/Susan Griggs Agency. 238 Robin Laurance. 239 John Sims. 240 Peter Keen/Susan Griggs Agency. 241 Bruno Barbey/Magnum. 242 Andrew De Lory. 243 Andrew De Lory. 244-245

K. Taconis/Magnum. **245** Bullaty/Lomeo/Image Bank. **246** Wisniewski/Zefa. **247** Morris Guariglia. **248-249** E. Sattler/Explorer. **249** Bullaty/Lomeo/Image Bank.

The Traveling Camera
250-251 John Hedgecoe. **254** l Dr. A. Berger/Daily Telegraph Colour Library, r Pat Morris/Daily Telegraph Colour Library. **255** l D. Williams/Daily Telegraph Colour Library, r R. G. Williamson/Daily Telegraph Colour Library. **256** t Anne Conway, b Michael Freeman. **257** l r Alain Choisnet/Image Bank. **258** l Robin Laurance. **259** l Michael Freeman, r John Garrett. **260** l Jake Rajs/Image Bank, r Vautier/de Nanxe. **261** l Ian Murphy, bl Richard Haughton, br Andrew De Lory. **262** l Bullarty/Lomeo/Image Bank, r Anne Conway. **263** t b Michelle Garrett. **264-265** All Adam Woolfit/Susan Griggs Agency. **266-267** All Harry Gruyaert/Magnum. **268-271** All Michael Freeman.

The Natural Landscape
272-273 Bill Brooks/Daily Telegraph Colour Library. **274** Reflejo/Susan Griggs Agency. **275** t Dennis Stock/Magnum, b Erich Hartmann/Magnum. **276-277** John Hedgecoe. **277** Paul Keel. **278** t John Sims, b Harald Sund/Image Bank. **279** Andrew De Lory. **280** John Cleare. **280-281** John Cleare. **281** John Garrett. **282** t b Michael Freeman. **283** t Dennis Stock/Magnum, b Michael Freeman. **284** t Adam Woolfit/Susan Griggs Agency, b Richard Dudley-Smith. **285** l Dennis Stock Magnum, r John Hedgecoe. **286-287** Jürg Blatter. **287** t Linda Burgess, b John Sims. **288** t R. Ian Lloyd/Susan Griggs Agency, b Michael Freeman. **289** Uli Butz. **290** Robin Morrison. **290-291** M. Moisnard Explorer. **291** t Francois Gohier/Ardea, b Robin Morrison. **292** l Michael Freeman, r Ernst Haas/Magnum. **293** t Ernst Haas/Magnum, b Ian Berry/Magnum. **294** Marc Riboud/Magnum. **295** t Ake Lindau/Ardea, b Andrew De Lory.

Animals and Plants
296-297 Jean-Paul Ferraro/Ardea. **298** Jean Philippe Varin Jacana. **298-299** Farrell Grehan/Susan Griggs Agency. **299** L. Lee Rue III/Image Bank. **301** t Jeff Foote/Bruce Coleman Limited. **302-303** Ian Murphy. **303** t Jean-Paul Ferraro/Ardea, b Ira Block/Image Bank. **304-305** Dennis Stock/Magnum. **305** t Horst Munzig/Susan Griggs Agency, c Max Hess, b Lionel Isy-Schwart/Image Bank. **307** Hans Reinhard/Zefa. **308** t b Eric Hosking. **309** t Wisniewski/Zefa, b Michael Freeman. **310** t B. & C. Calhoun/Bruce Coleman Limited. **311** Hans Reinhard/Bruce Coleman Limited. **312** t Robert P. Carr/Bruce Coleman Limited, b Michael Freeman. **313** Robin Laurance. **314** t Reflejo/Susan Griggs Agency, b Jeffrey C. Stoll/Jacana. **315** t b Michael Freeman. **316** David Muench. **316-317** Dennis Stock/Magnum. **318** Jean Paul Ferraro/Ardea. **319** b Viard/Jacana.

EXTENDING YOUR RANGE
321 Julian Nieman/Susan Griggs Agency. **322** Heinz Kluetmeier/Sports Illustrated. **323** All-Sport. **324-325** Tony Duffy/All-Sport. **325** Steve Powell/All-Sport. **326-327** Leo Mason. **328** Trevor Wood Picture Library. **329** Al Satterwhite/Image Bank. **330** Nancy Brown/Image Bank. **331** Graeme Harris. **332** Andrew De Lory. **333** Chris Alan Wilton. **334-335** Ken Griffiths.

Catching the Action
336-337 Adam Woolfitt/Susan Griggs Agency. **338** t Leo Mason, b Michelle Garrett. **339** t Robin Laurance, b Jerry Young. **340** All Michael Freeman. **341** Tony Duffy/All-Sport. **342** Jerry Yulsman/Image Bank. **343** t Steve Powell/All-Sport, bl bc br Derek St. Romaine/© Reed International Books Limited. **344** l Don Morley/All-Sport, r Canon UK. **345** Janeart/Image Bank. **346** All-Sport. **346-347** Fred Mayer/Magnum. **347** bl Horst Munzig/Susan Griggs Agency, br Graeme Harris. **348** t Sepp Seitz/Susan Griggs Agency, b Alastair Black. **349** Ernst Hass/Magnum. **350** John Cleare. **351** t Steve Powell/All-Sport, b Burton McNeely/Image Bank. **352-353** Adam Woolfitt/Susan Griggs Agency. **353** t Horst Munzig/Susan Griggs Agency, b John Kelly/Image Bank. **354** Adam Woolfitt/Susan Griggs Agency. **354-355** John Garrett. **356** t Tony Duffy/All-Sport, b Alain Courtois/Kodak. **357** t Jean Rochaix/Kodak, b Alex Webb/Magnum.

Creating Special Effects
358-359 Andrew De Lory. **360** t Robin Laurance, b Anne Conway. **361** t Jerry Young, b Richard Platte. **362** John Freeman. **363** t Robin Bath, b Ceri Norman. **364-365** Richard Oliver/Xenon. **365** t Lawrence Lawry, b John Sims. **366** t Geoff Gove/Image Bank, b Andrew De Lory. **367** t Andrew De Lory, b Francisco Hidalgo/Image Bank. **368** John Sims. **369** t Robert Eames, b Ed Buziak. **370** Ed Buziak. **370-371** Tony Jones/Robert Harding Picture Library. **371** l Mitchell Funk/Image Bank, r Richard Haughton. **372** Robin Bath. **372-373** Tom Grill/Susan Griggs Agency. **374** l Andrew De Lory, r Clive Boursnel. **375** Photri/Robert Harding Picture Library. **376-377** Ed Buziak. **377** t John Hedgecoe, b Geoff Gove/Image Bank. **378** Richard Platt (Band of 2nd Battalion, The Queen's Regiment). **378-379** Tim Stephens. **379** Michael Freeman. **380** Nick Boyce. **380** Richard Haughton. **380-381** Timothy Woodcock. **381** t Ian McKinnell, b Timothy Woodcock. **382** t Anne Conway, b Julian Calder. **383** t Julian Calder, b Michael Freeman. **384** l Andrew De Lory, r Chris Alan Wilton. **385** John Hedgecoe. **386** l Richard Haughton, r Alastair Black. **387** Alastair Black.

Special Conditions
388-389 John Cleare/Mountain Camera. **390** Alain Choisnet/Image Bank. **391** tl Ian Bradshaw, tr Max Hess, b Michael Freeman. **393-393** John Sims. **393** t Lionel Isy-Schwart/Image Bank, b Horst Munzig/Susan Griggs Agency. **394** Trevor Wood Picture Library. **395** tl bl Michael Freeman, r Ch. Pinson/Explorer. **396** George Wright. **397** tl John Cleare, tr John Sims, b A. Nadeau/Explorer. **398** tl Robin Laurance, tc Graeme Harris, tr Andre Chastel/Kodak, b John Hedgecoe. **399** Pete Turner/Image Bank. **400** l Michelle Garrett, r John Garrett. **401** t John Garrett, b Niki Mareschal/Image Bank. **402** l Donald E. Carroll/Image Bank, r Ellis Herwig/Image Bank. **403** t Gerard Champlong/Image Bank, b Vautier/de Nanxe. **404** t b Richard Haughton. **405** l Darryl Williams/The Dance Library, r Robin Laurance. **406-407** All Vautier/de Nanxe. **408** t c b All Flip Schulke/Planet Earth Pictures. **408-409** Warren Williams/Planet Earth Pictures. **409** t b Flip Schulke/Planet Earth Pictures.

Studio Techniques
410-411 Charlie Stebbings. **412** l Michael Melford/Image Bank, r Graeme Harris. **413** t Hele Pask, b Trevor Wood Picture Library. **414** Tony Stone Associates. **415** t Gered Mankowitz/Rembrandt Bros. Photo Studios, b Pete Turner/Image Bank. **416** All Michael Freeman. **417** All Michael Freeman. **420-421** Charlie Stebbings. **421** t Bob Croxford, b Peter Williams. **422** Tony Skinner. **423** t Nels, b Tony Skinner.

The Home Darkroom
424-425 Laurie Lewis. **434** Richard Platt. **436** Nick Meers. **439** All Clive Boursnell. **456** Tim Stephens. **457** Tim Stephens.

Presenting Your Pictures
458-459 John Garrett. **460-461** All John Garrett. **464** All Michael Freeman. **465** tl cl bl tr cr br Michael Freeman, tc cc bc John Garrett. **466-467** John Garrett.

Additional commissioned photography by John Bellars, Paul Brierly, Michael Busselle, John Freeman, Michael Freeman, John Garrett, Laurie Lewis, John Miller, Nick Scott, Tim Stephens, Frank Thomas, Victor Watts, Timothy Woodcock.

Artists David Ashby, Kuo Kang Chen, Gordon Cramp, Brian Delf, Roy Flooks, Tony Graham, John Hutchinson, Alun Jones, Edwina Keene, Aziz Khan, Richard Lewis, Haywood Martin, Coral Mula, Sandra Pond, Andrew Popkiewicz, Jim Robins, Alan Suttie

Retouching Roy Flooks, Bryon Harvey, O'Connor/Dowse

Typesetting by Hourds Typographica Ltd, Stafford, England and Dorchester Typesetting Group Ltd, Dorchester, England